Postcard History Series

Portsmouth

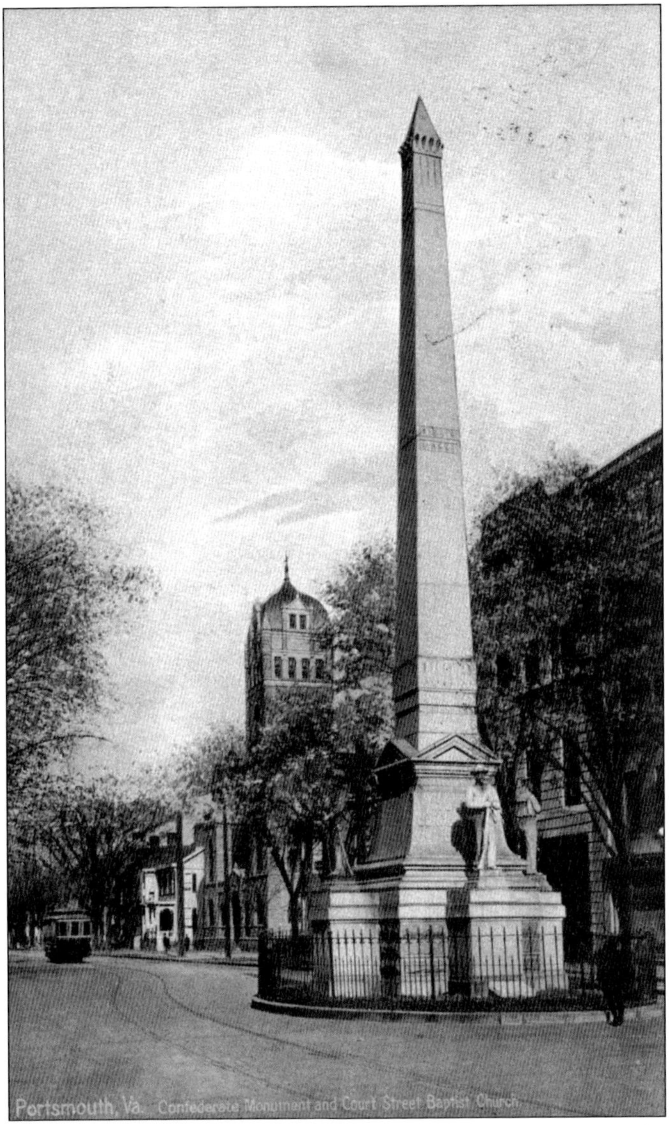

The Confederate Monument located in the center of Court Street was completed in 1881. It is one of three Confederate memorials that pay homage to the Confederate navy. The message on the back of this postcard reads, "this is a right pretty place, there is something new to see all the time." (Courtesy of author's collection.)

ON THE FRONT COVER: This image is of High Street as it appeared in the early 1900s, with horse-drawn wagons delivering and picking up goods from merchants such as A.C. Friedlin Wholesale Grocer (left). Portsmouth Street Railway's electric streetcars can be seen near the corner of High and Middle Streets. (Courtesy of author's collection.)

ON THE BACK COVER: This early postcard shows the Norfolk County Courthouse, located at the county seat in Portsmouth. After the city became incorporated in 1858, the courtrooms were divided between the city of Portsmouth and the county. This structure has been restored and is used by the Department of Museums as a gallery hosting various exhibits. (Courtesy of author's collection.)

POSTCARD HISTORY SERIES

Portsmouth

Keith and Pam Atkins

ARCADIA PUBLISHING

ISBN 978-0-7385-8234-4

Published by Arcadia Publishing
Charleston, South Carolina

Printed in the United States of America

Library of Congress Control Number: 2010940475

For all general information contact Arcadia Publishing at:
Telephone 843-853-2070
Fax 843-853-0044
E-mail sales@arcadiapublishing.com
For customer service and orders:
Toll-Free 1-888-313-2665

Visit us on the Internet at www.arcadiapublishing.com

We wish to dedicate this book to our parents, children, and grandchildren, who represent to us the past, present, and future in history.

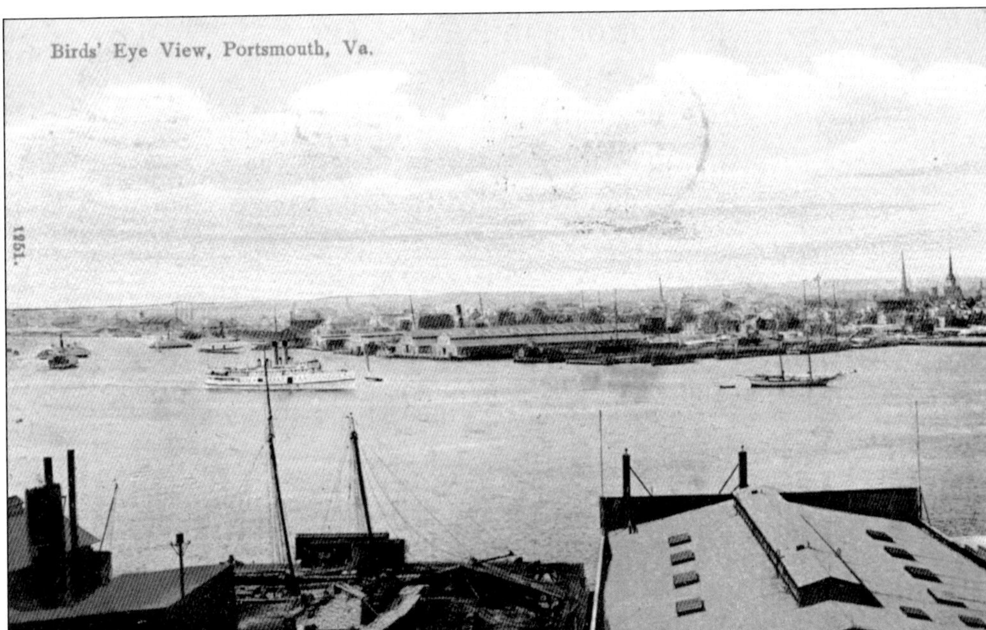

This is a bird's-eye view of the Portsmouth waterfront and skyline. The Norfolk Naval Shipyard can be seen on the left and the Seaboard Airline wharf and warehouses in the center. In the distance to the right are the steeples of Monumental Methodist Church and St. Paul's Catholic Church. (Courtesy of author's collection.)

Contents

Acknowledgments

We wish to recognize the endeavors of the individuals before us who spent countless hours sifting through various items and listening to stories from the citizens of Portsmouth; their intent was to provide a documented history of the city. No work related to the history of the city would be complete without Edward Pollock's *Sketchbook of Portsmouth* (1886), Richard C. Holcomb's *A Century with Norfolk Naval Hospital* (1930), or Marshall W. Butt's *Portsmouth under Four Flags* (1971), which were invaluable in noting the progress and events of the city through the years. *A Pictorial History of Portsmouth* (1975), by Robert W. Wentz Jr., and *Portsmouth—A Pictorial History* (1989), by Alf J. and Ramona H. Mapp, were essential for identifying locations depicted on the postcards. The daily accounts of life in the city provided by Mildred Holladay and Dean Burgess's *History of Portsmouth, Virginia* (2007) and Alan Flanders's *Bluejackets on the Elizabeth* (1998) provided insight into the relationship between the citizens and the military community since the founding of the city. Clay Shampoe and Thomas R. Garrett's *Baseball in Portsmouth, Virginia* (2004) and Dr. Robert Brooke Albertson's Images of America: *Portsmouth, Virginia* (2002) provided interesting snippets of local interest and events. We wish to acknowledge the past and present members of the Portsmouth History Commission, the Portsmouth Historical Association, and the African American Historical Society of Portsmouth for their efforts documenting and preserving the history of Portsmouth. We wish to thank the staff of the Wilson Memorial Room, especially Edie Carmichael, for providing assistance with our research in the library, and we also thank the Printing Center for their assistance in scanning the rare and fragile postcards in our collection. A special thank you to Al Cutchin, Dean Burgess, Ed Bottoms, and the friends and family members who allowed us to "pick their brains" for their knowledge of the city's past. Our heartfelt thanks to Jerome Johnson, without whose words of encouragement this book would not have been completed.

Unless otherwise noted, all images appear courtesy of the authors' collection.

Introduction

Once home to the Chesapeake tribe, the land now known as Portsmouth was abundant with wild game, and the river that flowed along the shore provided an ample amount of fresh fish and shellfish. The tribe flourished here well into the early 18th century. In 1716, a land grant of 239 acres was deeded to Col. William Crawford, a member of the militia and a loyal subject of the British Crown. A planter and ship owner, Crawford saw the potential of the land's natural harbor, and in 1752, he set aside 65 acres of his land for a town and commissioned Gershom Nimmo to survey it. Crawford's plan was presented to the general assembly of Virginia, and an act approved the design and the name Portsmouth for the new town. Crawford envisioned his town prospering, and with the harbor, Portsmouth would become a major naval and commercial port.

As the years passed, a shipyard was built in Gosport on the southern side of town. Through the years, it would grow to become the nation's largest naval shipyard as well as its oldest dry dock. Dry Dock No. 1 was completed in 1833 and is still in operation today. The annals of Naval history are full of the accomplishments of the working citizens of the shipyard. In 1862, workers built the nation's first ironclad warship, the CSS *Virginia*, which was originally the USS *Merrimac*. The first steel-hulled cruiser, the USS *Raleigh*, and the first steel-hulled battleship, the USS *Texas*, would be launched at the shipyard 30 years later. From 1920 to 1922, the USS *Jupiter* would be converted and commissioned as the USS *Langley*, the first aircraft carrier.

Construction of the Naval hospital began in 1827 and was completed in 1830. The hospital grew in size during World War I and again during World War II, but the major expansions of the facility took place in the 1950s and the 1990s and give it the distinction of being the oldest and largest naval medical center in the United States.

The nation's first lightship was anchored off Craney Island in 1820, and the officer in charge of the vessel was Capt. William Tee, who remained in command until 1859, when the lightship was replaced with a screwpile lighthouse. Portsmouth was the headquarters for the Sixth Life Saving District and the Fifth Lighthouse Service District from the 1870s and maintained a boat and buoy depot on the downtown waterfront. The Coast Guard, as it is known today, served in both world wars as part of the Navy; after World War II, the command in Portsmouth was named the Fifth Coast Guard District. After 100 years of service at its location on the Elizabeth River (adjacent to the Norfolk Naval shipyard) and under the command of the US Lighthouse Service and the US Revenue Cutter Service, the Fifth Coast Guard District moved to its new base of operations at Craney Island, where it all began.

Even during Colonel Crawford's lifetime, the city had become a major port. The coming of the railroads in the 1800s brought an increase of cargo to be loaded onto the ships, which were destined to sail to ports along the Atlantic coast and abroad. The coordinated plan of "where rail meets sail" became a reality in 1967, when the world's first completely planned container cargo port at Portsmouth Marine Terminals began operations at Pinners Point. The size of the facility has grown, and the APM Terminal is now in operation at West Norfolk. Recently, new rail lines have been laid to handle the flow of containerized and bulk cargo in and out of the city.

A city with so much commercial and military activity must have a brisk social life. Walking the streets of the many communities within Portsmouth, one can sometimes feel the presence of those who once called the city home. The city has always been, and remains today, a gracious host, offering hospitality to visitors. Through the years, many US presidents visited the charming city, including Andrew Jackson, Martin Van Buren, John Tyler, James K. Polk, Millard Fillmore, James Buchanan, Theodore Roosevelt, Franklin D. Roosevelt, and Harry S. Truman. There are plenty of celebrities and sports personalities whose hometown is Portsmouth. Whether singing, composing music, playing an instrument, making a hole in one, swinging a bat, making a basket, or scoring a touchdown, many of this country's best started out in Portsmouth. Opera singer Matilda Sissieretta Joyner Jones probably started her career singing in church. William "Bill" Deal of beach music fame could be heard practicing piano above Slim's Restaurant in his younger days. Golf legend J. Chandler Harper wouldn't admit that he lost to a "lefty" in his early days. Ruth Weston Brown had people dancing to her rhythm-and-blues hits of the 1950s. David Carr Glover had kids parading around the house to his arrangement "Mickey Mouse March." Charles "Mule" Peete dreamed of playing baseball, and he did play—for the Portsmouth Merrimacs and the St. Louis Cardinals. Tommy Newsome got his start in Cradock and made it all the way to the *Tonight Show* with Johnny Carson. Clarence "Ace" Parker excelled in athletics at Wilson High School and Duke University before moving to the pros, playing football for the Brooklyn Dodgers and the New York Yankees before moving on to baseball with the Philadelphia Athletics. With so much rising talent, the list of Portsmouth notables grows longer each year.

The architectural beauty and charm of the city's neighborhoods and downtown district has mostly remained intact since the 19th century. Neighborhoods such as Park View, Truxton, Cradock, Port Norfolk, and Olde Towne offer a sort of time capsule of when homes were built with decorative gingerbread and millwork trim. If these homes could talk, they would provide a history of the citizens and events that have shaped Portsmouth through the years. Although overshadowed by our neighboring city, Norfolk, which saw its name placed on military installations within the city by the federal government in 1862 (the Union had a Portsmouth Navy Yard and Hospital in Maine and New Hampshire), adding confusion for visitors, Portsmouth grew. However, the design of the city as Colonel Crawford had it laid out in 1752 was primarily retained. So you are invited and welcomed, with greetings from Portsmouth—the hidden jewel of history in Virginia.

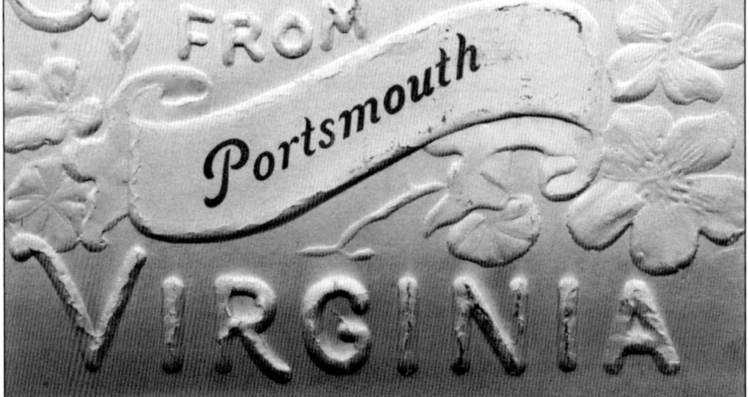

This embossed card, postmarked 1911, offers salutations from Portsmouth, Virginia. The sender writes, "We are having some beautiful weather here. I am having a dandy time. Today is a real sweet day."

One

Greetings and Welcome to Portsmouth

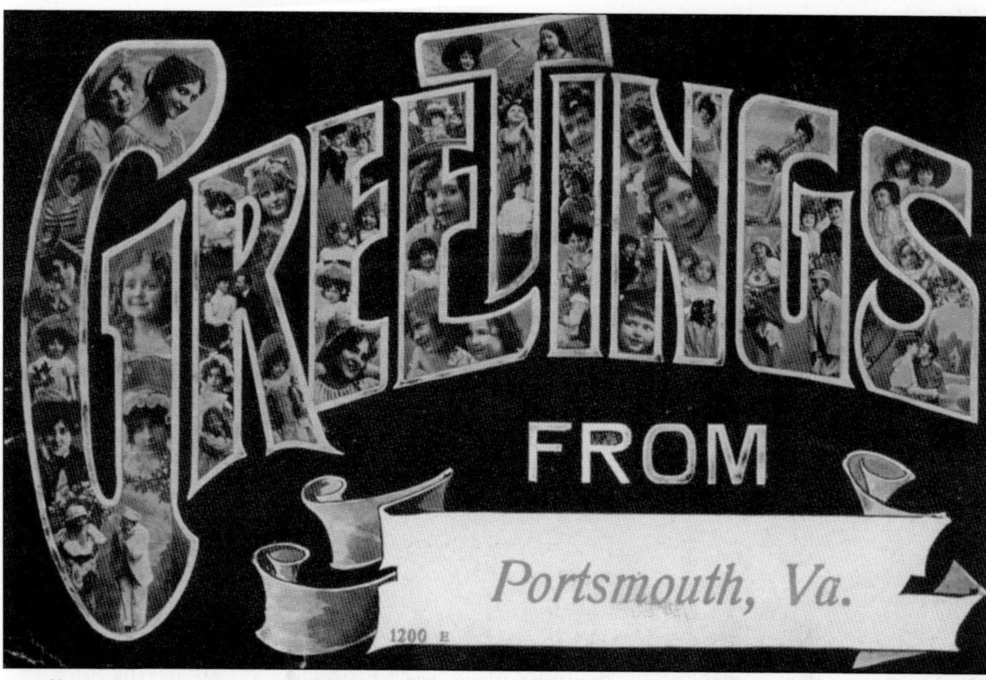

A collage-design postcard could be ordered by merchants and stationery shops with the name of the city and state preprinted on the front. Visitors would buy these cards to send to friends and family, advising them that they had arrived and where they were staying. In 1909, the sender of this card writes, "had a very pleasant trip down, will let you know about my boardinghouse later."

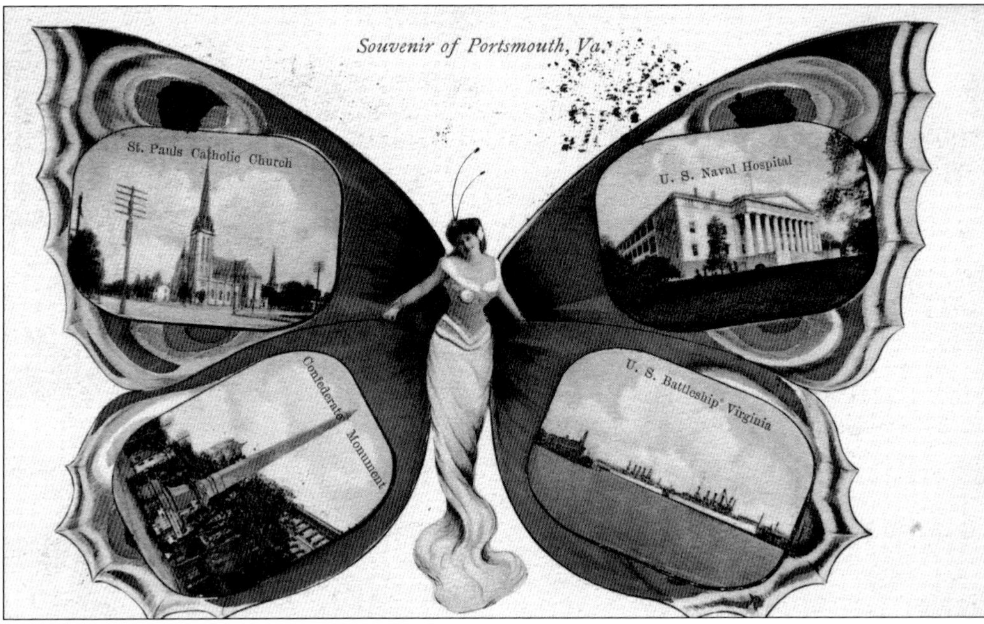

This is a "Souvenir of Portsmouth, VA" postcard, printed during the Jamestown Exposition Celebration of 1907. This very popular butterfly design depicted scenes around the city that were visited by tourists during the celebration. The visitors of 1907, as today, would be awestruck by the number of Naval and commercial vessels navigating the Elizabeth River.

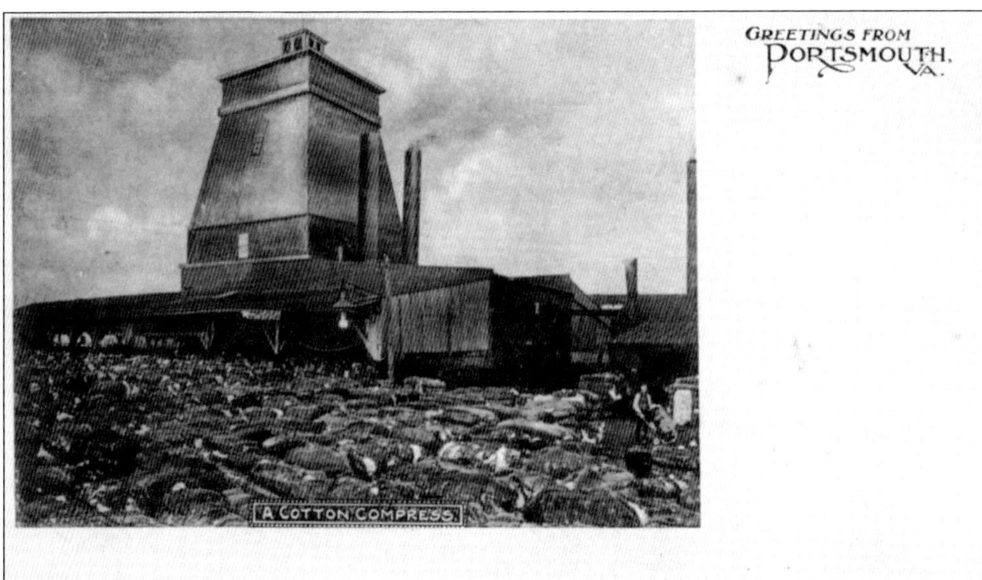

During the early 1900s, it was said that Portsmouth was the largest exporter of cotton along the Atlantic Coast. Cotton was compressed and stored for shipment at Heath and Smith, which was located on Water Street near the Seaboard Airline wharves. In 1915, a major industry within the city was the Portsmouth Cotton Oil Refinery, which produced oil from raw cottonseed.

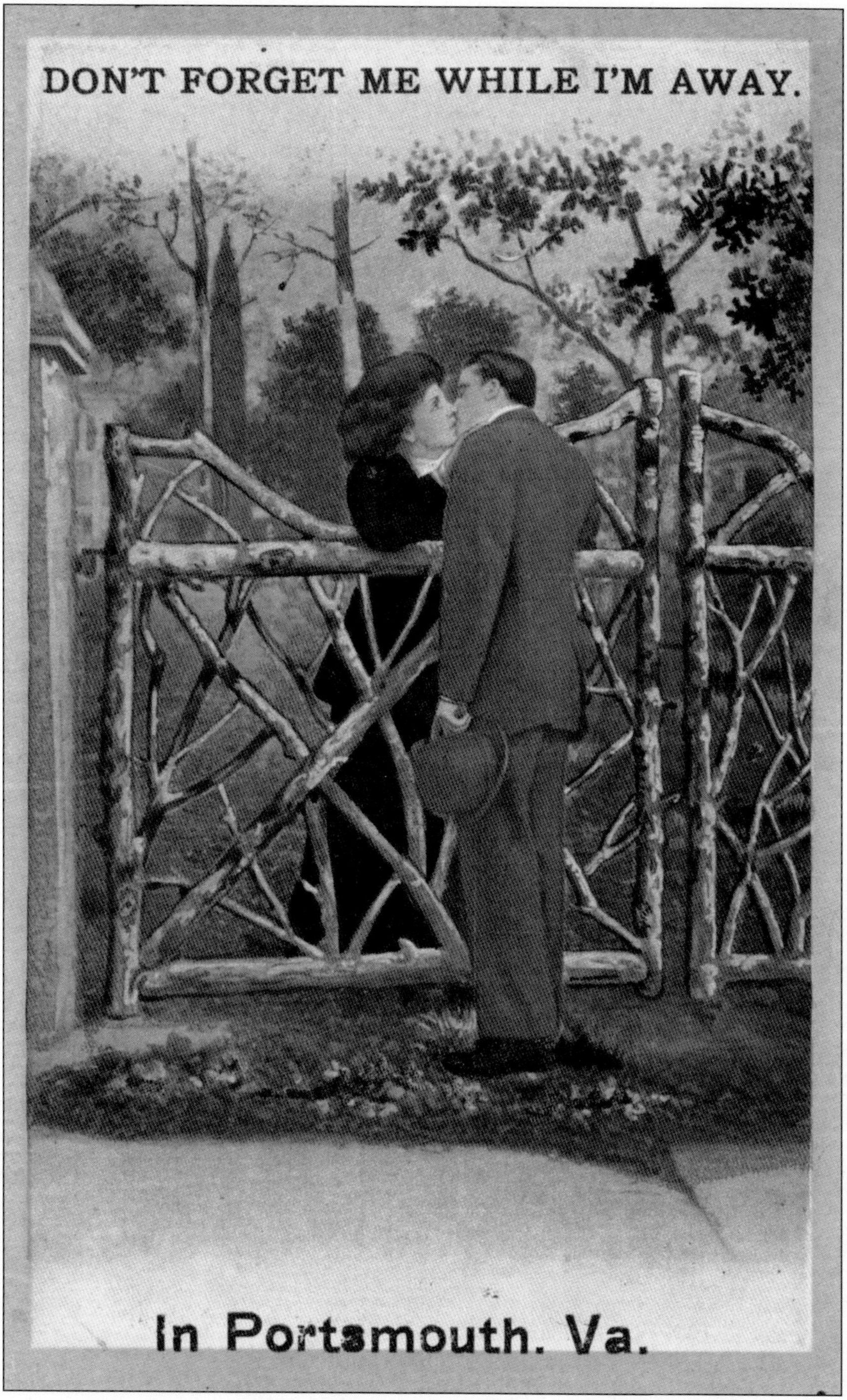

Greeting and romantic postcards with the locale printed on the front were often used by the sender in the early 1900s to boast of where they were moving or visiting. This card is not postmarked, but the sender possibly sent it in January 1918, when a severe snowstorm blanketed Portsmouth. Even the Elizabeth River was frozen solid. On the back was written, "We are completely snowed under."

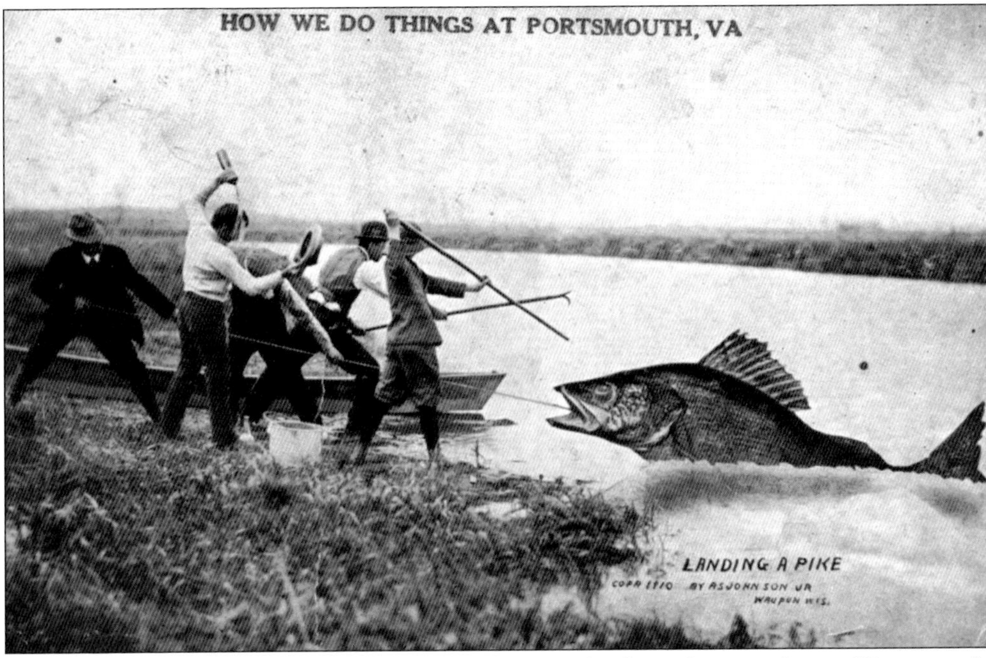

The fishing and seafood industry has always been a staple along the waterfront of Portsmouth. Fresh fish, crabs, and oysters were brought in daily to the piers that lined Scott's Creek, Pinners Point, West Norfolk, and Port Norfolk. This example of an "exaggeration" postcard does not give the location of this "secret fishing hole."

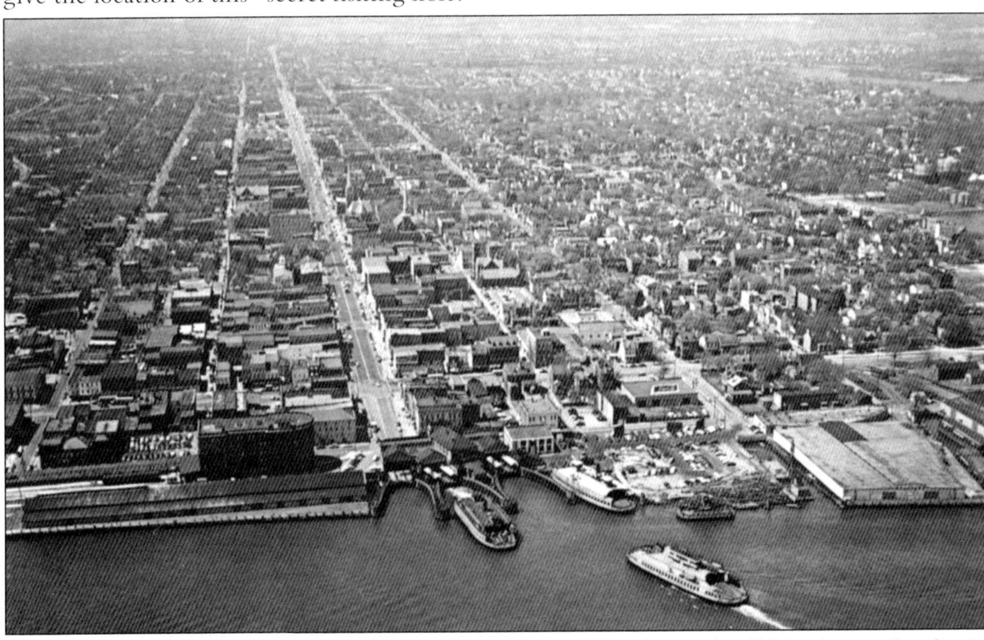

This aerial view of the city along the Elizabeth River in the early 1950s shows the ferries running between Portsmouth, Norfolk, and Berkley. The Seaboard Airline Railroad was still in operation at this time, as noted by the train on the tracks behind the terminal building next to the ferry landing. The docks (pictured on the right side) were busy unloading and loading freight, and High Street was bustling with shoppers on a typical weekday.

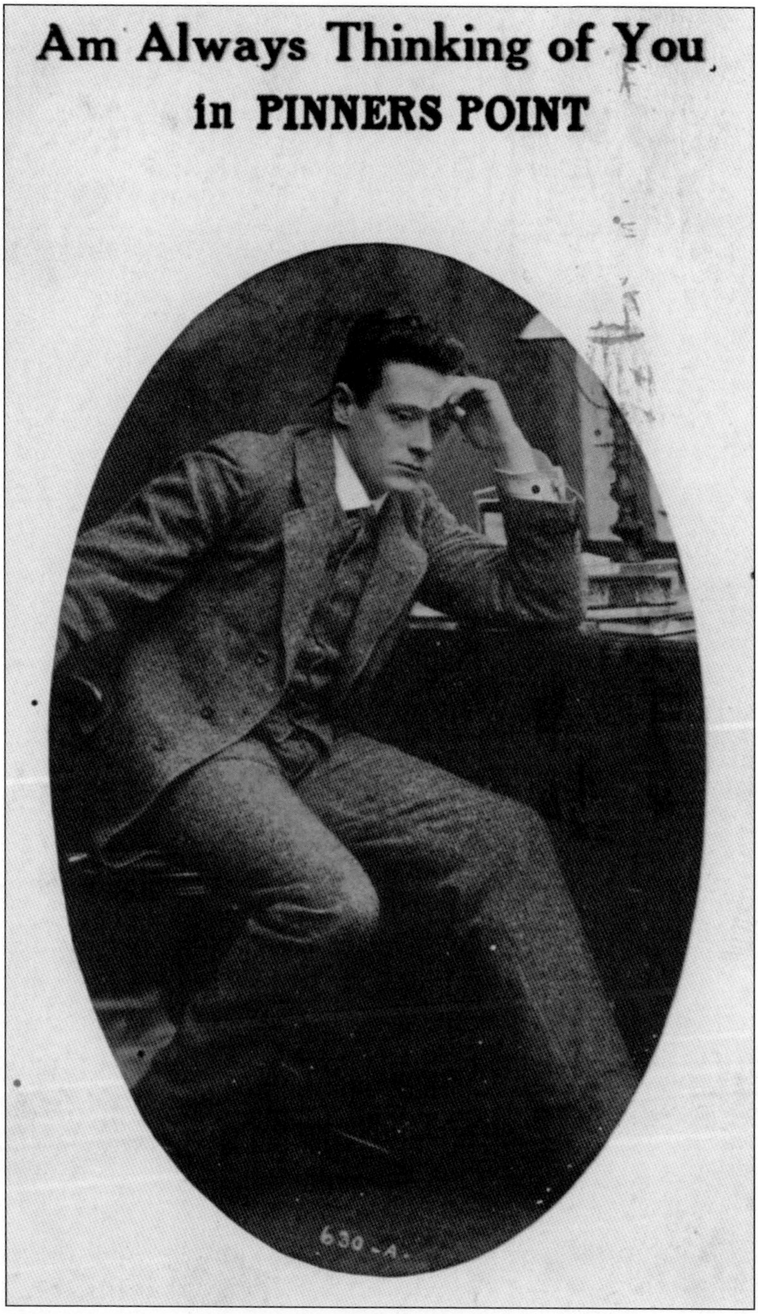

Since the late 1800s, Pinners Point has been the center for rail and ship cargo in the city. The flow of freight brought in by train and car barges was easily transferred to waiting steamers and freighters for shipment to ports along the East Coast and overseas. Through the years, the cargo and port facility has modernized and grown in size. All that remains from the earlier days is Sugar Hill, a small African American community where stevedores, who handled the loading and unloading of cargo, once lived. The sender of this card, postmarked in 1914 and sent to a female friend in Norfolk, reads, "Hello, worried how are you today, there you are enjoying life. I am feeling very lonely and alone."

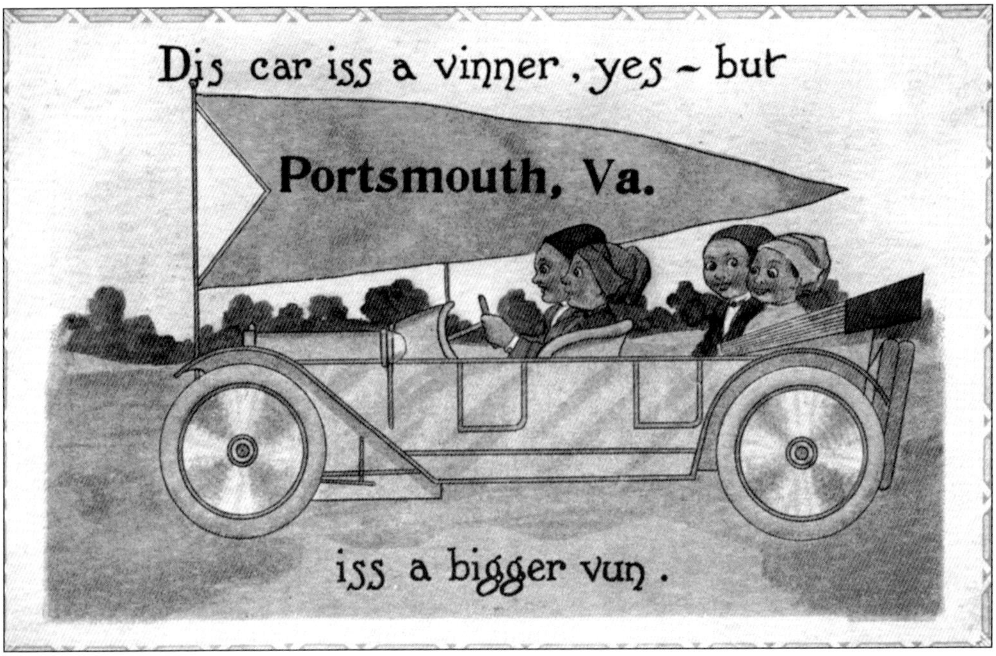

In the early 1900s, most people did not own cars, and so they traveled by train or boat. At each depot and office, there was always an array of postcards they could quickly purchase, writing a brief message to send before they boarded another train or boat. The sender of this card must have disembarked from a steamship and gone directly to the Seaboard Airline Railroad ticket office, because she writes, "Arrived here in time to get the train this morning."

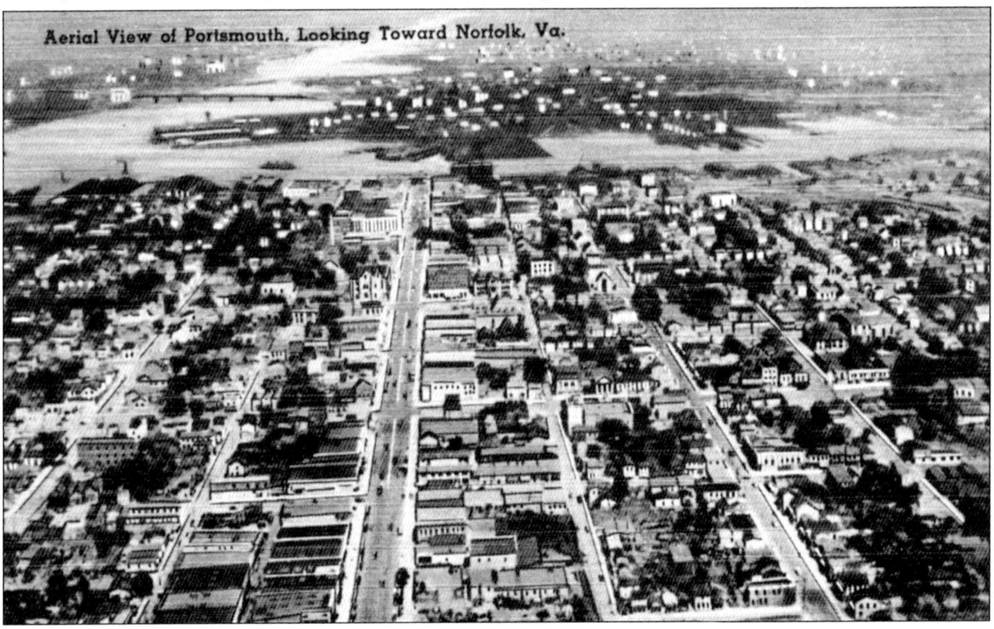

This early aerial view of downtown Portsmouth shows most of the residential section known as the Southside (Newtown), which is located near the Norfolk Naval Shipyard in Portsmouth. During this time, there were still a number of private residences along High Street, shown near the bottom of this postcard.

Two

Let's Go Downtown

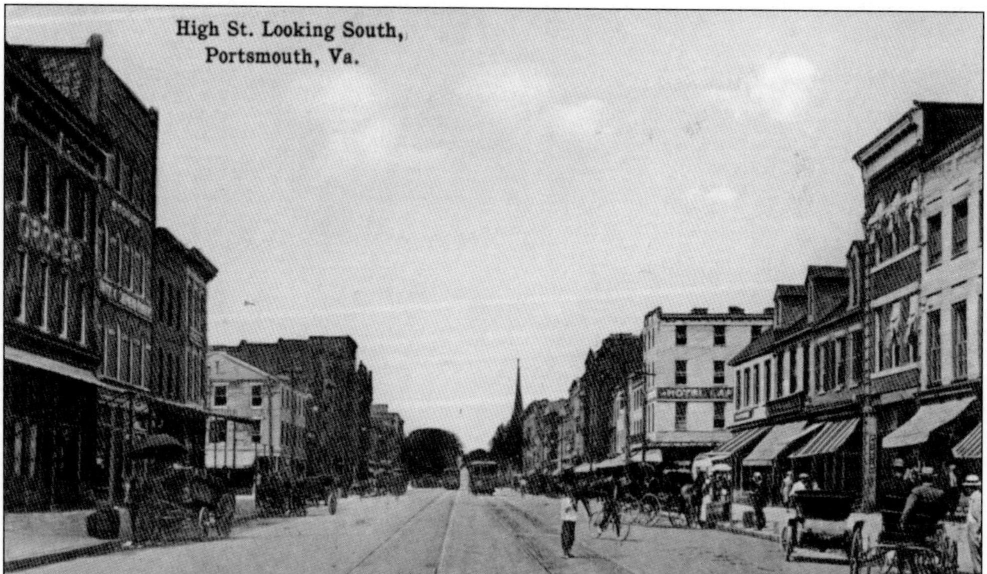

An early-1900s view of the stores along High Street shows the Western Union telegraph office, Wise Cigar and News Company, the Beacon Restaurant, Hanger Drug Company, and the Hotel Lafayette on the right side of the street. The single car parked at the curb most likely belonged to Dr. George Carr, a resident who introduced the first automobile to the city. On the left side of the street, the wagons being loaded are in front of A.C. Friedlin Wholesale Grocer and the Portsmouth Storage Company.

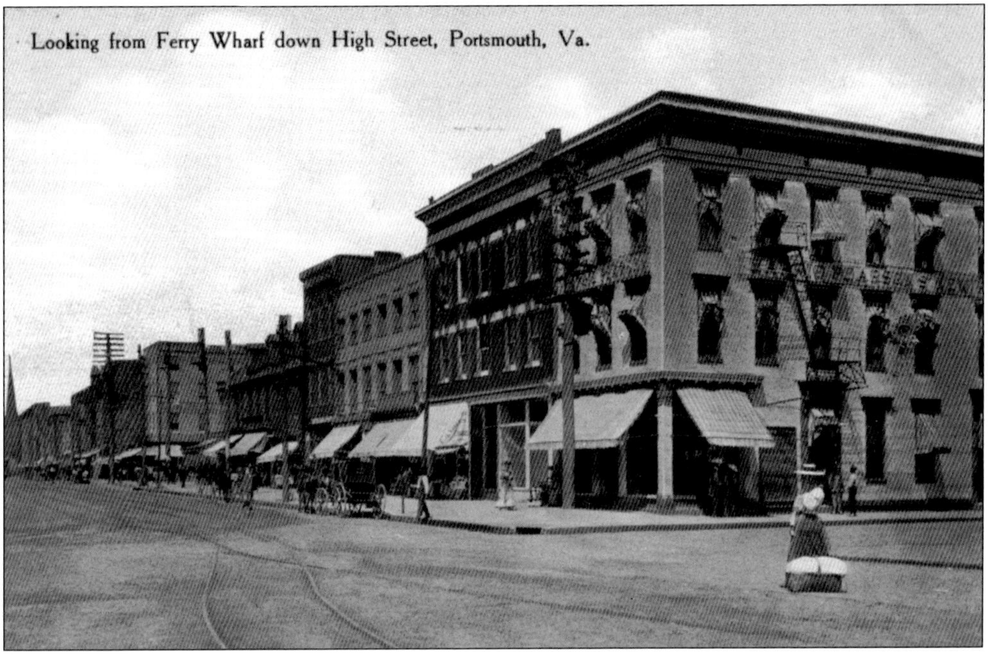

A woman, who has apparently come across the Elizabeth River on the ferry, stands at the intersection of High and Water Streets. Pearson's Hotel, the offices for the *Daily Record*, and William A. Fiske Printing Company are to her right.

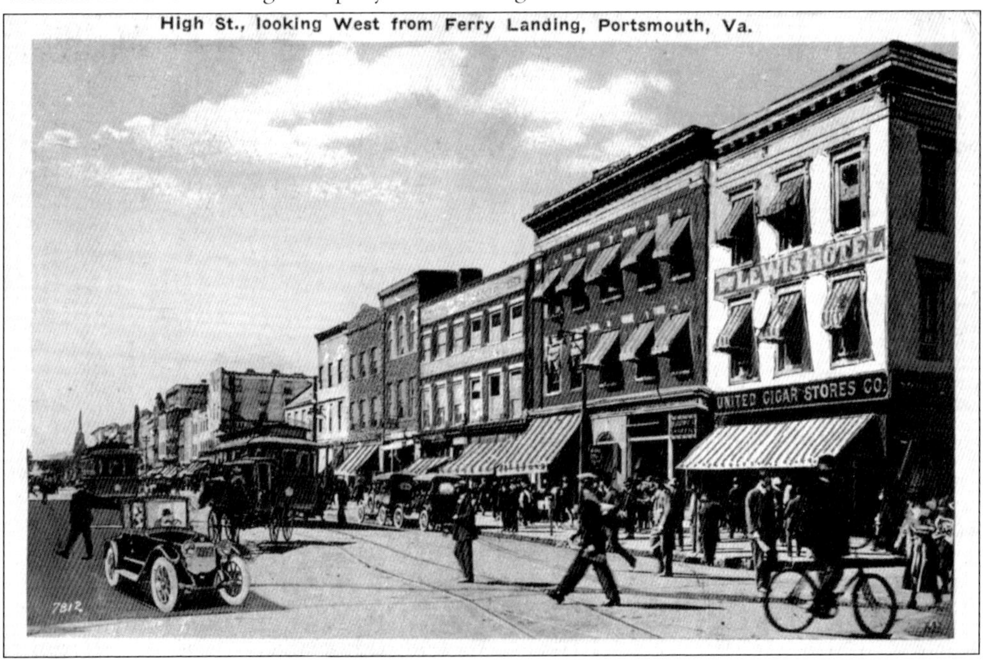

People are hurrying along High Street to avoid the horse-drawn wagons, electric streetcars, and bicycles in this scene from 1916. The Lewis Hotel and United Cigar Store were in business where Pearson's Hotel had been in earlier days. Whenever possible, photographers would take a picture with a sailor in the frame, like the one in the center, because then sailors would buy the postcards to send home.

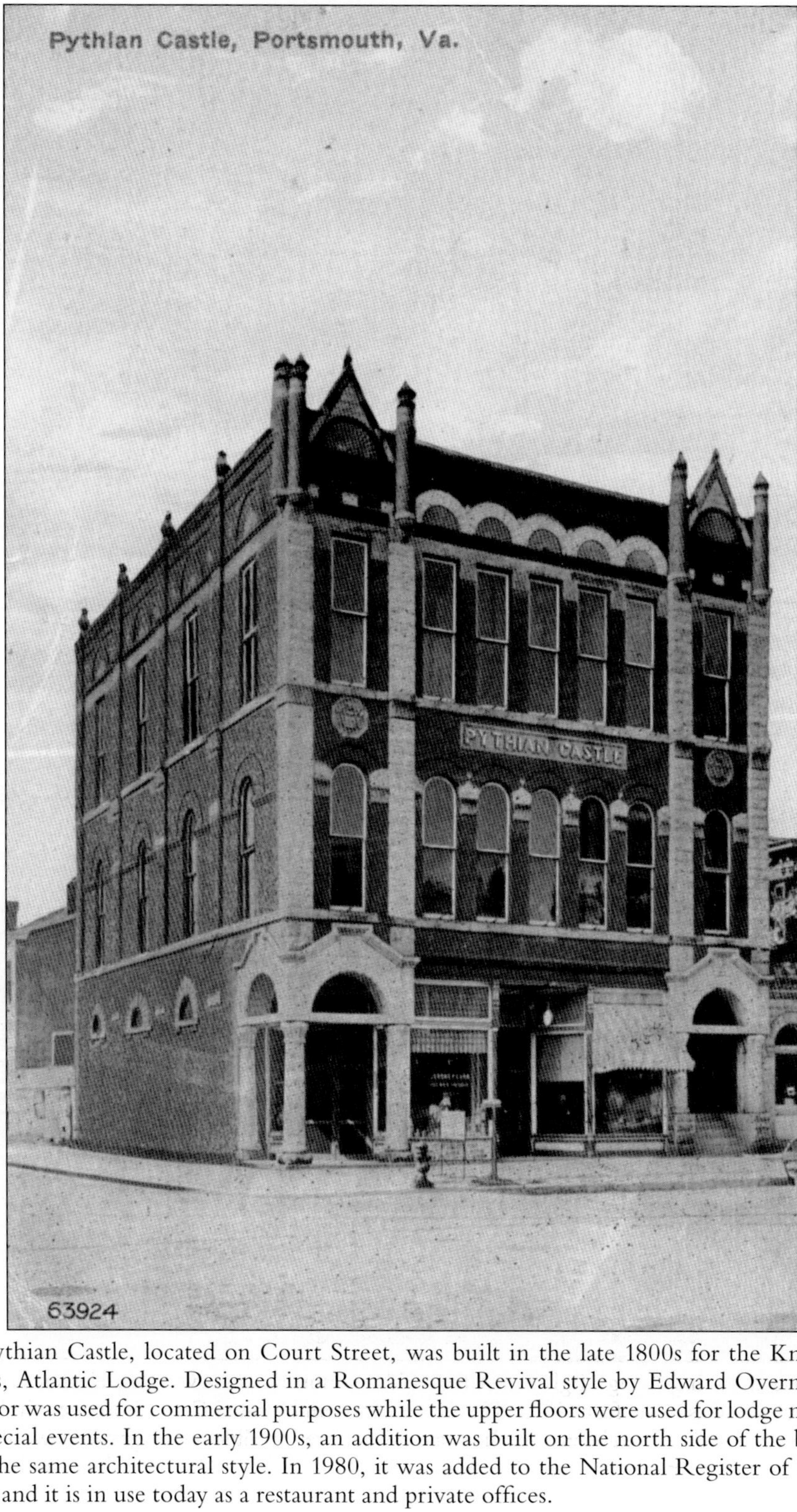

The Pythian Castle, located on Court Street, was built in the late 1800s for the Knights of Pythias, Atlantic Lodge. Designed in a Romanesque Revival style by Edward Overman, the first floor was used for commercial purposes while the upper floors were used for lodge meetings and special events. In the early 1900s, an addition was built on the north side of the building using the same architectural style. In 1980, it was added to the National Register of Historic Places, and it is in use today as a restaurant and private offices.

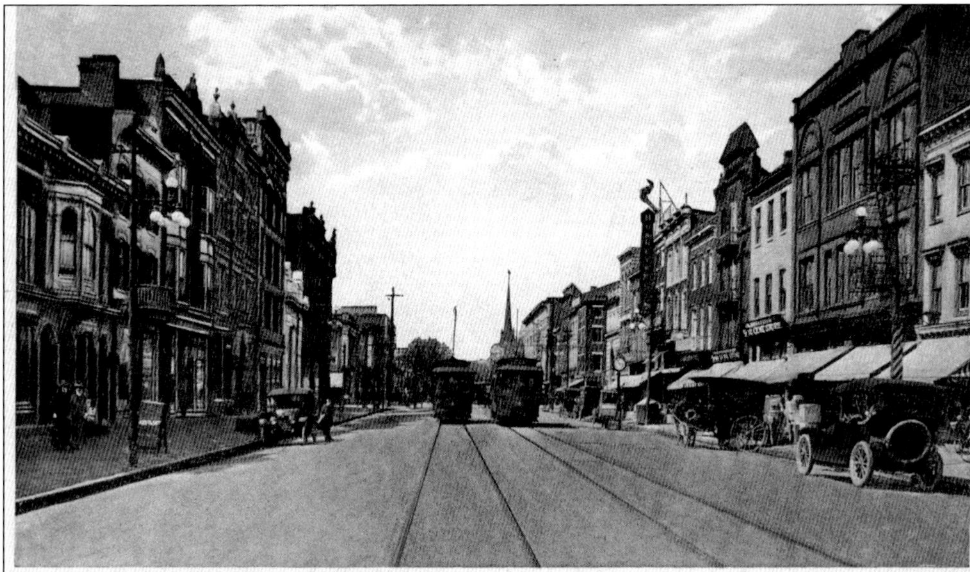

HIGH STREET, LOOKING WEST, PORTSMOUTH, VA.

The mailer of this card, sent in 1919, writes, "I am having a nice time down here and the weather is nice and quite warm." The author may have enjoyed shopping at Hofheimer's Shoe Store or F.W. Woolworth's Department Store or selected a variety of teas from the C.D. Kenny Tea Company. While strolling and looking in the shop windows, the sender could have admired the latest furniture designs at M.M. Crockin Furniture Company.

103:-HIGH STREET LOOKING EAST, PORTSMOUTH, VA.

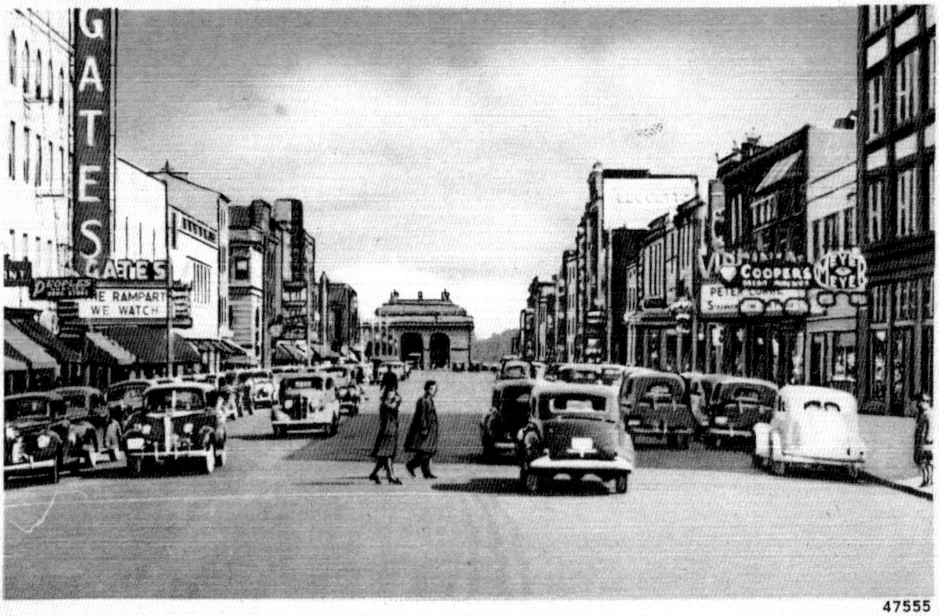

47555

During 1940, the citizens of Portsmouth were keeping their attention on the war in Europe, while the Norfolk Navy Yard was preparing for the possible arrival of damaged British warships. In that year, the Gates Theatre was showing *The Ramparts We Watch*, a World War I drama, while across the street at the Virginia Theatre, audiences could see *Stranger on the Third Floor*, a suspense-thriller starring Peter Lorre.

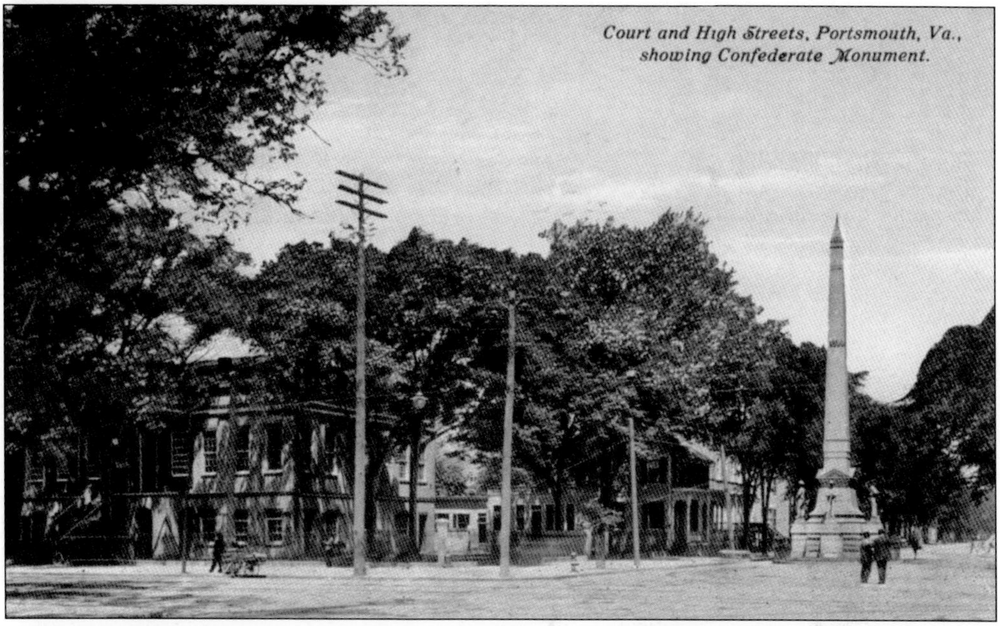

This card offers a pleasant view of the Confederate Monument and the 1846 Portsmouth Courthouse. The house located behind the courthouse was the residence of Col. James Langhorne, who served in the state senate for the district. At the corner fence post there is a cannon with the muzzle buried that is said to commemorate the Battle of Craney Island in the War of 1812.

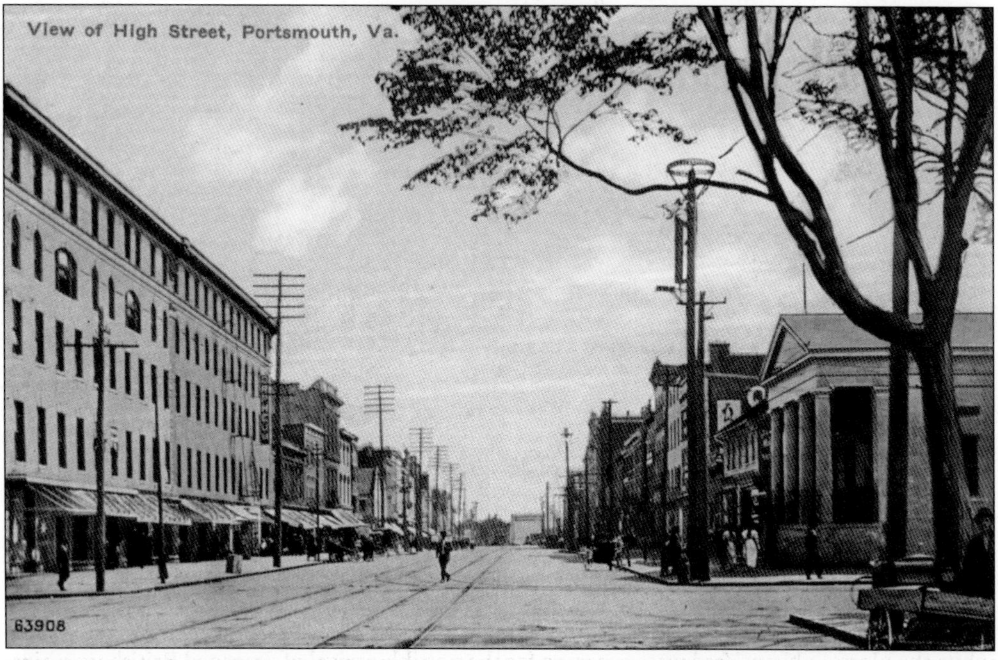

This is a scene from 1910, with the Ocean House Hotel to the left. The hotel was host to Pres. Franklin Pierce and Pres. John Tyler during their terms in office. The Greco-Roman-style building to the right is the post office, and next to it is the Portsmouth Tavern, which was razed in 1911 to accommodate the construction of the New Kirn Building.

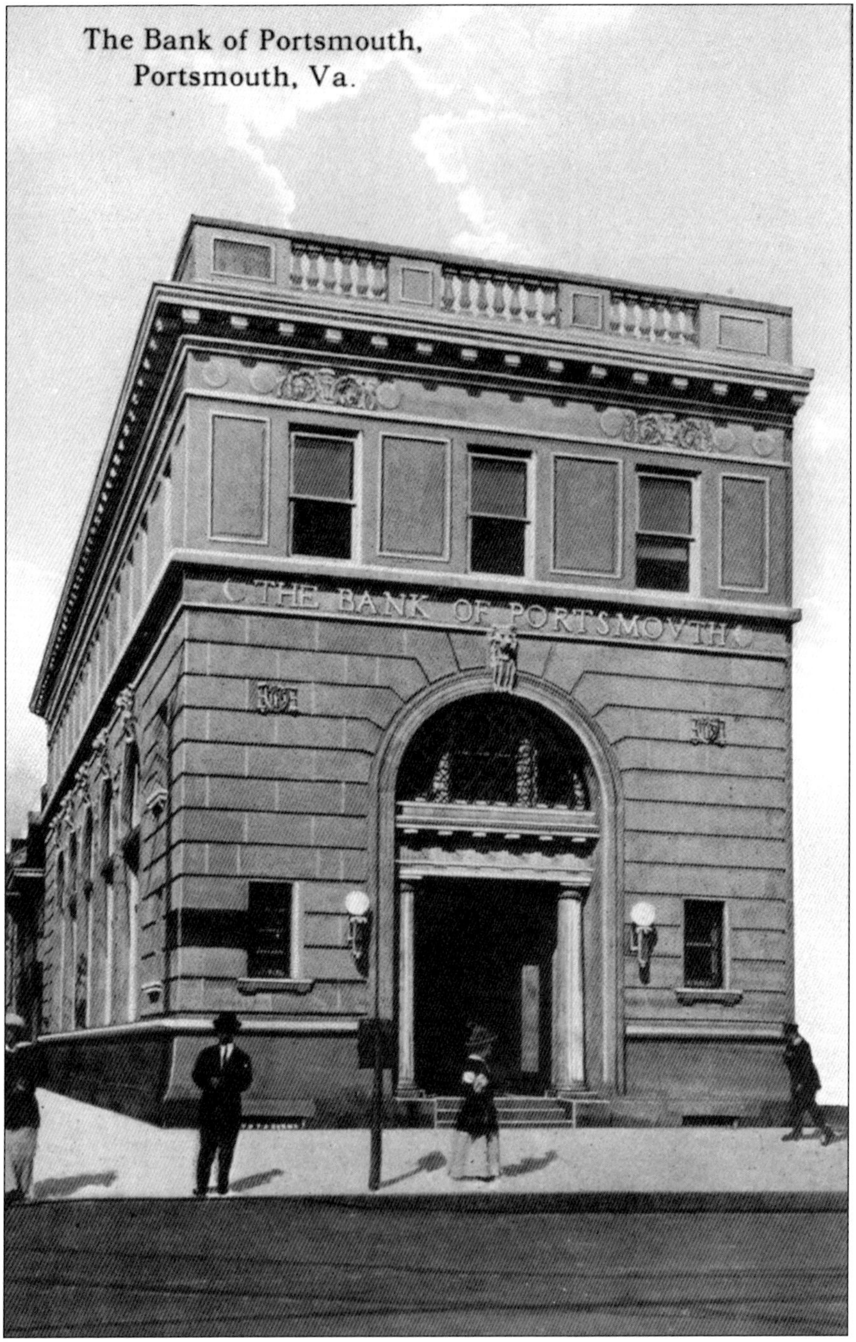

The Bank of Portsmouth was established at 205 High Street in 1867 by L.R. Watts and remained at that location until the early 1900s, when it relocated to its new building at the corner of High and Middle Streets. In June 1919, the Bank of Portsmouth merged with American National Bank, which was organized and instituted by a 27-year-old resident of the city named Frank D. Lawrence. The building remained at its location until it was razed in the early 1970s. One of the original lion's head pediments was placed in the Memorial Arch at the Marquis de Lafayette Park on Crawford Street.

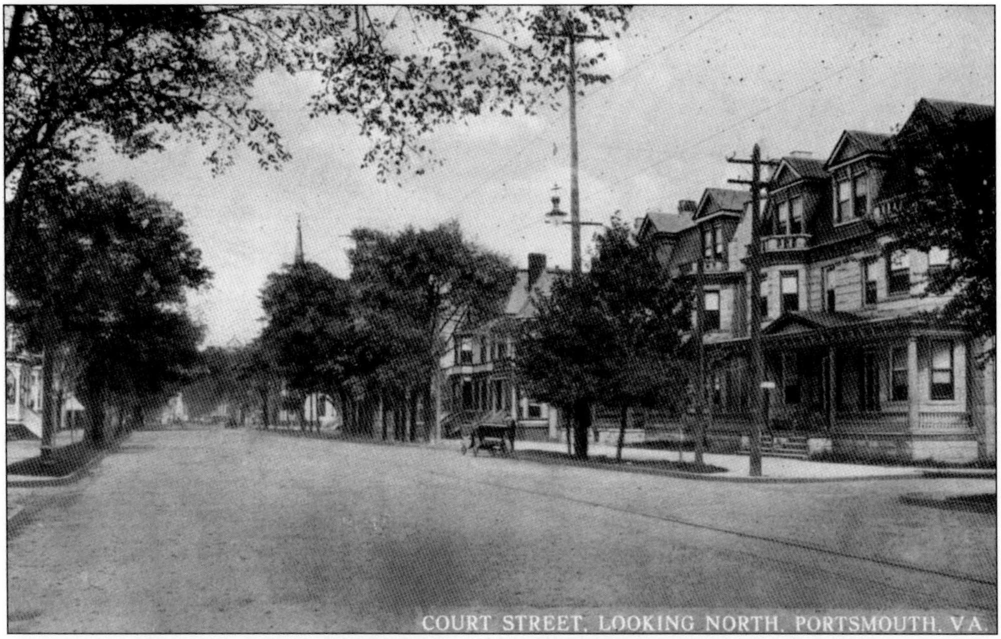

This quaint residential scene depicting Court Street on the Southside in 1913 looks north towards High Street. The steeple above the trees is that of First Presbyterian Church, located at the corner of Court and King Streets. The homes were razed in the late 1940s to make way for the construction of the Downtown Tunnel.

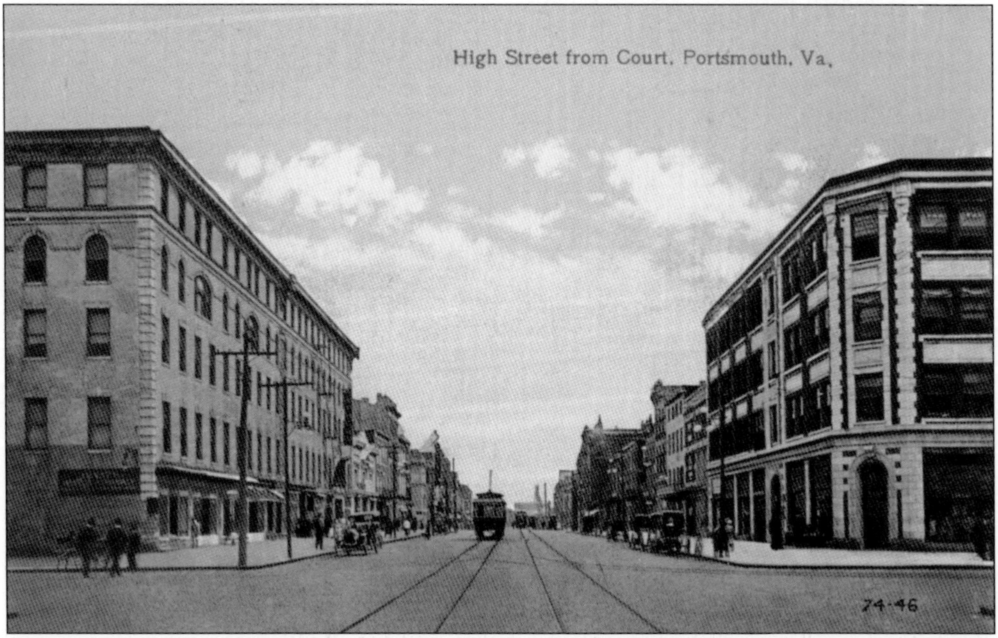

This pre-1914 view of High Street looks eastward, with the Ocean House Hotel and Orpheum Theatre on the left. Trant's Pharmacy was one of the many shops that occupied the first floor of the hotel. The New Kirn Building, to the right, was completed in 1911 and provided shops on the ground floor and offices for doctors, lawyers, and other professions on its higher floors. The building is still in use.

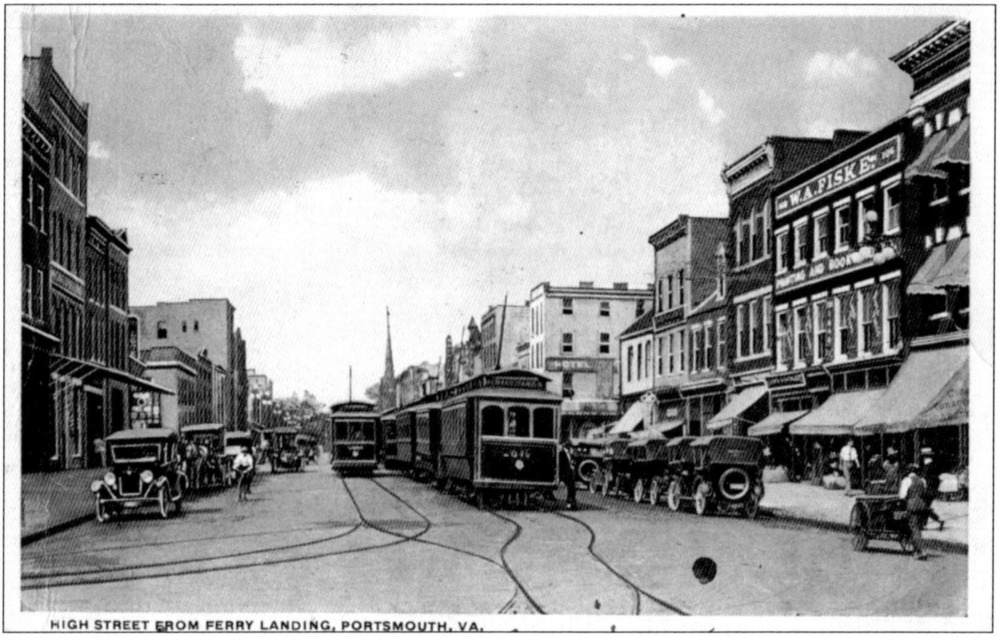

A busy scene of High Street in 1918 illustrates the growth the city was experiencing from the Norfolk Naval Shipyard's increased workforce. The sign on the front of the streetcar designates the destination as the "Navy Yard." The sender might have been a sailor or marine preparing to ship out, as the message states, "I leave tomorrow for somewhere, but where it is, I don't know."

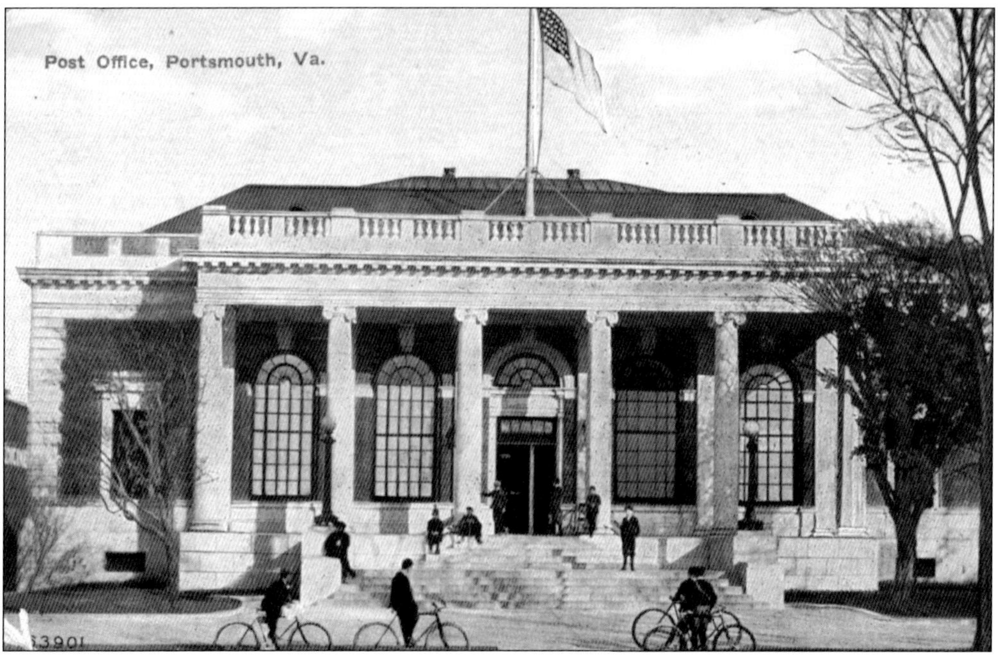

In 1908, the newly constructed post office opened to the public at the corner of Court and King Streets. It remained in service at this location until the completion and opening of the new federal building in 1961. In 1963, the city opened a publicly managed library at this location. Mail carriers, like the two at the bottom of this picture, often rode bicycles to deliver mail.

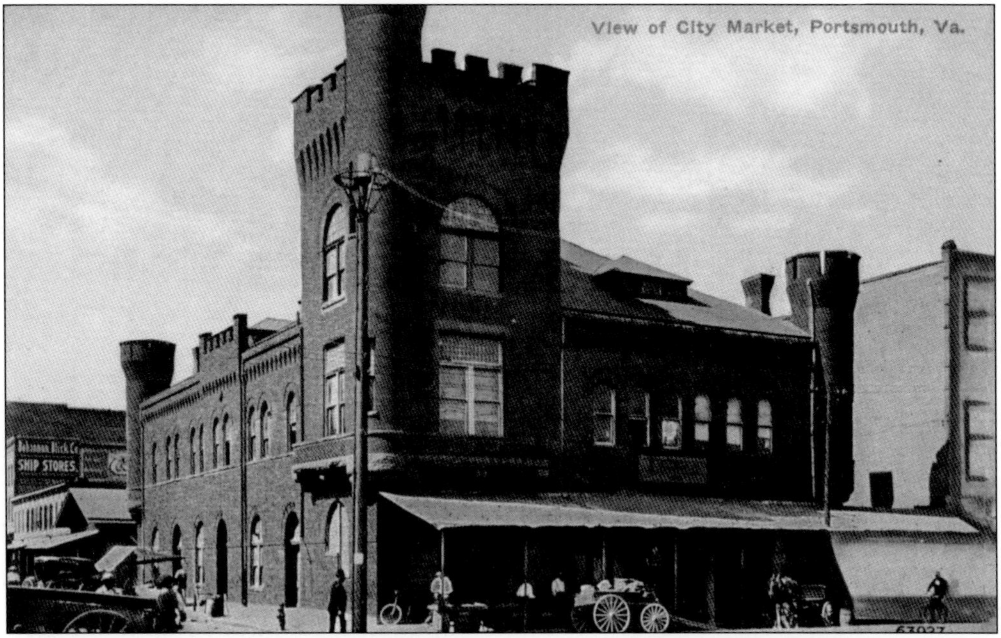

The City Market (originally named the Seaboard Market and Armory) was donated to the city in 1893 by the Seaboard Airline Railroad. It was located on Crawford Street between King and County Streets, where butchers sold a large variety of fresh meats and fowl. Hawkers would line the streets around the market selling fresh vegetables and goods from their wagons and carts. The African Americans pictured in the lower left were there either as laborers or sellers of seafood or produce.

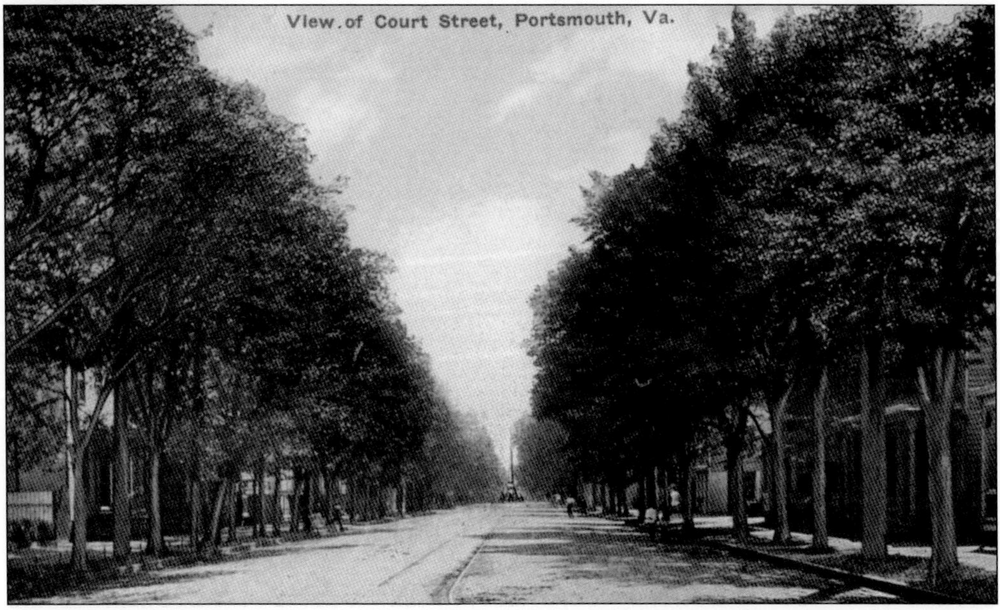

This picturesque view of Court Street shows the southern view from the Elizabeth River, looking towards High Street. The trees provided shade as well as a scenic view for commuters riding the streetcars back and forth to the Norfolk Naval Hospital and Park View. The Confederate Monument can be seen in the distance.

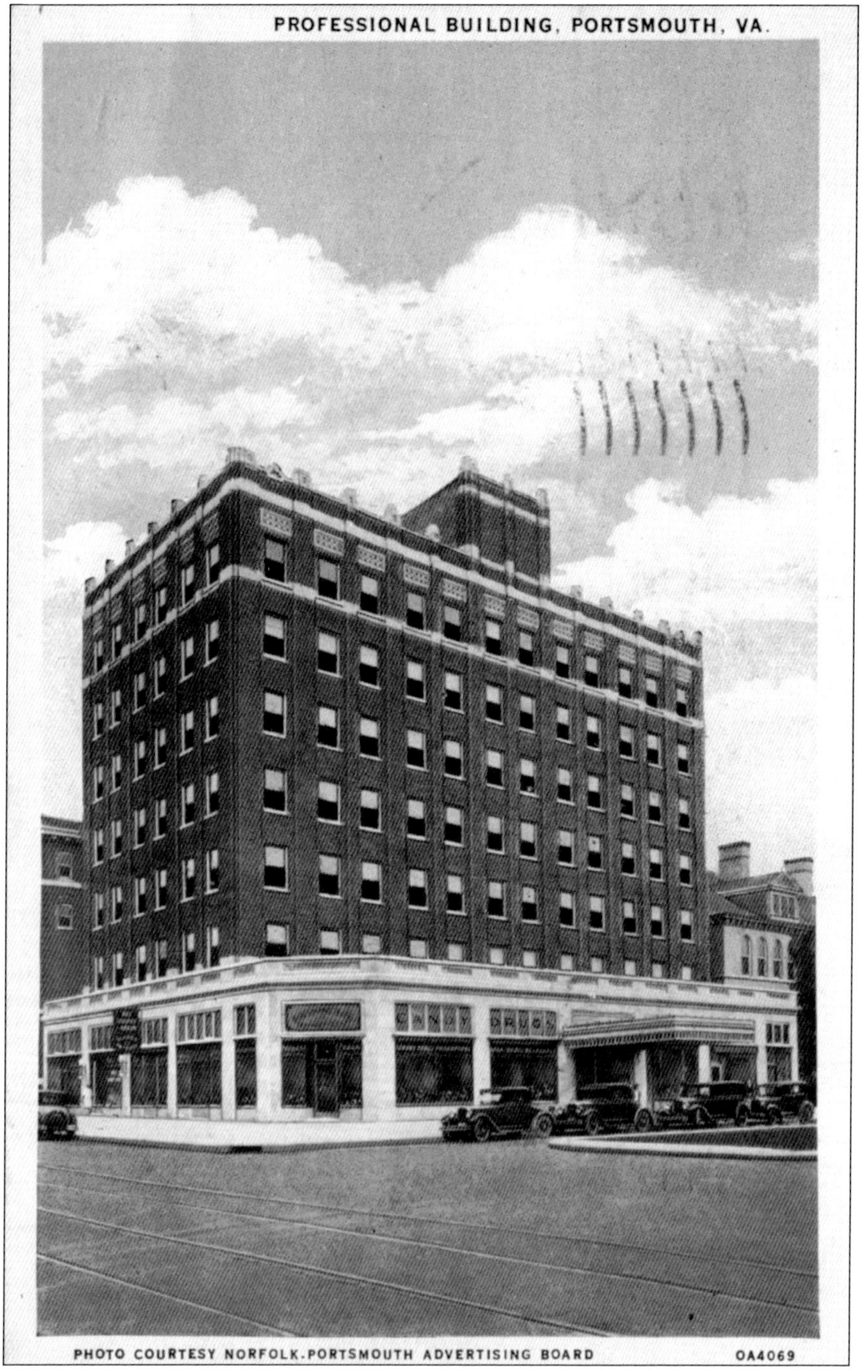

The Professional Building, located at the corner of Washington and High Streets, was completed in 1920. First floor occupants were the Washington Pharmacy, Cooper Optical Company, Model Barber Shop, and the Portsmouth Savings and Loan Company. The upper floors had offices for dentists, doctors, and other professions. The grassy median in front was asphalted at a later date, and the building remains in use today. Briggs School, located to the right of the building, was lost to a fire in the 1960s.

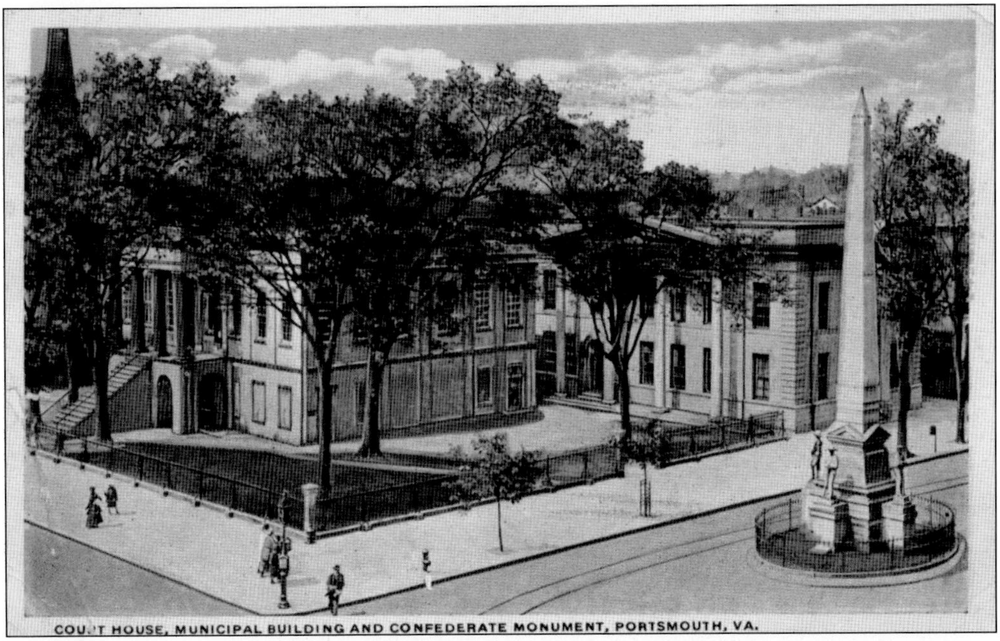

This scenic view includes the Confederate Monument, courthouse, and municipal building from the 1920s. The Municipal Building was constructed in 1912 and remained in use until the 1960s, when it was torn down. On the corner is one of the first stoplights in the city, installed in 1926. The sender wrote, "will let you know about chance to work here, there has been plenty so far."

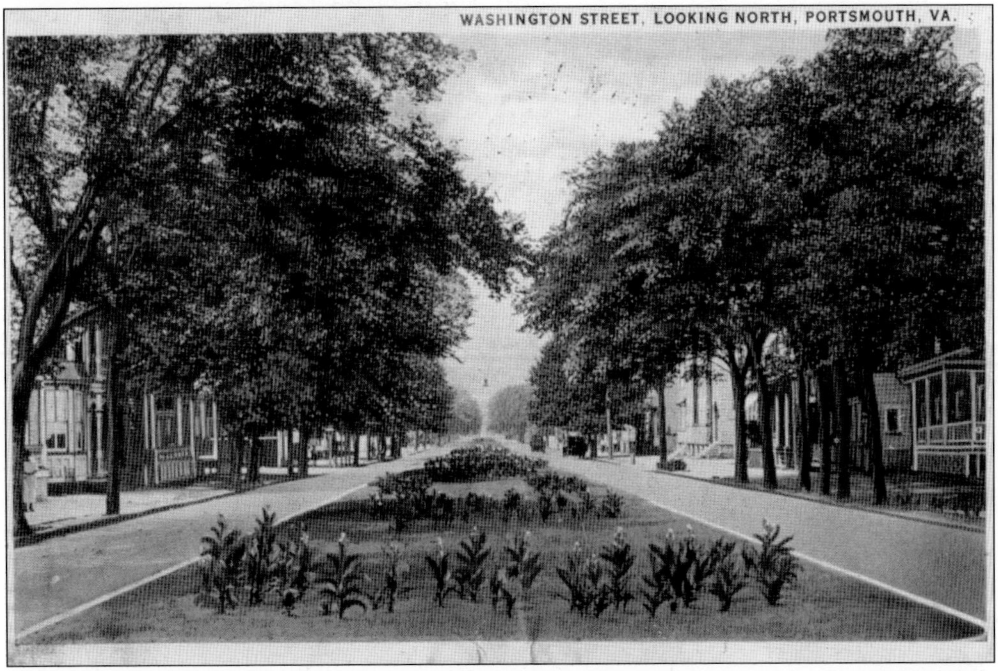

The tree-lined view of Washington Street in 1924, looking towards Swimming Point, looks very much as it does today. The grass-covered median, with calla lilies and ornamental plants, remains well tended by the residents in the historical Olde Towne district.

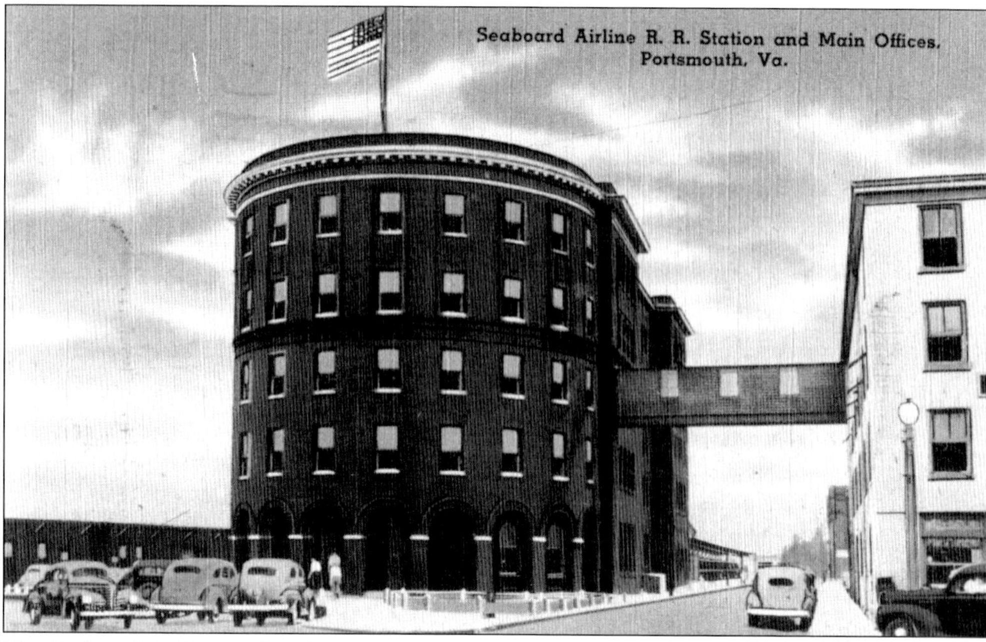

The Seaboard Airline Railroad Station and its main offices were built in 1894 but suffered a fire in 1906. During the restoration, an additional two stories were added to the structure. The enclosed overhead walkway connected it to the building across Water Street, which housed J. and E. Mahoney Liquor Dealers and later the offices and press of the city's newspaper, the *Portsmouth Star.*

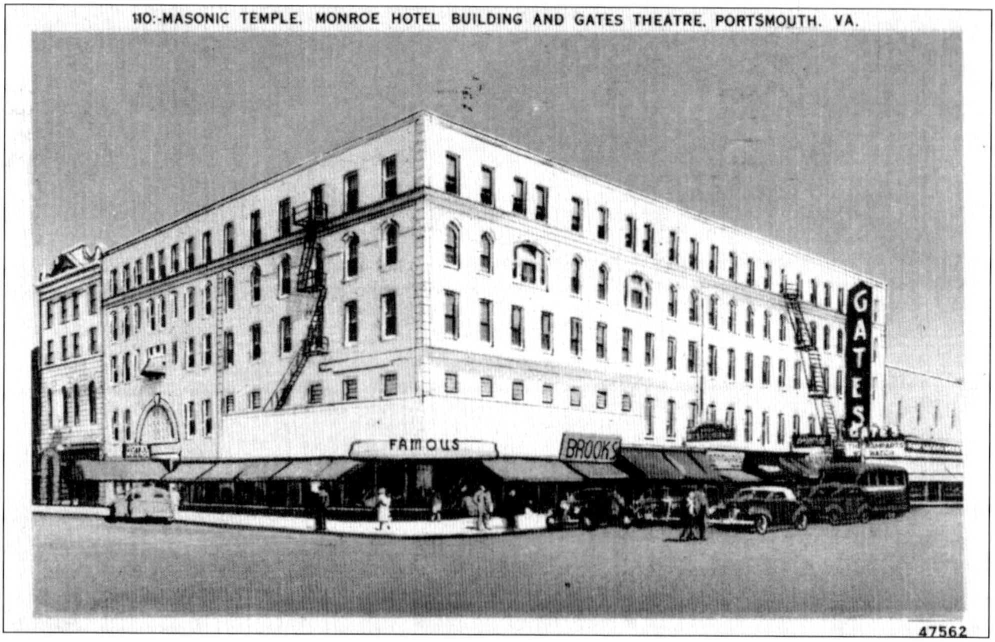

A city landmark was lost in 1957 when the Hotel Monroe (formerly the Ocean House) became engulfed in flames and reduced to rubble. The Famous, a store that had been on the first floor, was rebuilt on the location as a four-story women's apparel store and was acclaimed as "the South's foremost ladies' specialty shop." The sender writes, "We are having a grand time and have so many places to go."

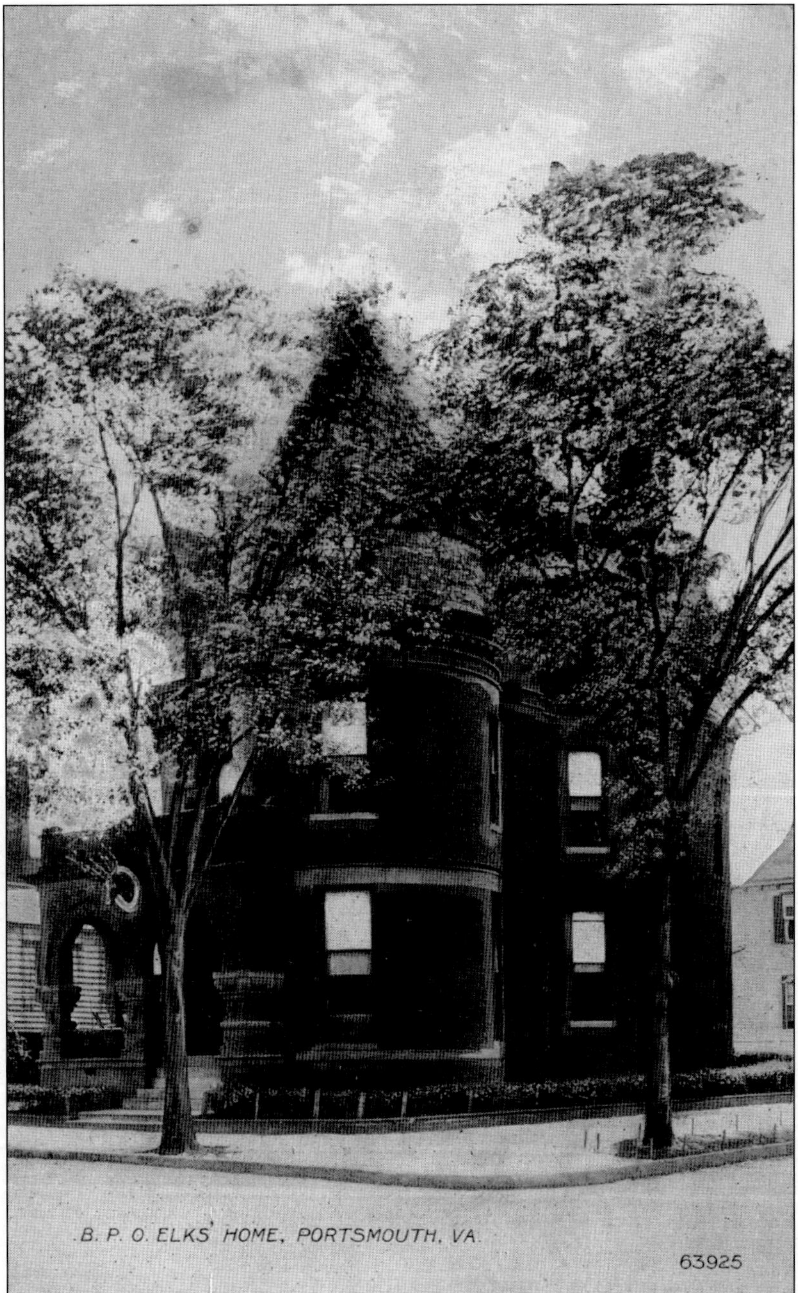

In1894, this Romanesque Revival residence was built by Beverly A. Armistead for his daughter Laura C. Armistead. It was converted into the Elks Home and Club in the early 1900s by the Benevolent and Protective Order of Elks (BPOE) Lodge No. 82. The addition of an auditorium on the North Street side of the building, with the Elks symbol between the arches, was host to various civic functions and holiday events. The silhouette of the building was used in the 1970s as that of "Madblood Manor," the castle of *Doctor Madblood*, a locally produced late-night horror show. The building's interior was remodeled into apartments in the 1970s, leaving the exterior intact, including the tile sidewalk with the Elks symbol embedded in concrete at the entrance.

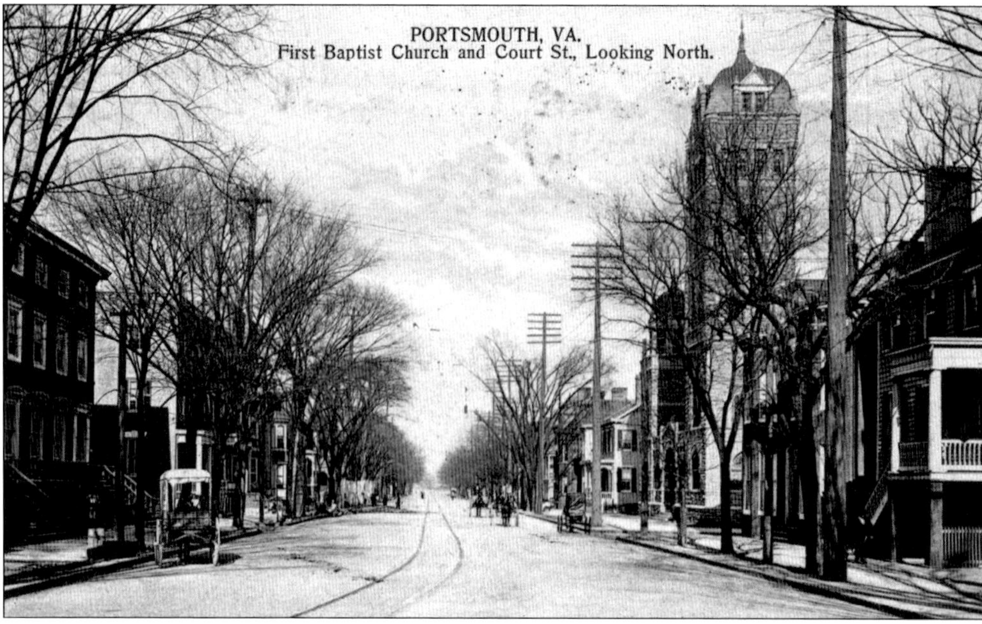

A view of Court Street in 1910, looking north towards Crawford Bay, misidentifies the structure as First Baptist Church. It is Court Street Baptist Church, which was the first Baptist church in the city. The first house on the left was built in 1859 for the daughters of William H. Wilson. Having survived the Civil War, it was used during World War I to house and entertain members of the military who were away from home. In later years, it was the Catholic Club, which housed a local social organization.

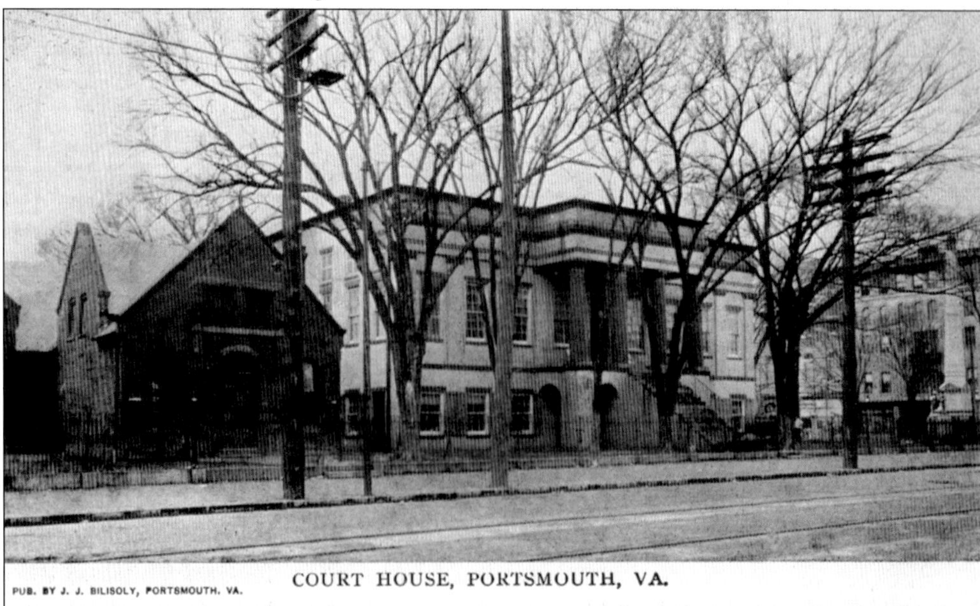

Winter had begun to set in when this image of the courthouse and the clerk of court's office was taken in the early 1900s. The cupola that once graced the roof of the courthouse is missing but was replaced during the restoration of the building. In 1970, it was placed on the National Register of Historic Places.

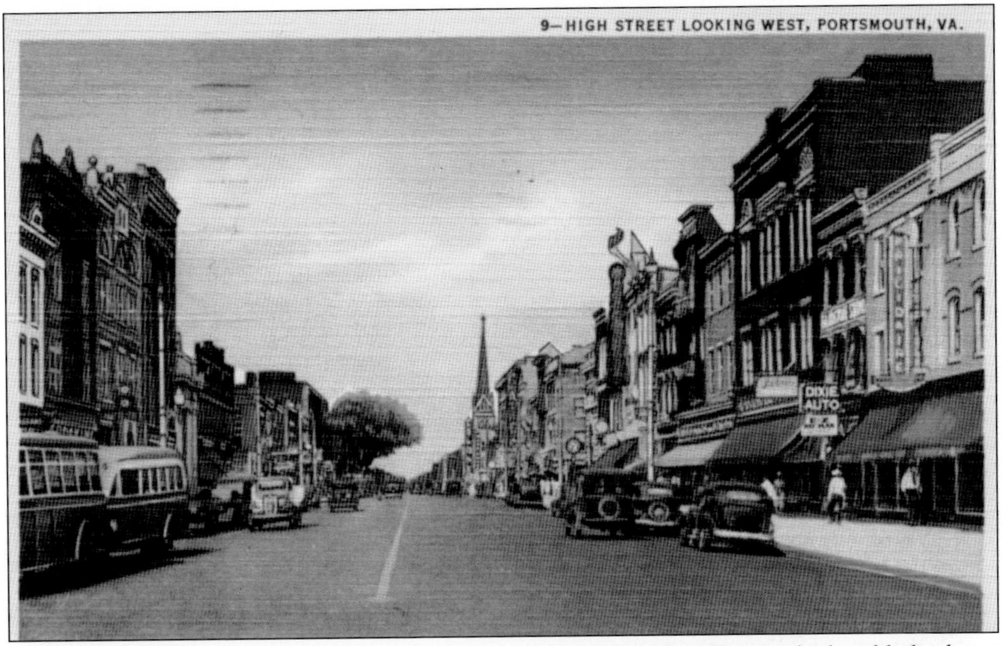

This card, postmarked 1942, provides a view of Morris' Music Shop, which sold the latest appliances, record players, and radios. For those wanting a sweet treat or lunch, Fantone's Ice Cream Bar and Luncheonette or the soda bar at W.T. Grant Company were in walking distance. The sender writes, "This place is full of men in uniform, I never saw such a sight; the people here are very sociable."

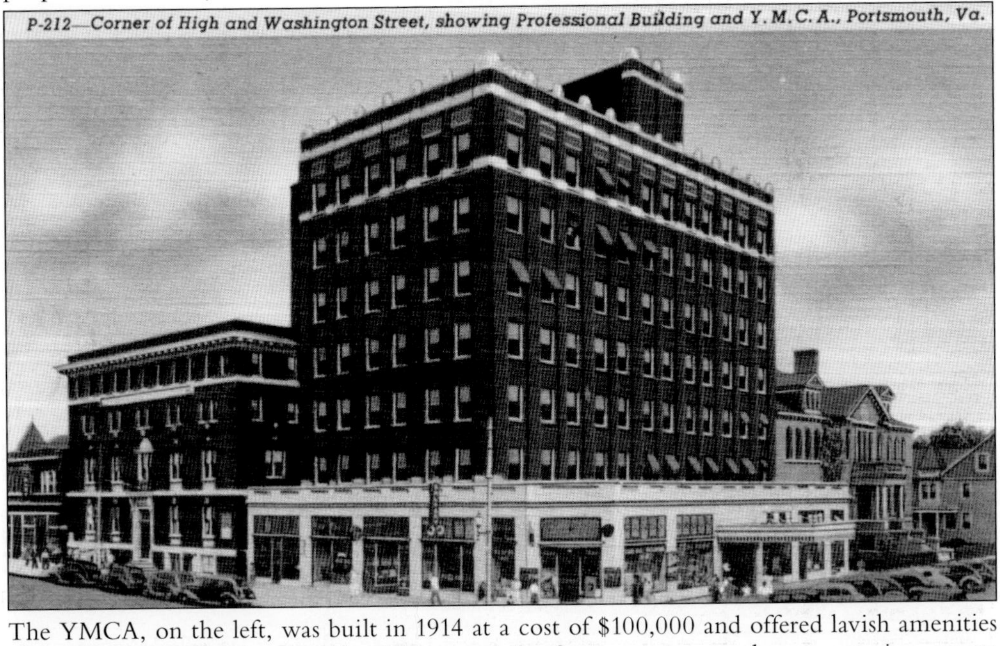

The YMCA, on the left, was built in 1914 at a cost of $100,000 and offered lavish amenities throughout the building. Marble steps graced the front entrance, and upon entering, guests were greeted in a grand hall with an ornate fireplace. An indoor racetrack with bleachers, billiard game rooms, and a swimming pool in the basement were available to the public. After restoration and renovation, the building is now apartments.

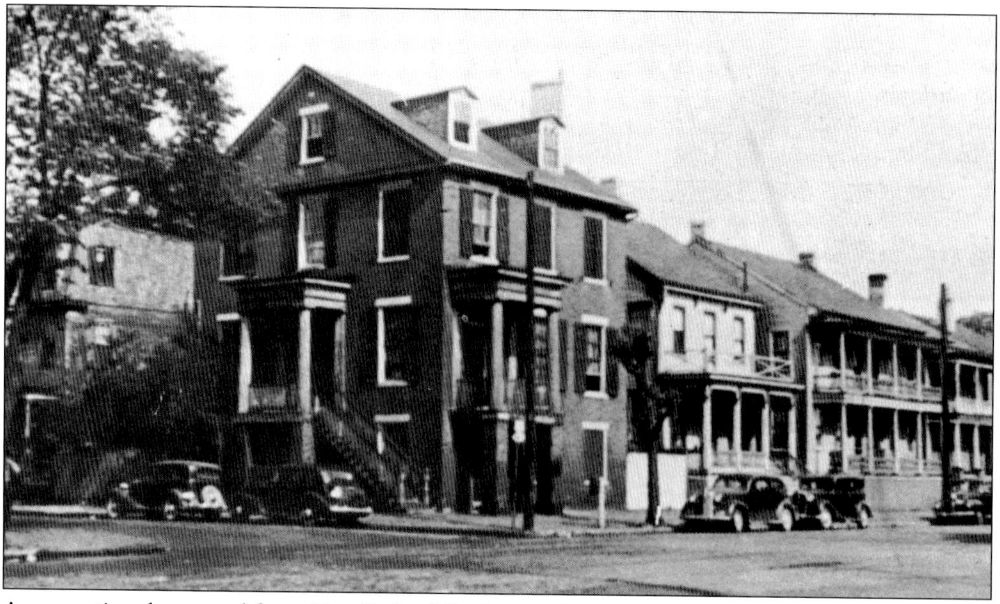

A promotional postcard from First Federal Savings and Loan Association of Portsmouth shows a view of the corner of London and Crawford Streets in the 1930s. The house on the corner, built in 1841, was the home of William Murdaugh. During the Civil War, after Union forces had occupied the city, it was commonly referred to as the Pass House because the provost marshal used it as his headquarters, and any Portsmouth resident who desired to travel outside the city required a "pass."

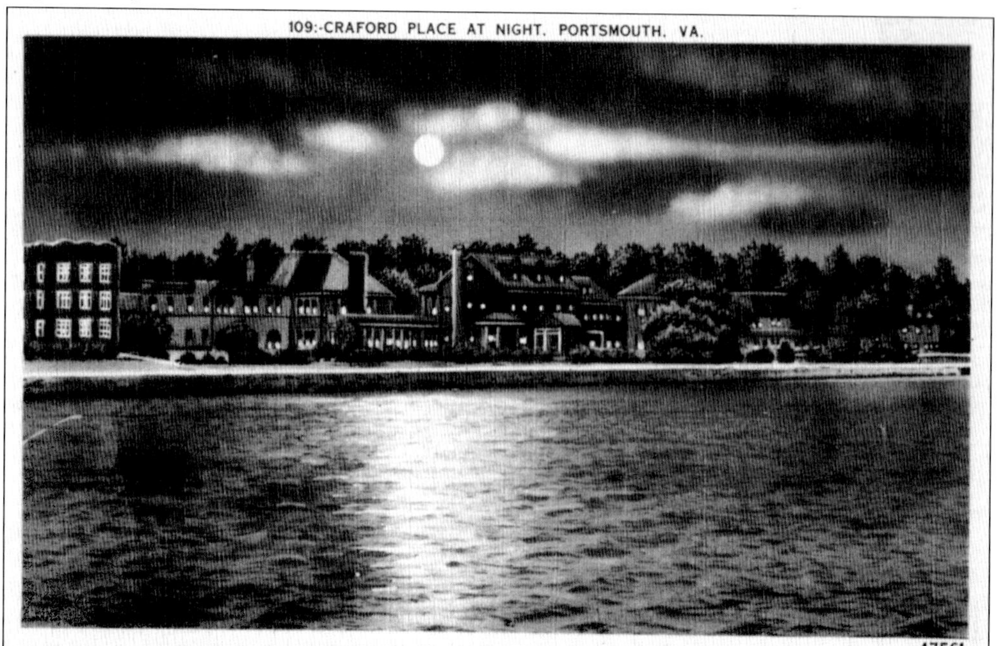

Crawford Bay in the 1930s is featured in this moonlit view of Crawford Place (Swimming Point). The neighborhood, with its picturesque homes and beautifully landscaped yards, provided a beautiful view across the Elizabeth River towards Norfolk. One of the homes in this community includes parts of one of the early homes of Col. William Crawford.

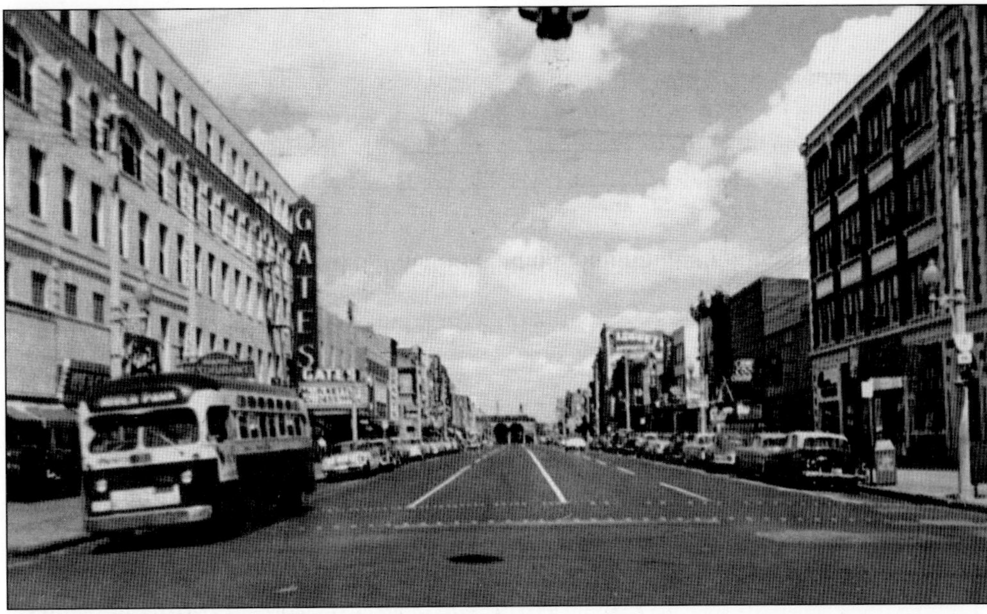

This image of High Street was postmarked in March 1958, the year after the Hotel Monroe (the large building on the left) and 13 other businesses were lost in a major fire. The ferry terminal in the distance sits vacant after the Norfolk County and Portsmouth Ferry service ceased operations in 1955. A Portsmouth Transit Company bus is leaving downtown with passengers going to River Park.

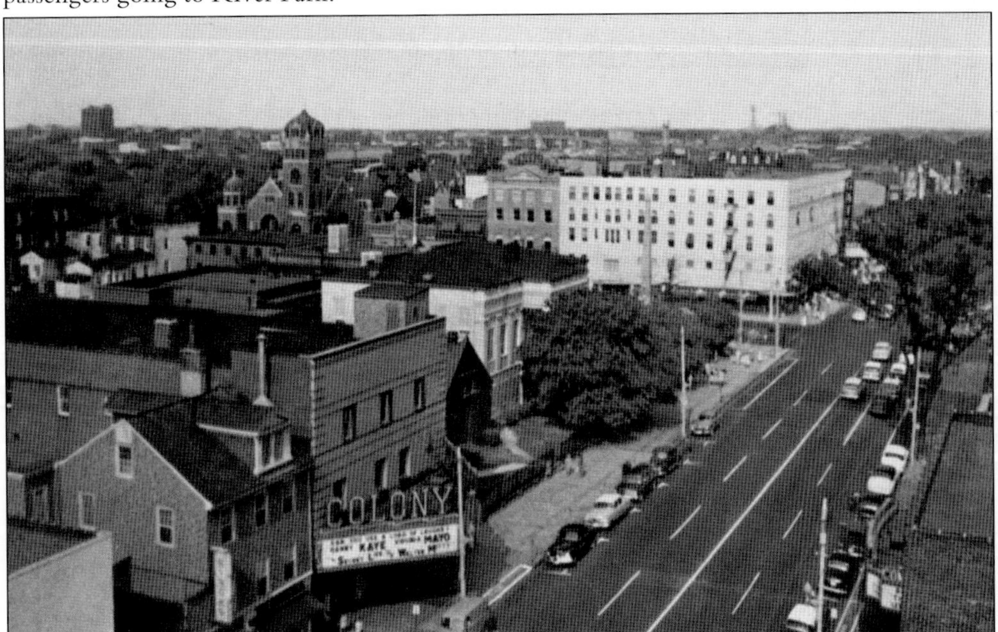

An aerial view of the city in the early 1950s, taken from the Hotel Governor Dinwiddie, provides a glimpse of Warner's Women's Wear, next to the Colony Theatre. The Colony Theatre opened in the 1930s and was the first in the city to show motion pictures in color. Located beside the theater were the offices for the clerk and treasurer of Norfolk County and the city.

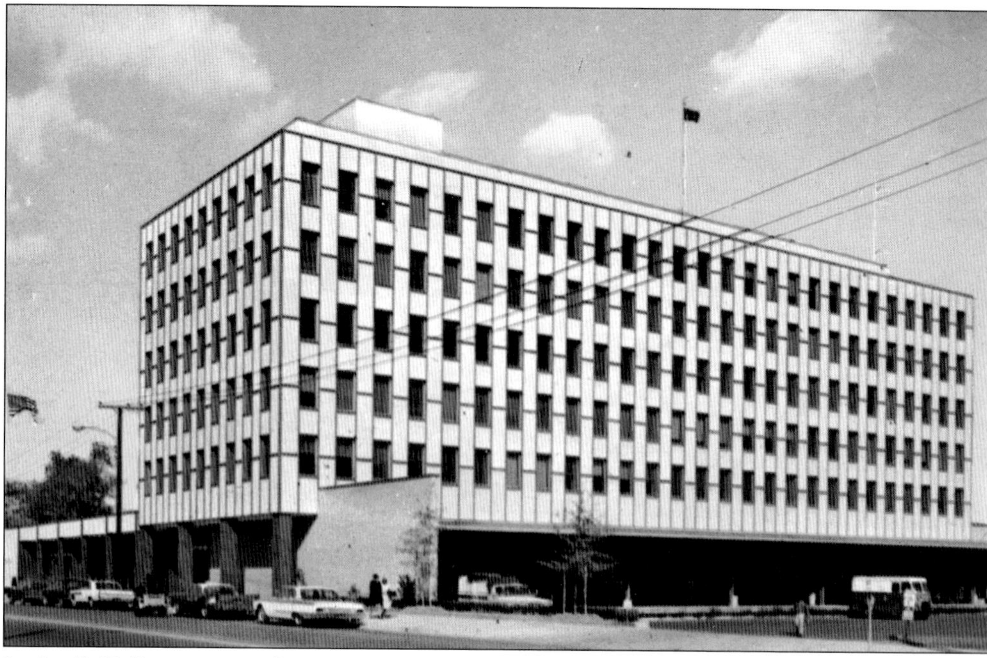

In April 1961, at a cost of $3.5 million, the Federal Building opened to serve the citizens of Portsmouth. The post office, Fifth District Coast Guard Headquarters, and various federal offices remain in service at this location. Note the Portsmouth Police Department's three-wheel motorcycle (lower left) checking for parking violations.

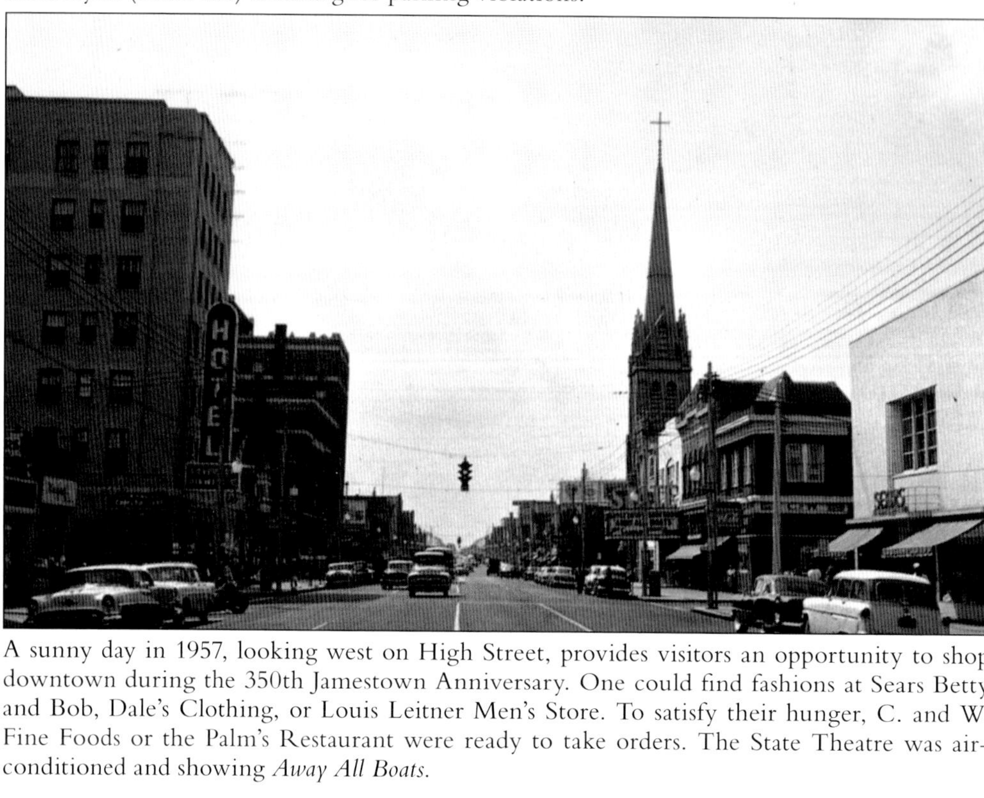

A sunny day in 1957, looking west on High Street, provides visitors an opportunity to shop downtown during the 350th Jamestown Anniversary. One could find fashions at Sears Betty and Bob, Dale's Clothing, or Louis Leitner Men's Store. To satisfy their hunger, C. and W. Fine Foods or the Palm's Restaurant were ready to take orders. The State Theatre was air-conditioned and showing *Away All Boats.*

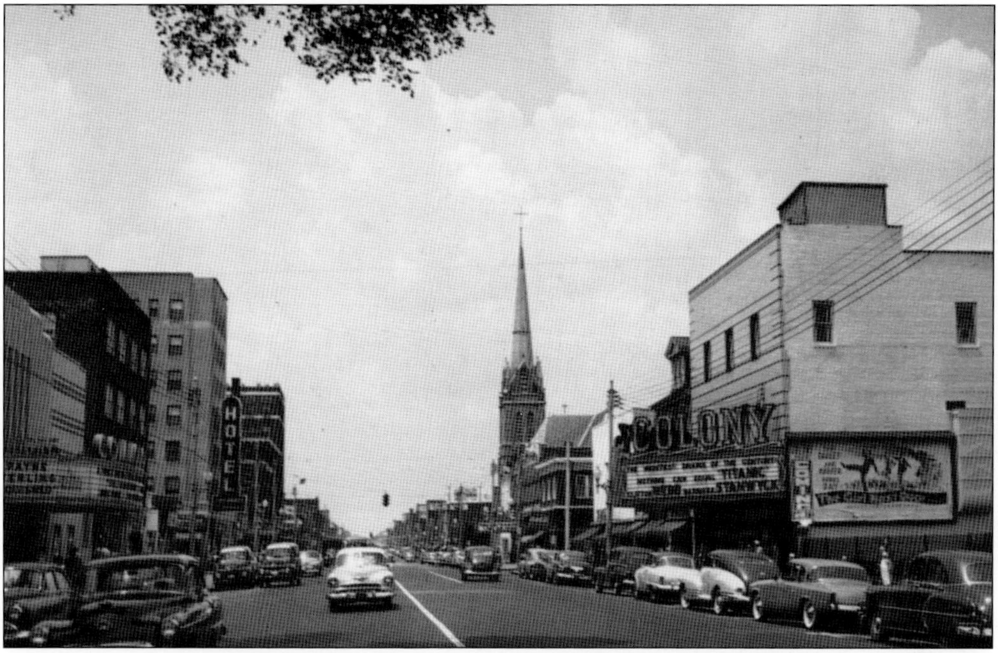

The Commodore Theatre, on the left, opened as the flagship of the Wilder chain of theaters in November 1945. William "Bunkie" Wilder had it built in the art deco style, with elaborate furnishings and state-of-the-art equipment. After closing in the 1970s, the Commodore remained vacant until it was restored and reopened in 1989. The building is on the National Register of Historic Places and the Virginia Landmark Register.

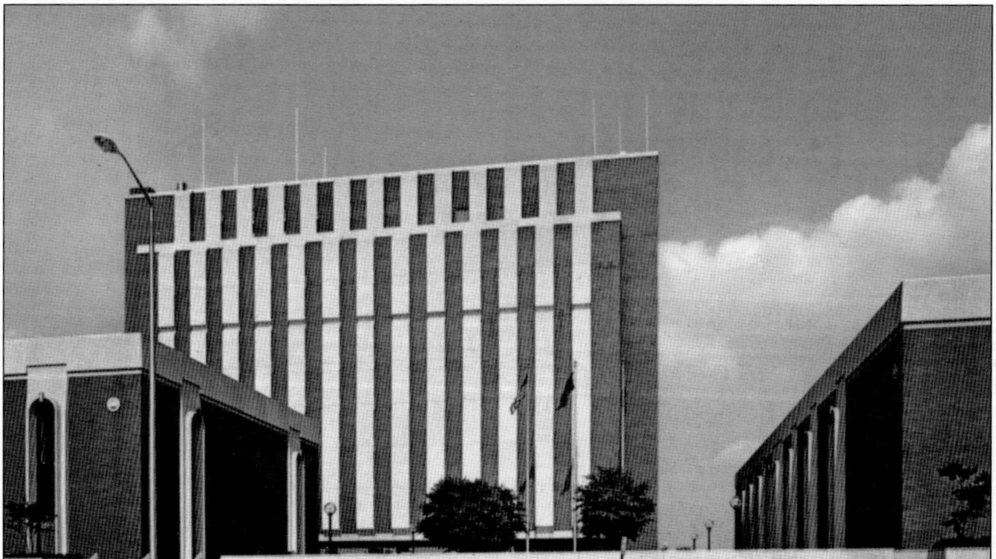

The 1846 Portsmouth Courthouse had become too small to handle the requirements of the city, and there was no room for expansion. Portsmouth's growth and progress required a combined judicial facility within the city. In 1970, Mayor Jack P. Barnes dedicated the Portsmouth Civic Center, which organized the courts, police headquarters, and city jail in one location on Crawford Street.

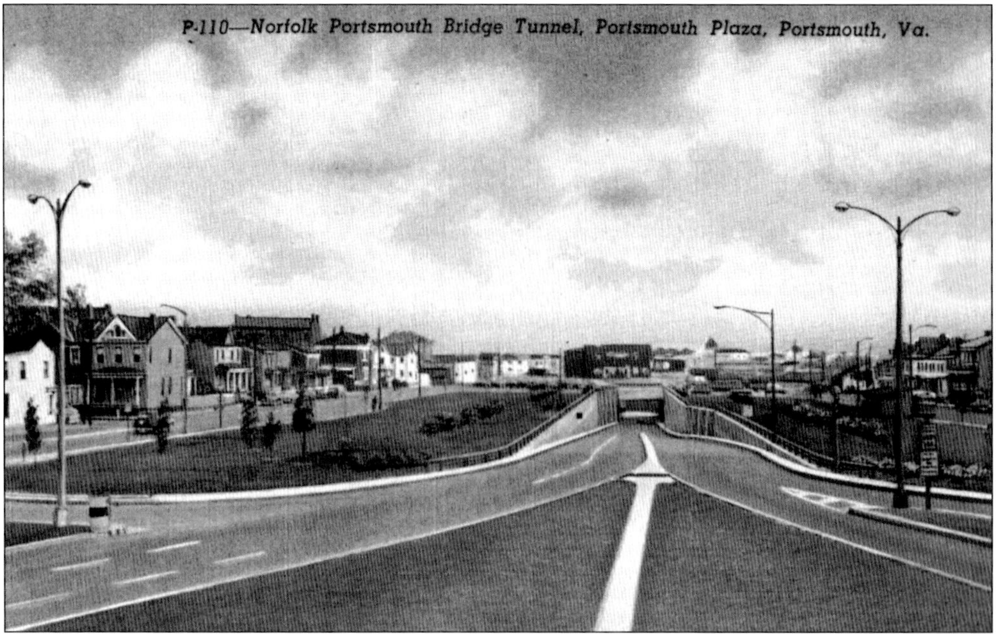

The Norfolk-Portsmouth Bridge Tunnel was completed in May 1952 and brought an end to the Norfolk County and Portsmouth Ferries in August 1955. Portsmouth's bicentennial was celebrated along with the opening of the tunnel. Both were major events in 1952. The residential section on the right, Southside (Newtown), was later torn down to make room for a second tunnel.

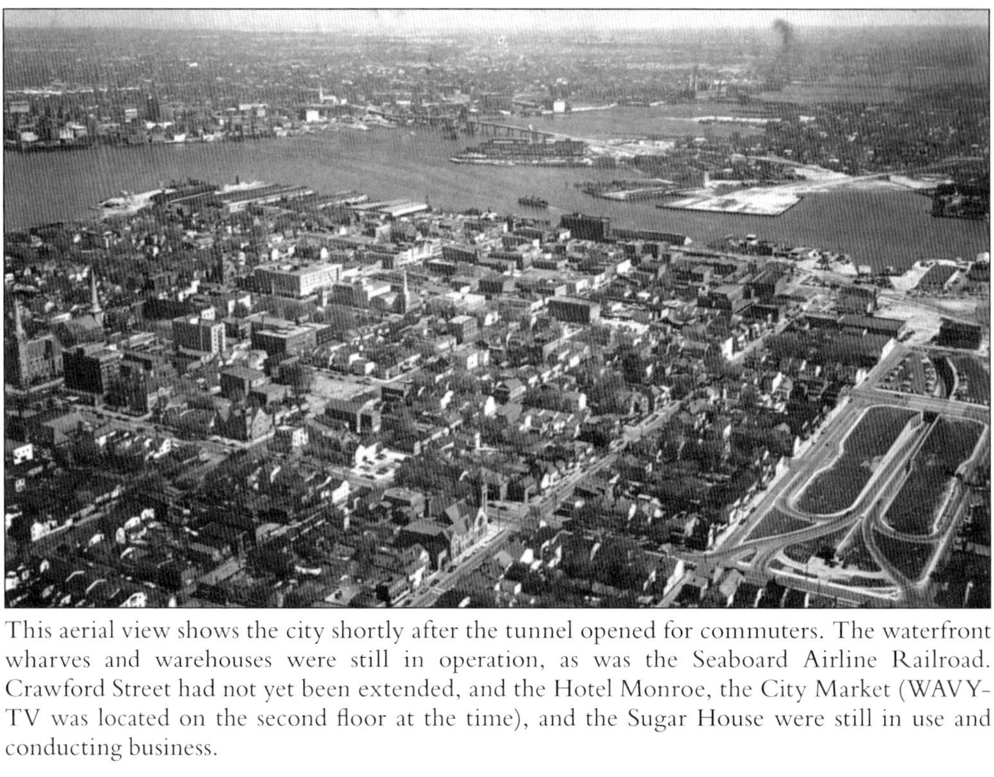

This aerial view shows the city shortly after the tunnel opened for commuters. The waterfront wharves and warehouses were still in operation, as was the Seaboard Airline Railroad. Crawford Street had not yet been extended, and the Hotel Monroe, the City Market (WAVY-TV was located on the second floor at the time), and the Sugar House were still in use and conducting business.

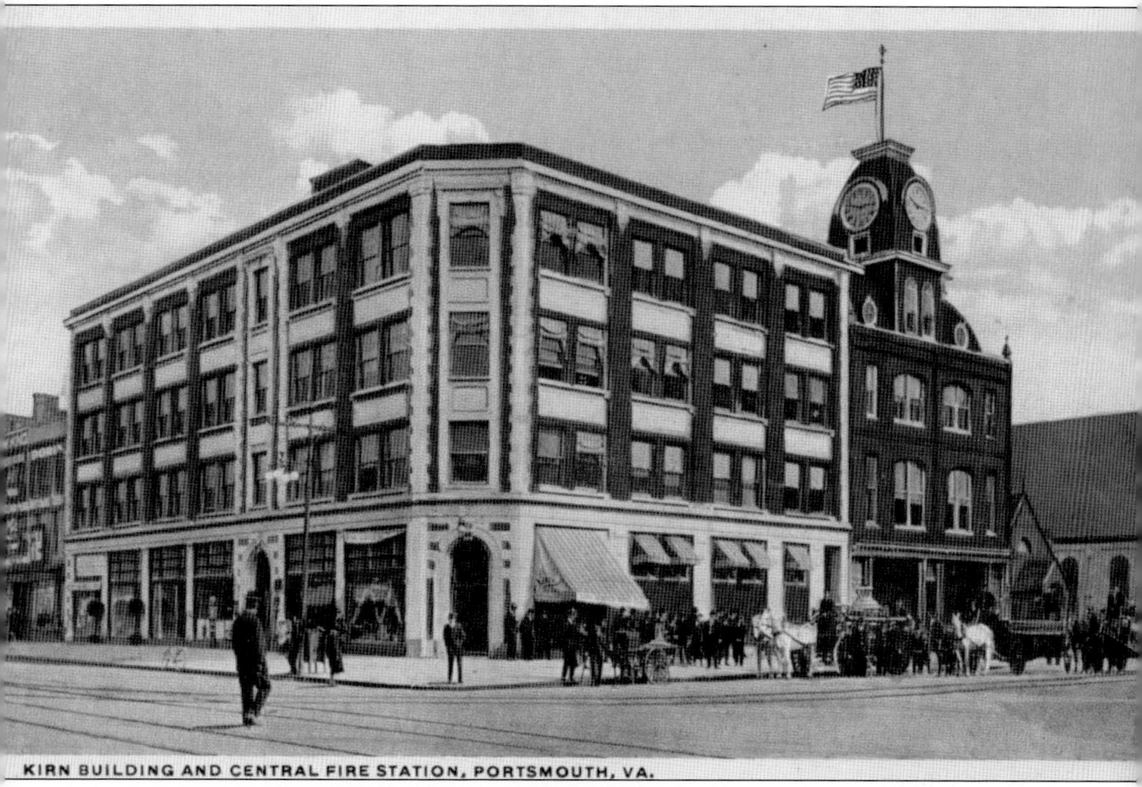

This view shows the new Kirn Building and Central Fire Station in the early 1900s. Note the fire department displaying its equipment. The fire steamer truck was that of Chamber's Fire Company No. 2, and the wagon to the rear with ladders was that of the Portsmouth Hook and Ladder Company No. 1. In 1916, the two fire companies, along with the other independent fire companies in the city, were organized and became members of the Portsmouth Volunteer Firemen's Association. The fire station occupied the first and second floors, while the city hall occupied the upper floors. During the mid-20th century, both buildings were restored, and they now have businesses on the first floor and professional offices on the upper floors. Postmarked in 1918, the sender mailed this card as a landmark guide, writing, "They will see this at the corner where they are to turn at High and Court Streets. I don't think they will need this, for I am pretty sure I can meet them."

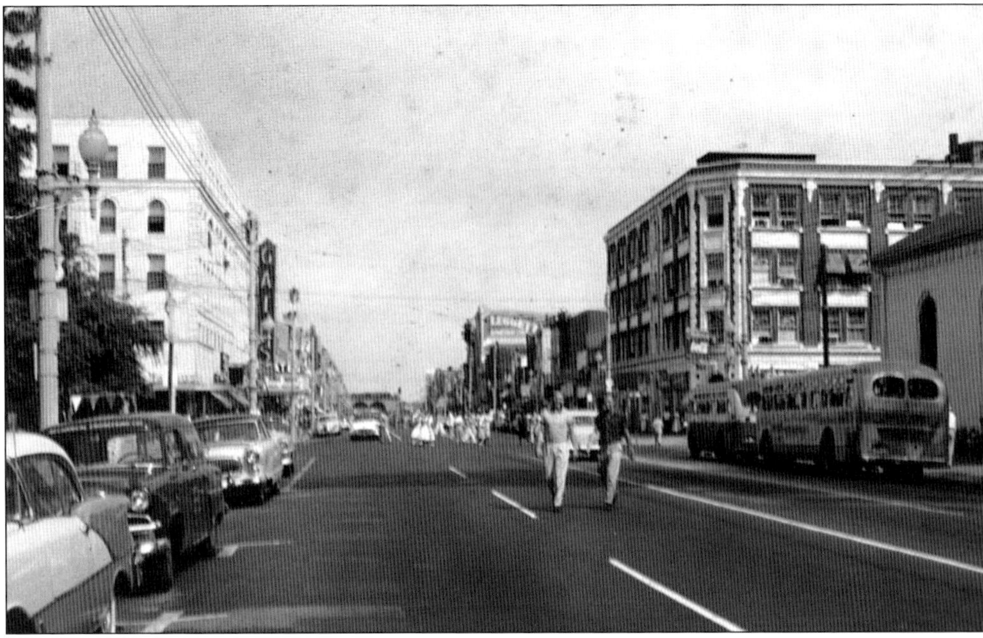

Walking across High Street was not a major problem during the 1950s, as a large number of city residents relied on the Portsmouth Transit Company and the Community Motor Bus Company for transportation, resulting in less traffic. There were always a number of benches located in front of the courthouse (left) and next to Trinity Church (right) for waiting commuters or residents looking for a spot to sit and chat about current events.

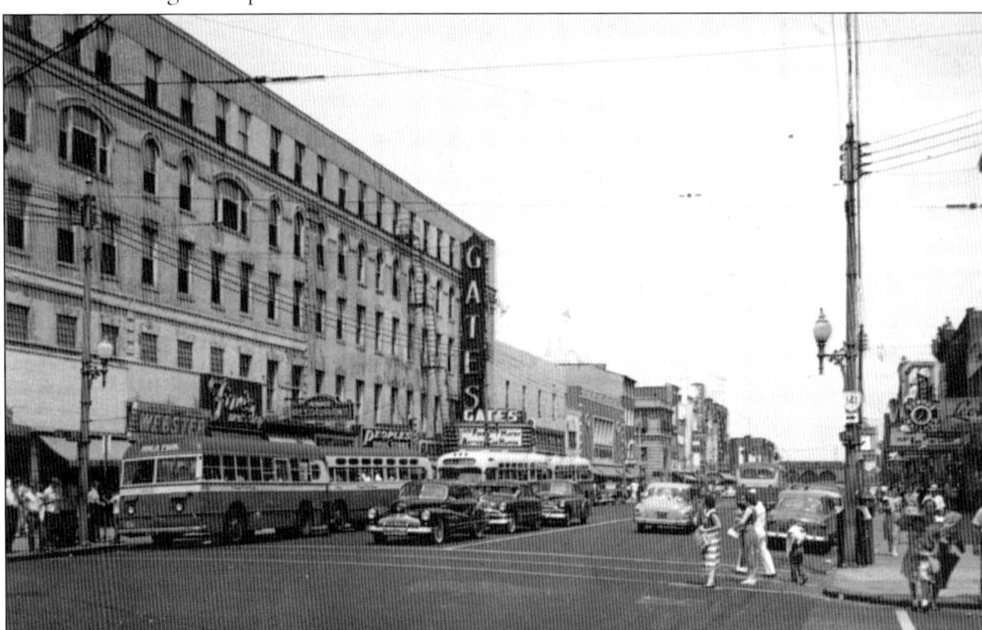

High Street, the main thoroughfare of the city, has run the length of Portsmouth since it was surveyed and a layout of the city was drawn by Gershom Nimmo in 1752. The street begins at the Elizabeth River and runs a distance of six miles, stretching to the city line in Churchland, which was annexed in 1968.

Three

Churches, Schools, and Hospitals

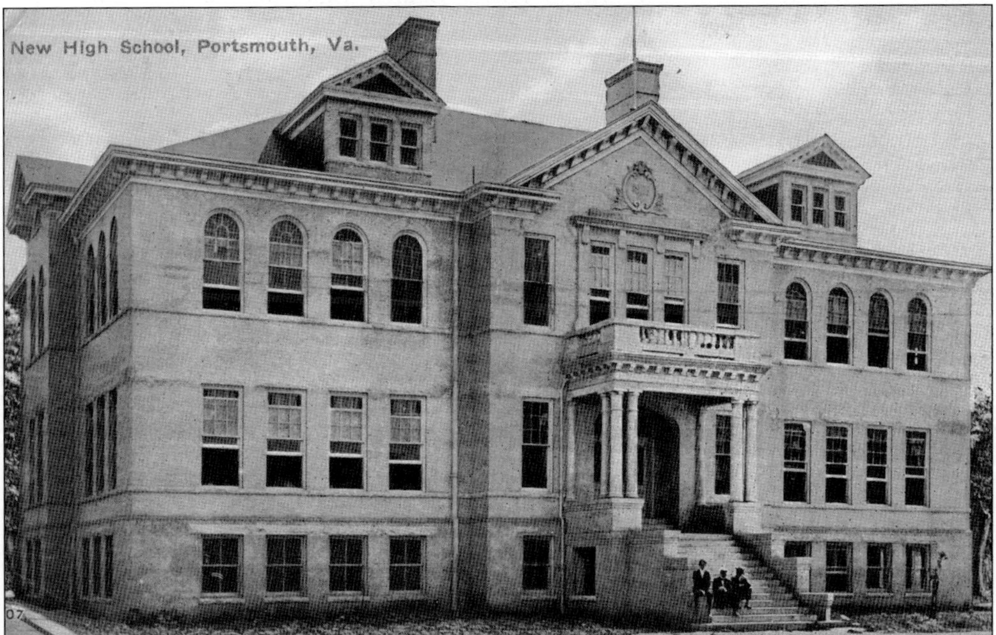

Portsmouth High School, on the east side of Washington Street, opened in 1909 to accommodate the children residing downtown. The name was later changed to Briggs School in honor of Frank Briggs, a long-term member of the school board. In later years, it served as offices for the school board until it was lost in a fire in the 1960s. The three young men sitting on the front steps are rather well dressed, the one in the center sporting a straw boater.

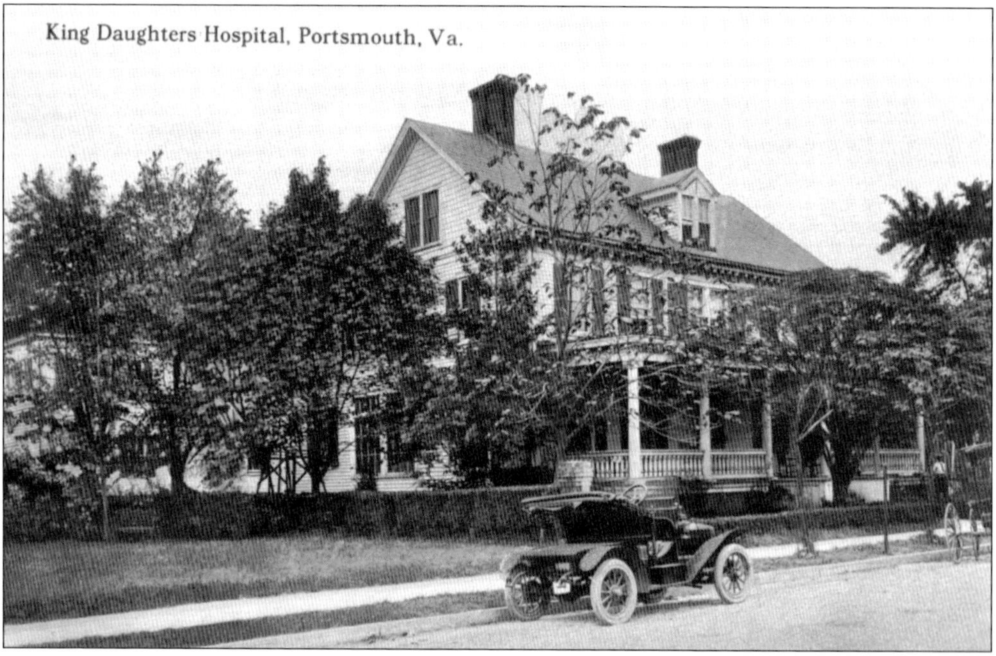

In 1903, the Daughters of the King Ladies Auxiliary purchased this residence on Emmett Street from Dr. William Schmoele and converted it into the second King's Daughters Hospital. In later years, this location was razed to make way for a larger hospital and health clinic.

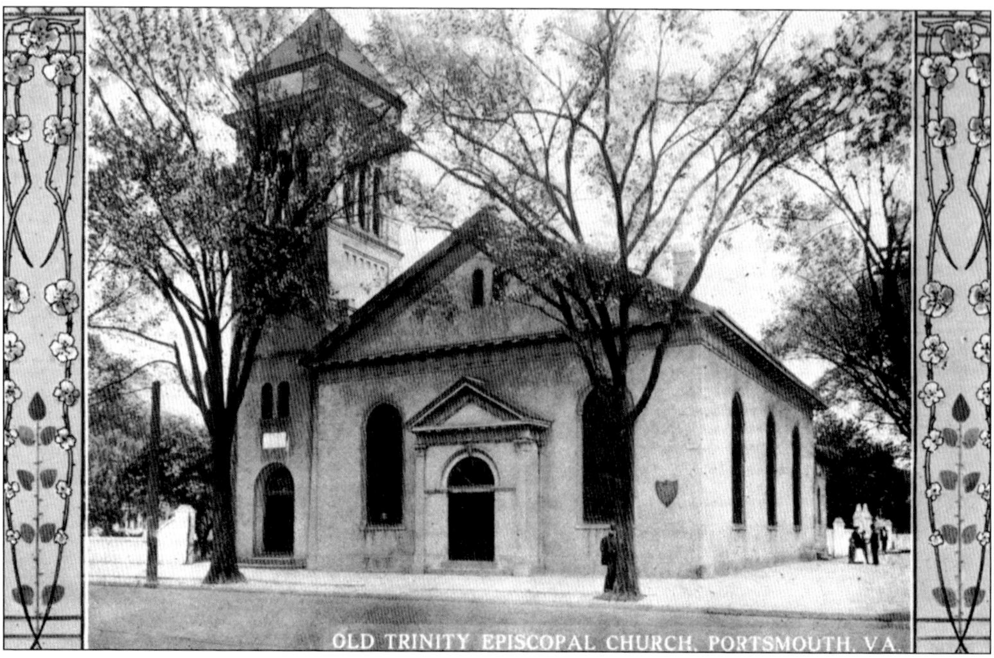

Trinity Episcopal Church, shown as it appeared in 1907, was founded in 1761 with Col. William Crawford serving on the church's first vestry. During the 1820s, after falling into disrepair, the church was torn down and rebuilt around the original nave. The sanctuary was restored in the 1900s, and in 1973, it was placed on the National Register of Historic Places.

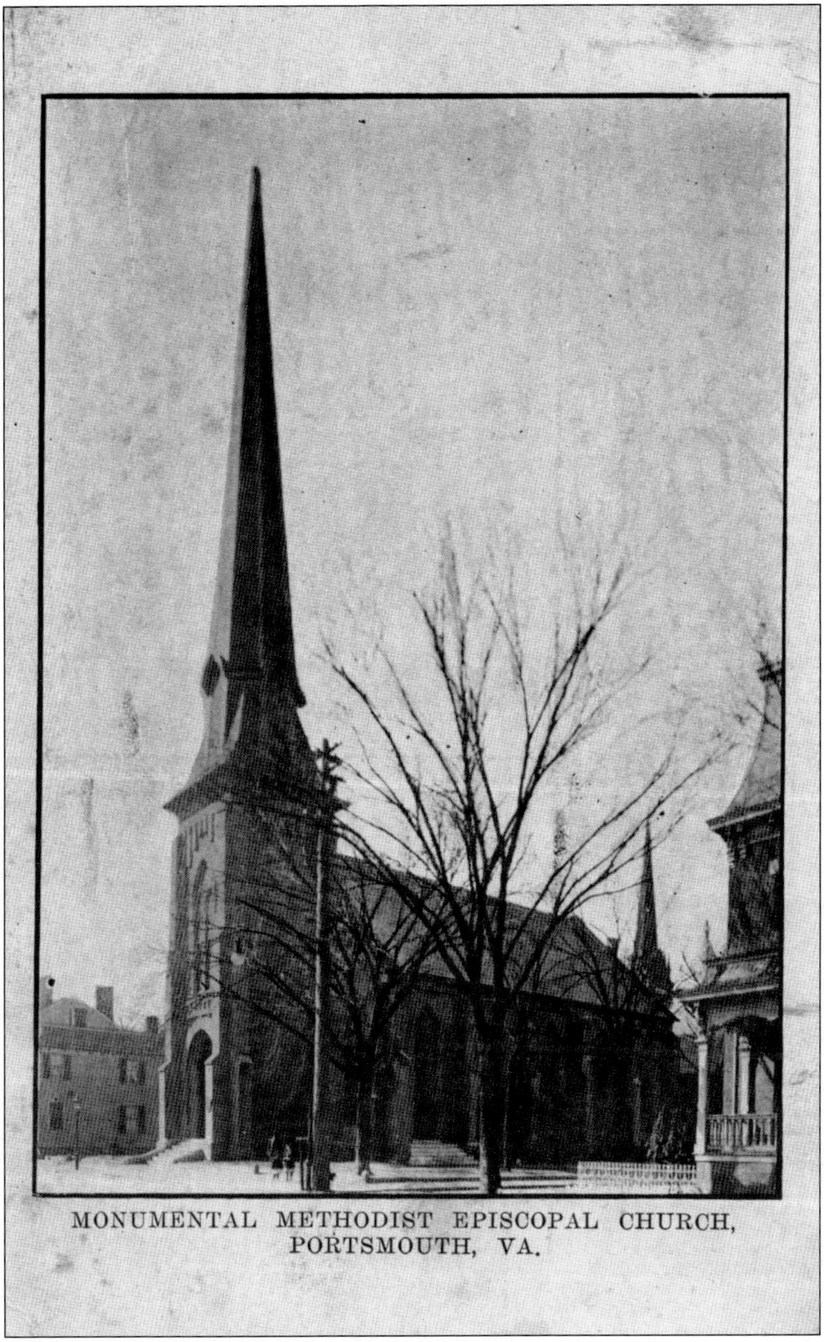

This wintery view shows Monumental Methodist Episcopal Church (Monumental United Methodist Church) in the early 1900s. The church was built at this location in 1876. Its history dates back to 1772, and it is claimed to be the oldest Methodist congregation in the South and third oldest in the nation. The first Sunday school in the city was established by its members in 1818. One of the most notable members of the congregation was John L. Porter, the designer and builder of the first ironclad ship, the CSS *Virginia*. The church is on the Virginia Landmarks Register and the National Register of Historic Places.

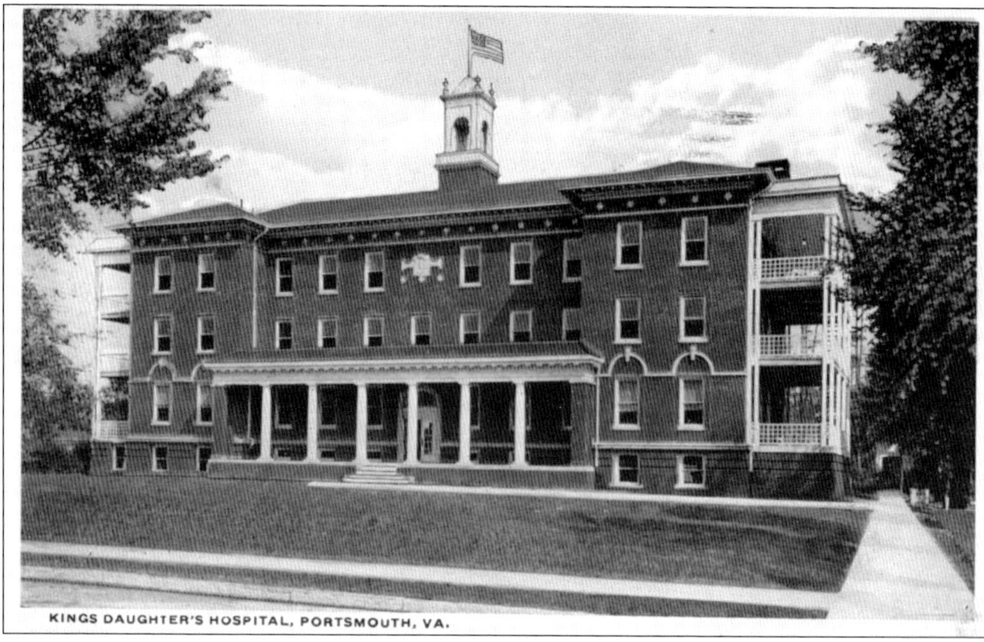

Kings Daughter's Hospital on Fort Lane was completed in 1914 with two modern operating rooms. The first surgical procedure there was an appendectomy performed by Dr. J.D. Collins. An addition was added during 1943 on Leckie Street, increasing patient accommodation to 240 beds. During the 1960s, the hospital underwent a major expansion, and the name was changed to Portsmouth General Hospital.

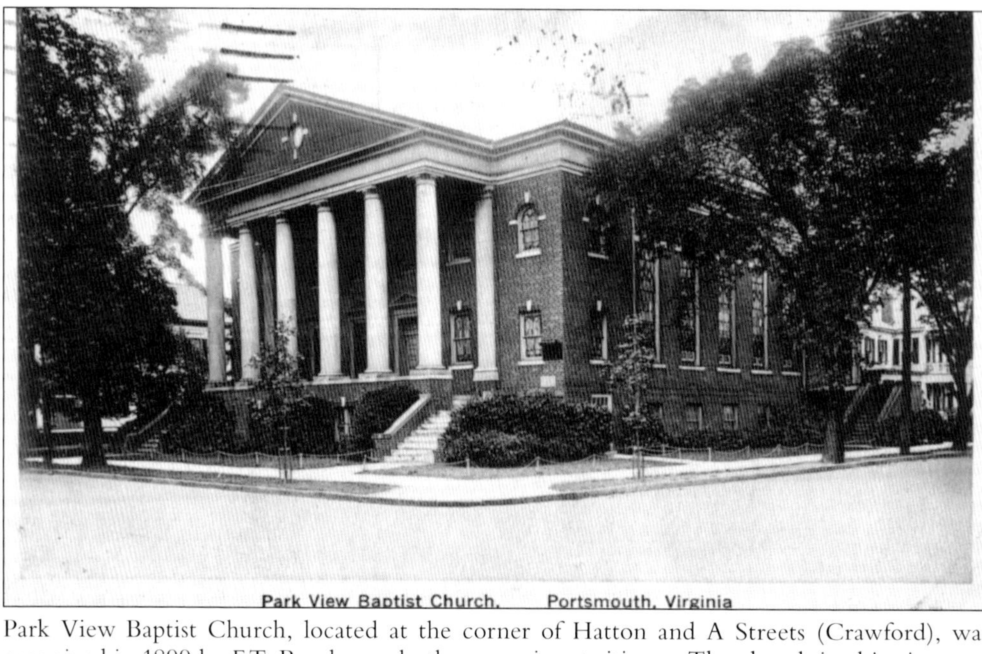

Park View Baptist Church, located at the corner of Hatton and A Streets (Crawford), was organized in 1899 by F.T. Beazley and other prominent citizens. The church in this view was built in 1924, and the congregation held its first services here in 1925. During World War II, the church opened its doors to young local women and members of the military away from home as a place to meet and socialize.

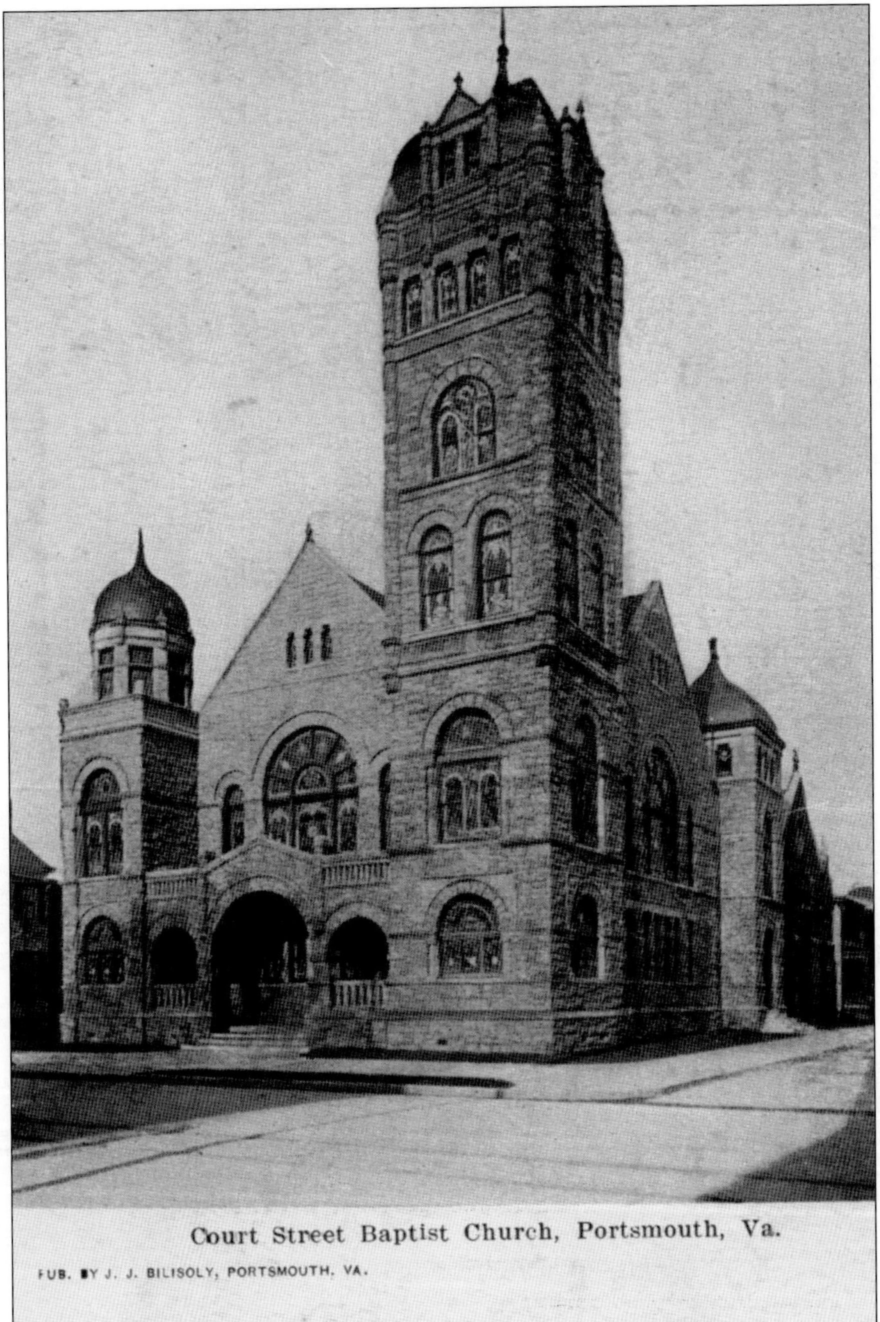

Court Street Baptist Church was founded in 1789 and was originally called the Portsmouth and Norfolk Baptist Church. In the early 1800s, it was renamed Portsmouth Baptist Church, and in 1855, the congregation changed the name to Court Street Baptist Church, a name it has retained for the past 155 years. The building pictured on this card was built in the Byzantine Romanesque style, and in May 1903, the congregants held their dedication services. The ebullient architectural design is contrary to other Baptist churches and is one of two in this style built in the United States.

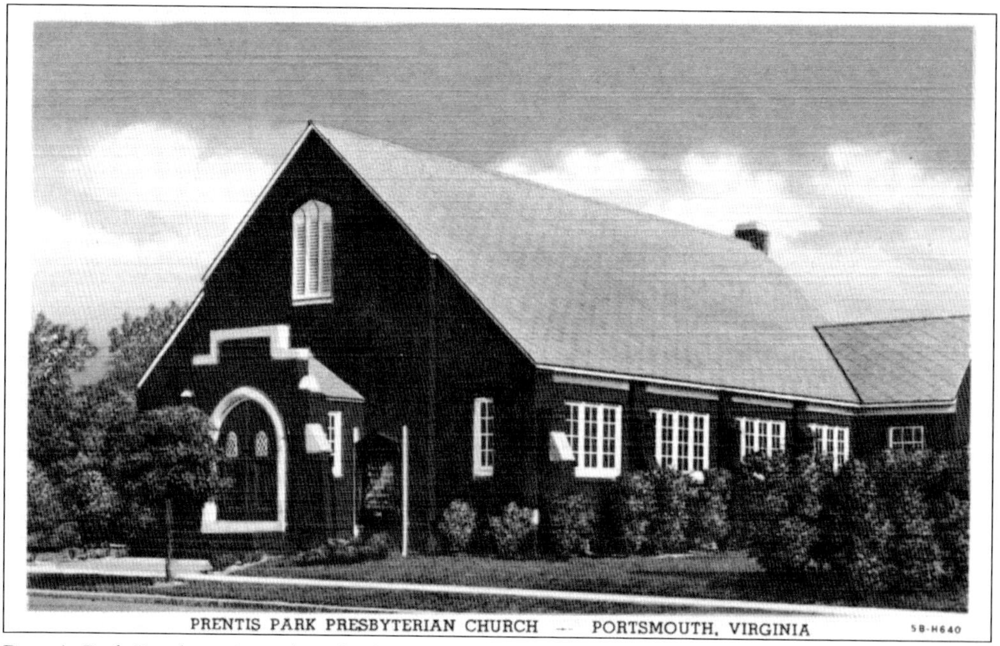

Prentis Park Presbyterian Church, founded in 1916, was located at the corner of Palmer Street and Deep Creek Boulevard. In the early days of the church, it was proclaimed as "a fellowship of many denominations worshipping and working together." The church merged its membership with the membership of First Presbyterian Church (Court Street) in 1967. Today, the building is affiliated with another denomination.

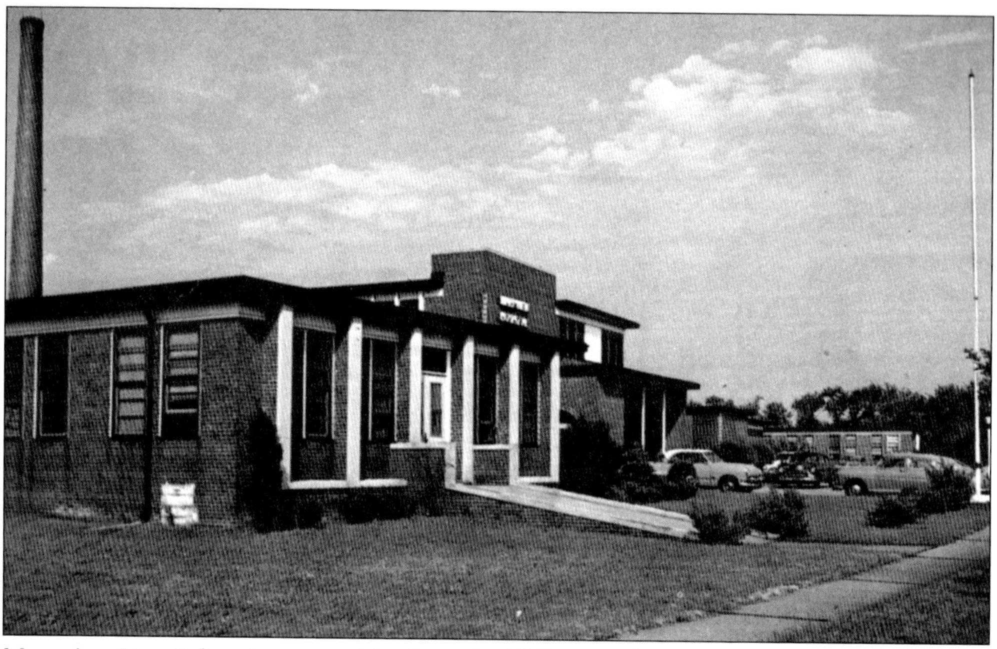

Maryview Hospital, as it appeared in the early 1950s, was the major hospital for the city and parts of Norfolk County. This view is of the west wing (maternity and pediatrics). Like many hospitals throughout the country, Maryview experienced a large increase in the delivery of babies after World War II.

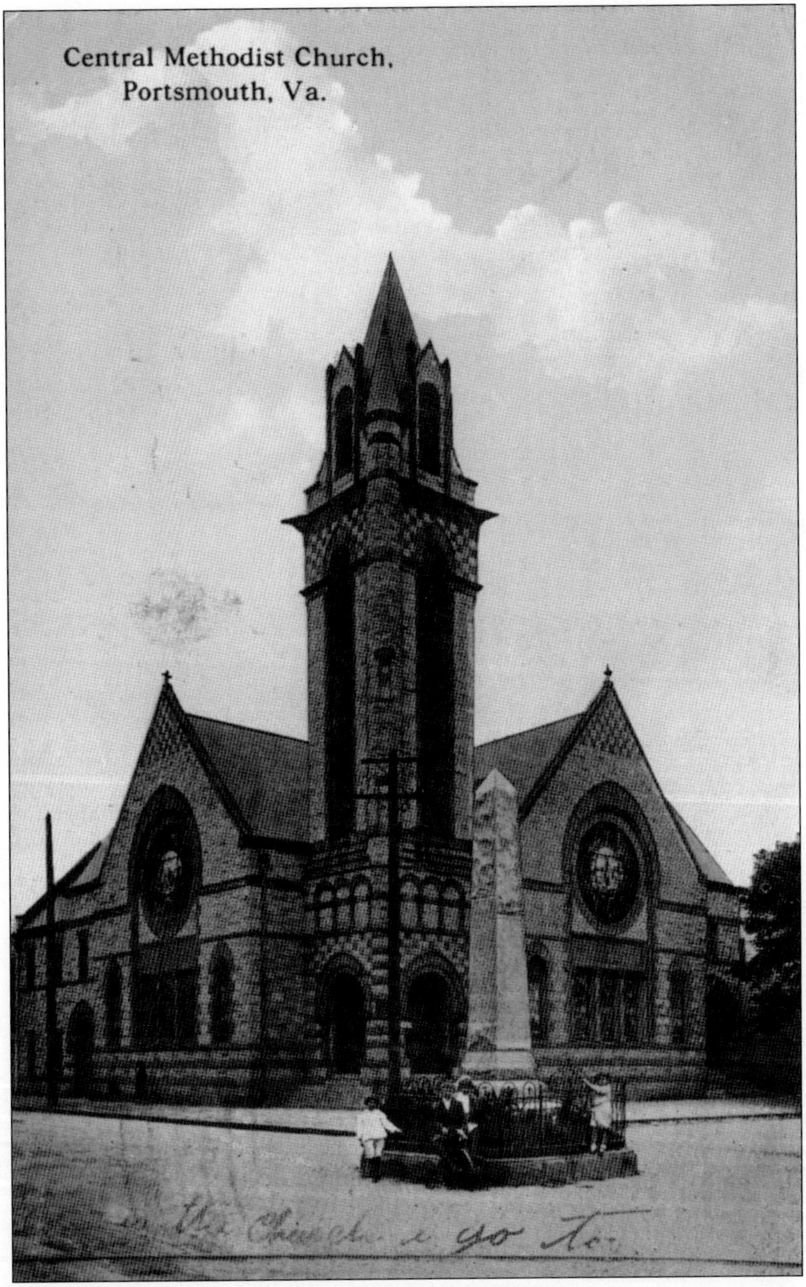

Central Methodist Church, as it appeared in the early 1900s, was located on the corner of Washington and South Streets. The church was dedicated in November 1902 and was active until the congregation relocated to Norfolk County (Chesapeake). Since that time, the church has been the home of several African American congregations. The old church still sits vacant, and restoration work has not been completed. The person who sent the card, who obviously worked at one of the manufacturing plants in the city, writes, "Had a busy morning at the plant and a very busy afternoon in town with railroad people, saw Ruth Gay, she works at the Seaboard Airline. There is a dinner tonight in honor of the visitors from Savannah to which I am invited."

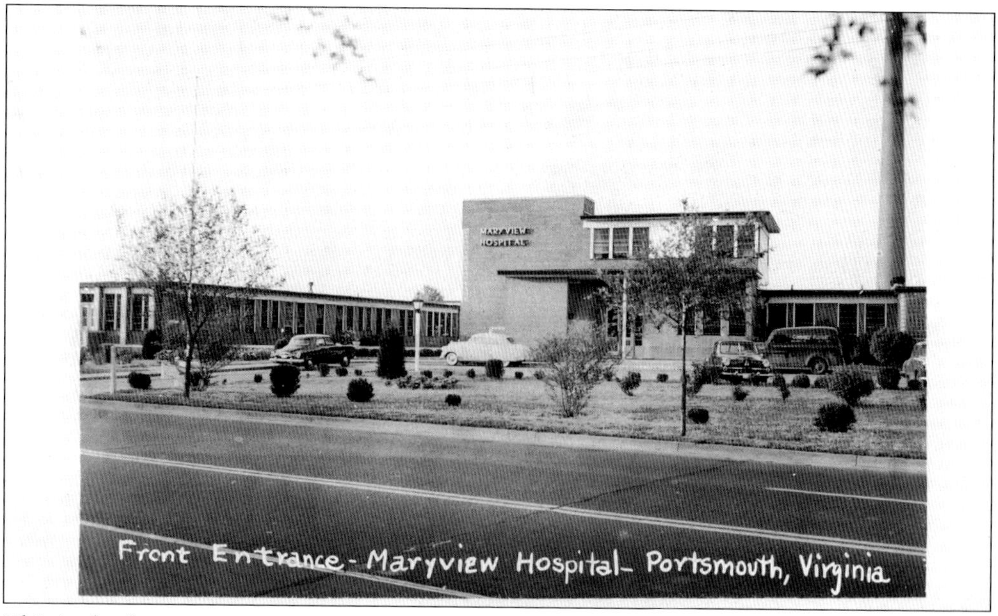

This is the front entrance to Maryview Hospital as it appeared in July 1952. Maryview was founded in 1945, when the federal government saw the need for a large medical facility in Portsmouth to accommodate the sizeable number of shipyard workers and their families. After World War II, the main mission was for the care and needs of polio victims. A panel truck parked in front was delivering flowers from Collery Florist located on High Street.

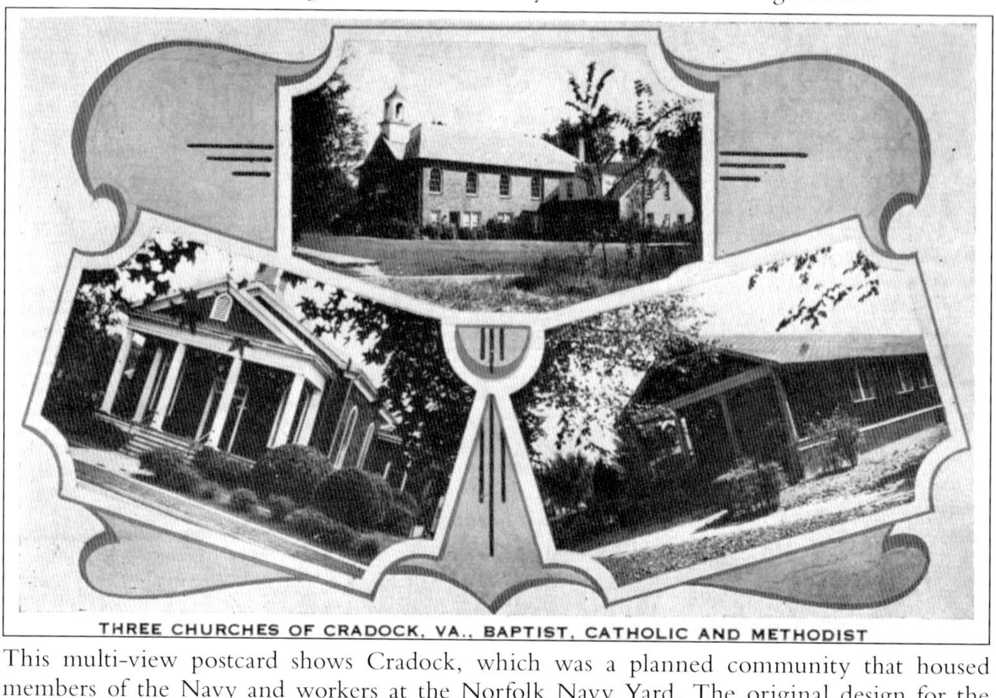

This multi-view postcard shows Cradock, which was a planned community that housed members of the Navy and workers at the Norfolk Navy Yard. The original design for the community included lots for municipal facilities, retail businesses, and churches. Cradock Baptist Church, Holy Angels Catholic Church, and Cradock Methodist Church were some of the first congregations to build churches in Cradock.

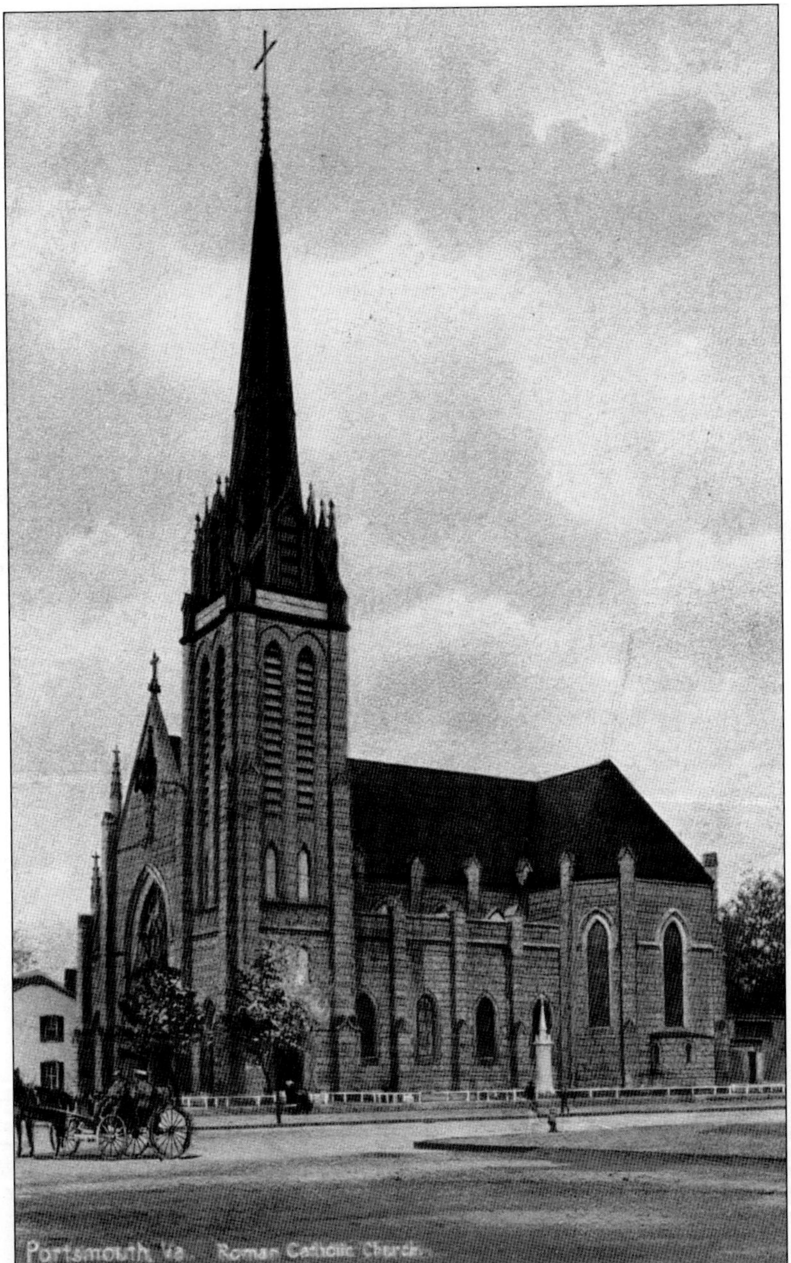

St. Paul's Catholic Church, located at the corner of High and Washington Streets, was dedicated in 1905. This church, built in the Gothic Revival style, was the fifth to be constructed at this location. The cathedral-style sanctuary contains hand-fired, stained-glass windows that were manufactured by Meyer and Company of Munich, Germany. It is acclaimed as one of the finest Catholic churches built in the South. Distinctive features of the church are the copper-clad steeple, which soars 200 feet above the sanctuary, and the statue of St. Paul above the Washington Street entrance. The church is on the National Register of Historic Places and the Virginia Landmarks Register. The horse and buggy passing by the church was probably owned by one of the more affluent families of Portsmouth at the time.

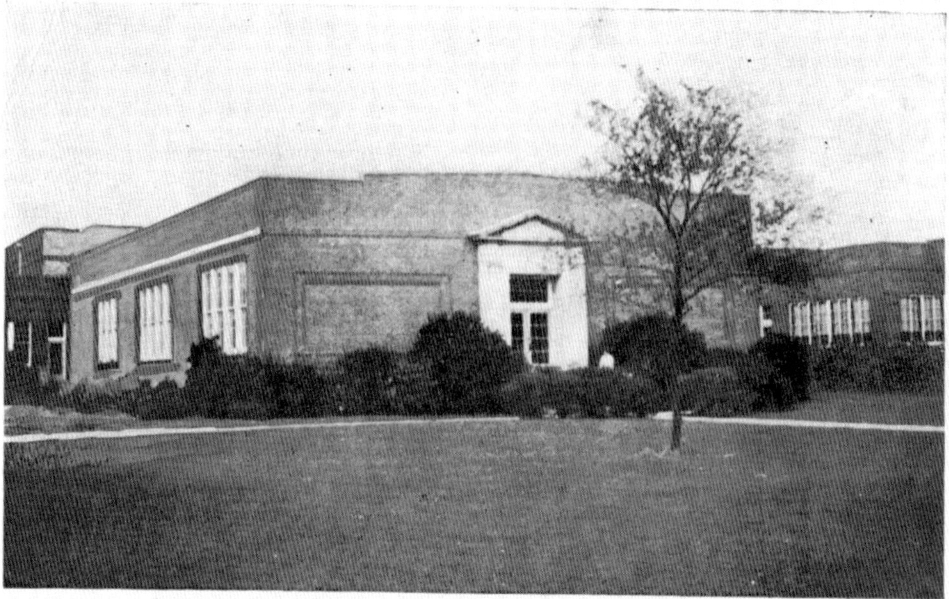

THE CRADOCK GRADE AND HIGH SCHOOL, CRADOCK, VA.

Construction began in 1918 for the Cradock Grade and High School. The first school session was in 1920 and included 16 teachers and 546 students. Students were only required to complete grades one through 11 in order to graduate, but that was changed in 1940 when an additional year was added to the curriculum.

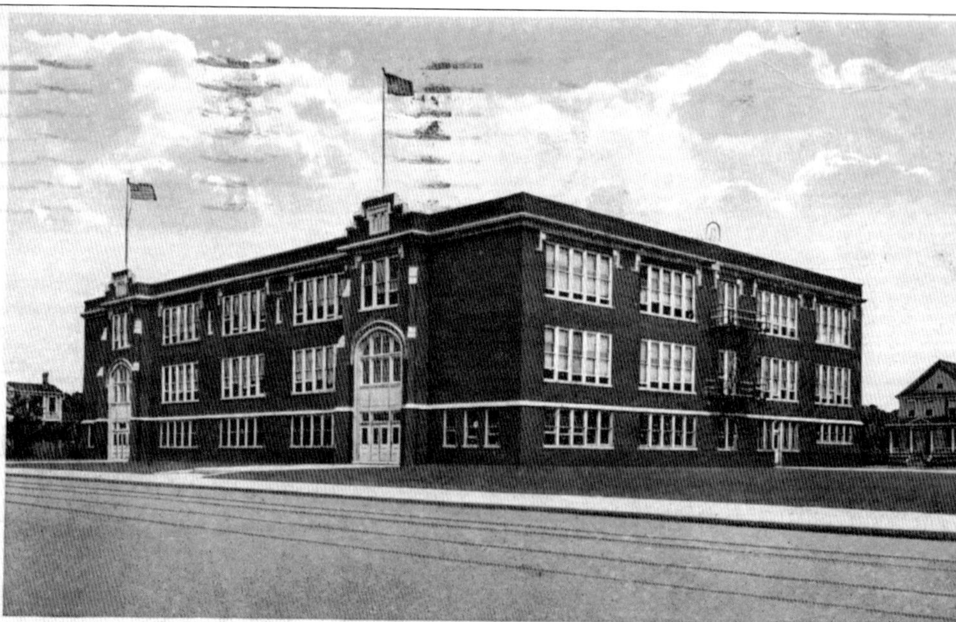

NEW HIGH SCHOOL, PORTSMOUTH, VA.

The cornerstone for the new Portsmouth High School was laid in May 1917, and the school opened in September 1919. It was proclaimed in the *Portsmouth Star* as "the newest of the many educational institutions in Portsmouth and [was] recognized as being the finest and most complete public school building in Virginia." The school was named for a native Virginian and the 28th president of the United States, Woodrow Wilson.

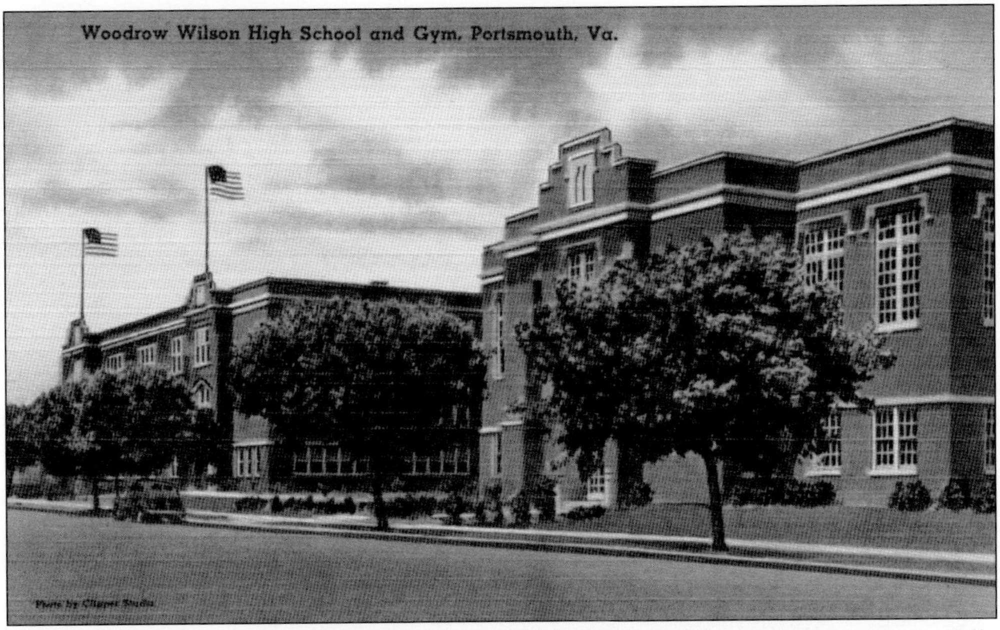

When it opened in 1917 as Portsmouth High School, the building did not contain a fully functional gymnasium. In 1919, the school's name was changed to Woodrow Wilson High School, and in the early 1930s, a separate building was completed that housed the physical education department and gymnasium. Ernie Wild, the athletic director and coach of the school, was honored in later years when the school board bestowed his name on the facility.

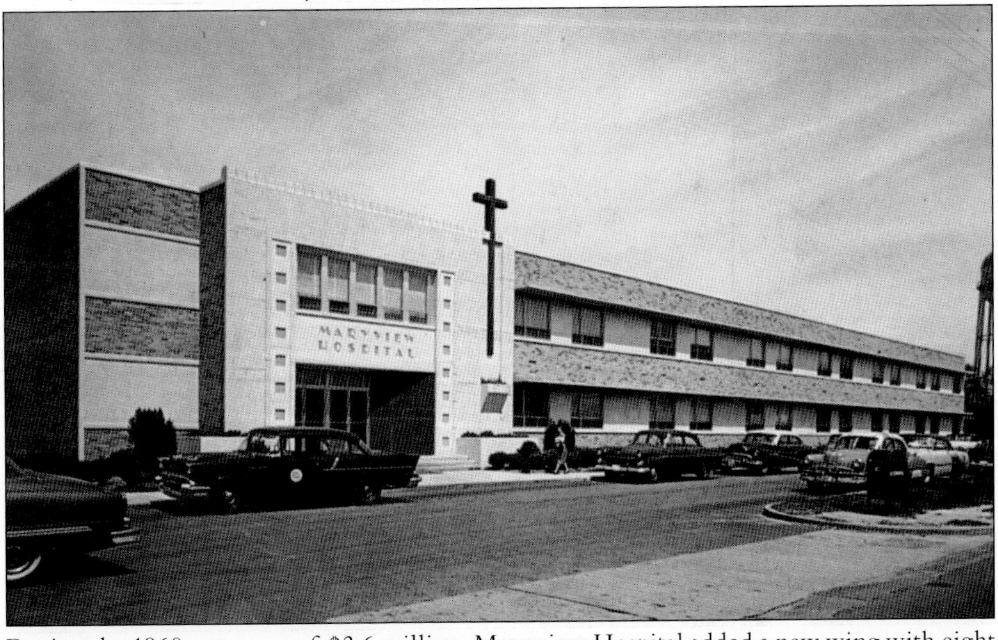

During the 1960s, at a cost of $3.6 million, Maryview Hospital added a new wing with eight operating rooms to the existing facility, and the wing was dedicated on December 7, 1968. The black sedan parked at the front entrance was a city vehicle, possibly used by the public health clinic or coroner's office. The sender of this card writes, "Having a nice time, quite historical around here."

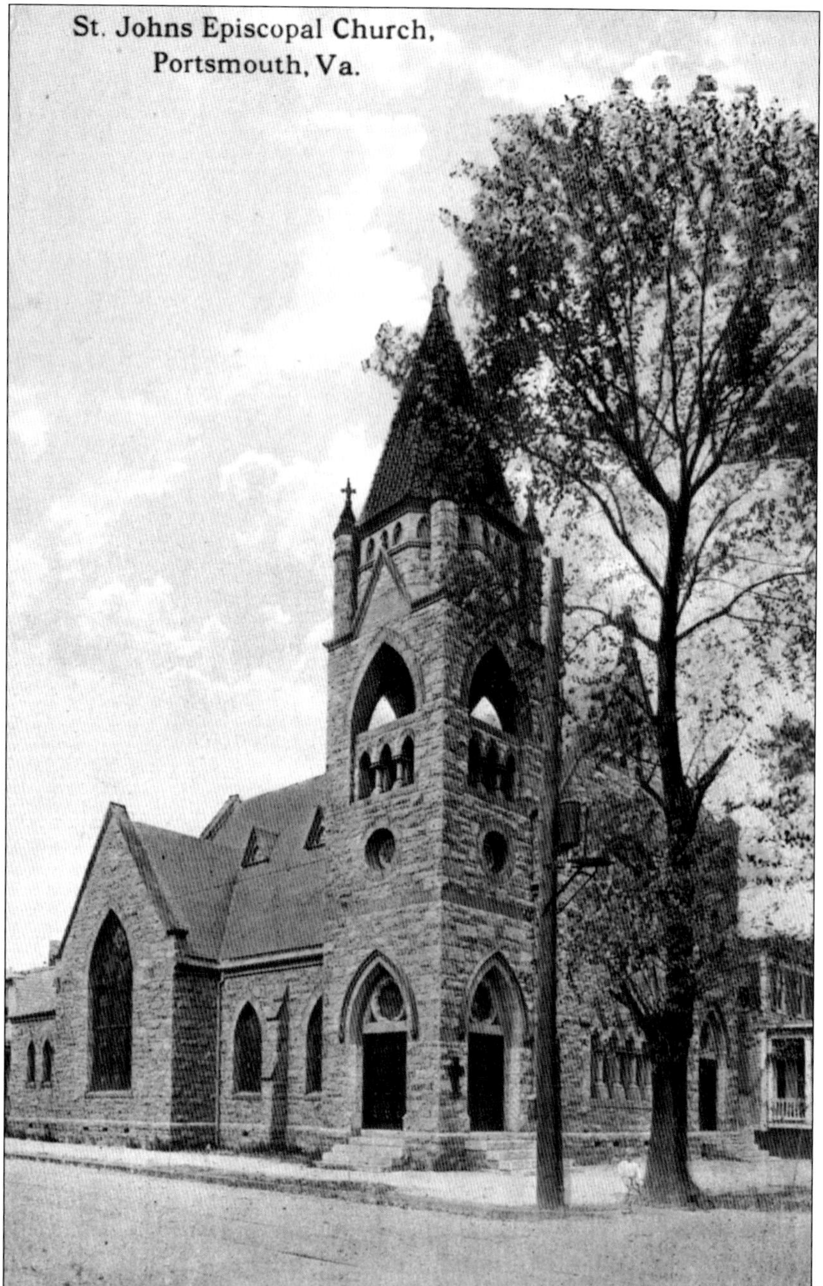

St. John's Episcopal Church, at the corner of London and Washington Streets, was built in 1897, and the congregants held their first service at this location in September 1898. The exterior of stone was constructed in a magnificent Gothic style designed by Charles Cassell, an architect in the city as well as a member of the church vestry. A baptismal font fashioned from an oak pillar that was taken from the frigate USS *Constitution* was donated to the church by Commodore Lewis Warrington and remains in the sanctuary today. The stained-glass window of Christ ("Come unto Me") by Tiffany and Company was installed in 1907. Very faintly, an unidentified child can be seen next to the tree, possibly a member of the congregation or the photographer's child.

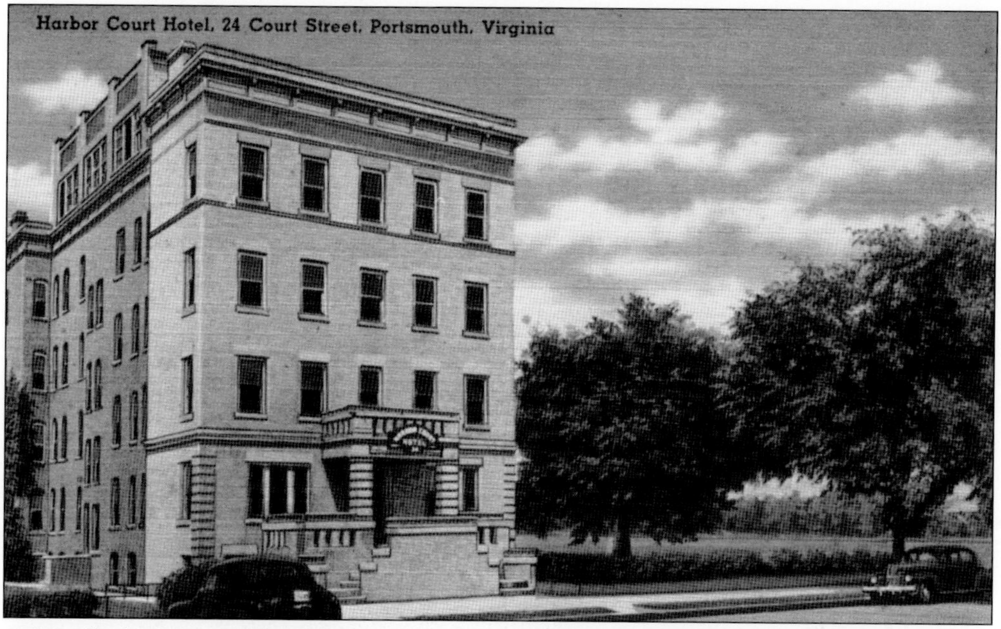

Originally built as the Waverly Apartments in the early 1900s, the use of this building was constantly changing. Due to an increase in 1908 of female staff assigned to the Norfolk Naval Hospital, female nurses were housed here and ate their meals in the café on the first floor. After some modifications, it opened as Parrish Memorial Hospital in 1921 and remained in service as a hospital until January 1945. The remodeled building, as seen in this view, was opened as the Harbor Court Hotel.

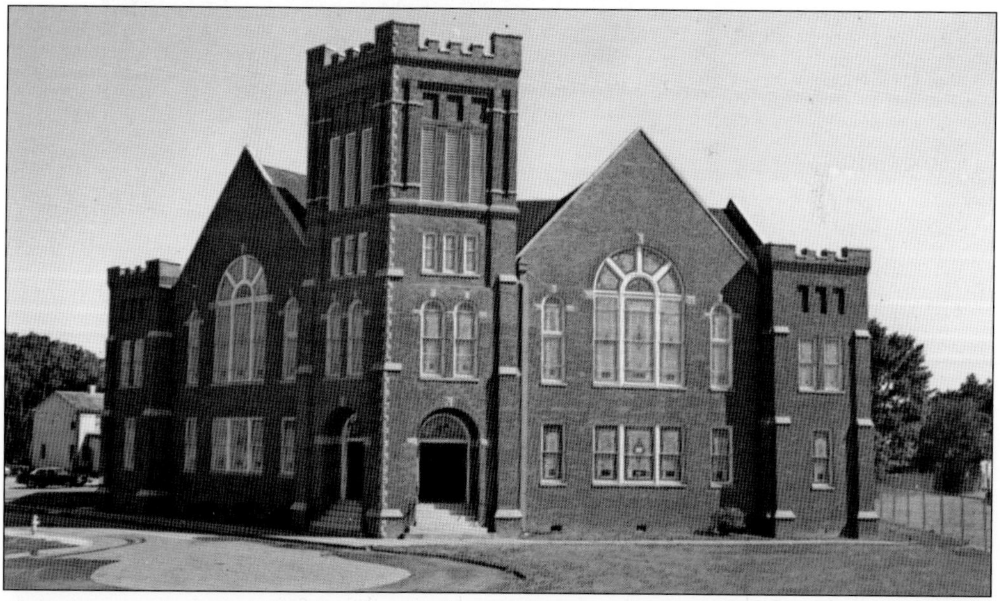

Constituted as Scottsville Baptist Church, the congregation changed the name to Cavalry Baptist Church in 1898. Built in 1918 on Glasgow Street, the Gothic Revival–style sanctuary, with its castellated parapets and bell tower, was constructed of brick and stone. With the numerous stained-glass windows gracing all of the exterior walls, the interior is aglow with tranquil colors on a sunny day.

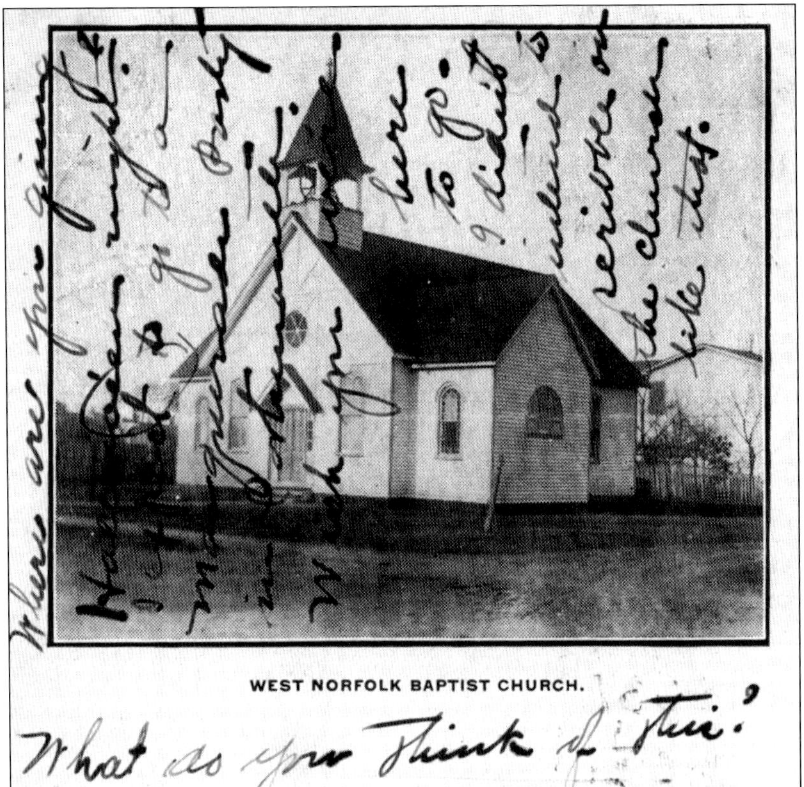

The village of West Norfolk was laid out with 58 lots by the West Norfolk Land Development Company in 1890. West Norfolk Baptist Church, shown at the corner of Mariner and Monroe Avenues, was established in 1891, and the sanctuary was built in 1895. Located on the Elizabeth River, the village supported a number of industrial and maritime businesses. Virginia Chemical Company, West Norfolk Lumber Company, and Planters Manufacturing Company relied on the Atlantic and Danville Railroad as well as the number of coastal schooners that sailed in and out at the docks. Though the businesses have been shuttered and closed, the church remains intact and active today.

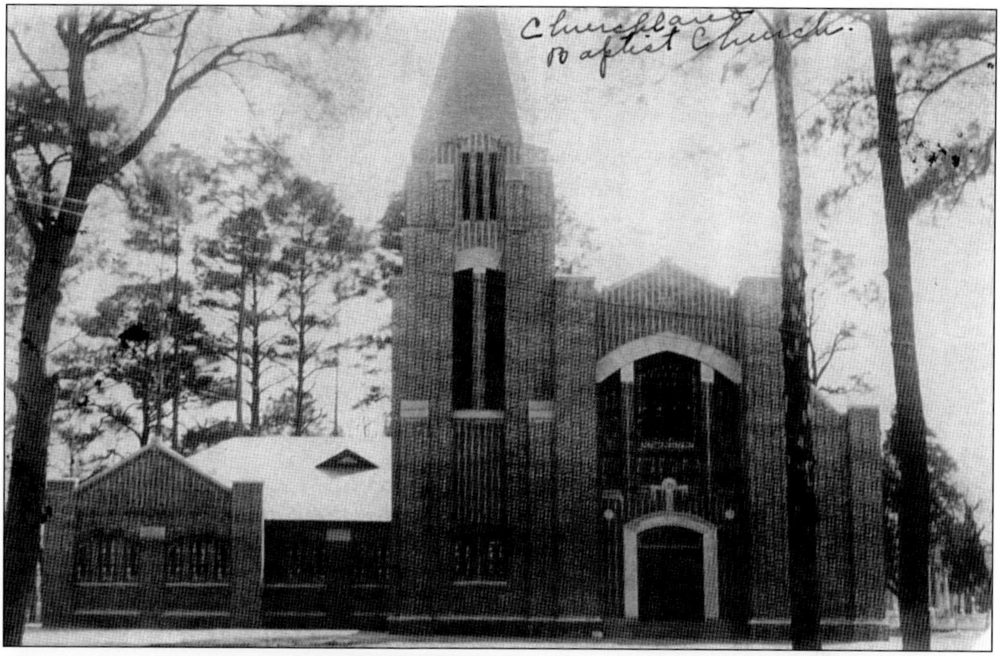

This real photo postcard, postmarked in 1911, shows Churchland Baptist Church as it appeared shortly after the dedication of the new sanctuary and parsonage. Founded as Shoulder's Hill Baptist Church in 1785, the church relocated to this donated parcel of land and built its first sanctuary on this site in 1829. The name was changed to Churchland Baptist Church during the 19th century, and in the 1960s, a new sanctuary was built. (Courtesy of Churchland Baptist Church.)

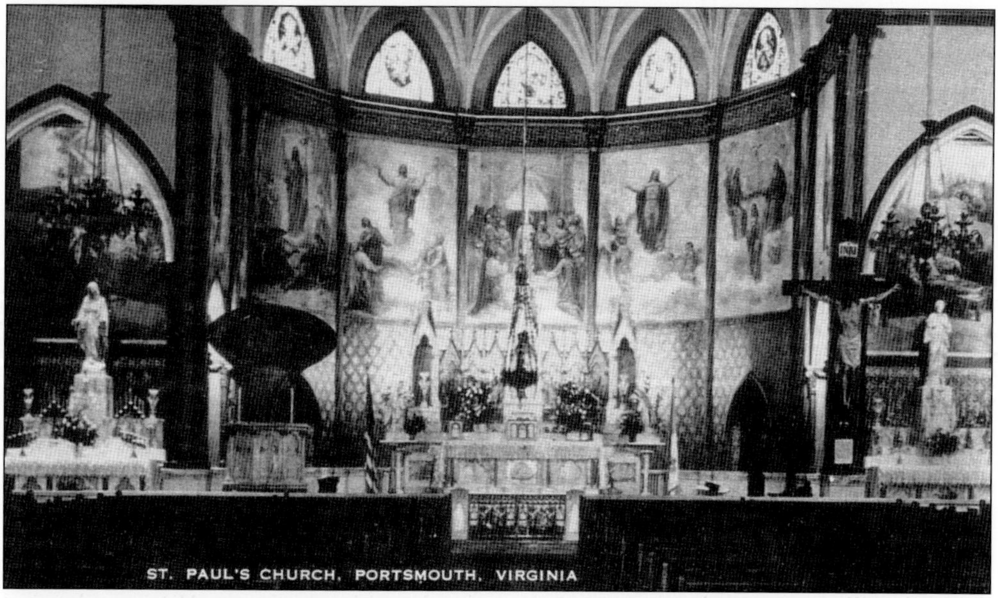

An interior view of St. Paul's Catholic Church shows the magnificent fresco paintings on the walls that adorn the sanctuary, gifts of the Parker and Maupin families. The magnificent sculptures, ornate decorations, and numerous memorial windows were gifts of church families and parishioners. It has been claimed that the decoration of the church was not completed until the early 1930s.

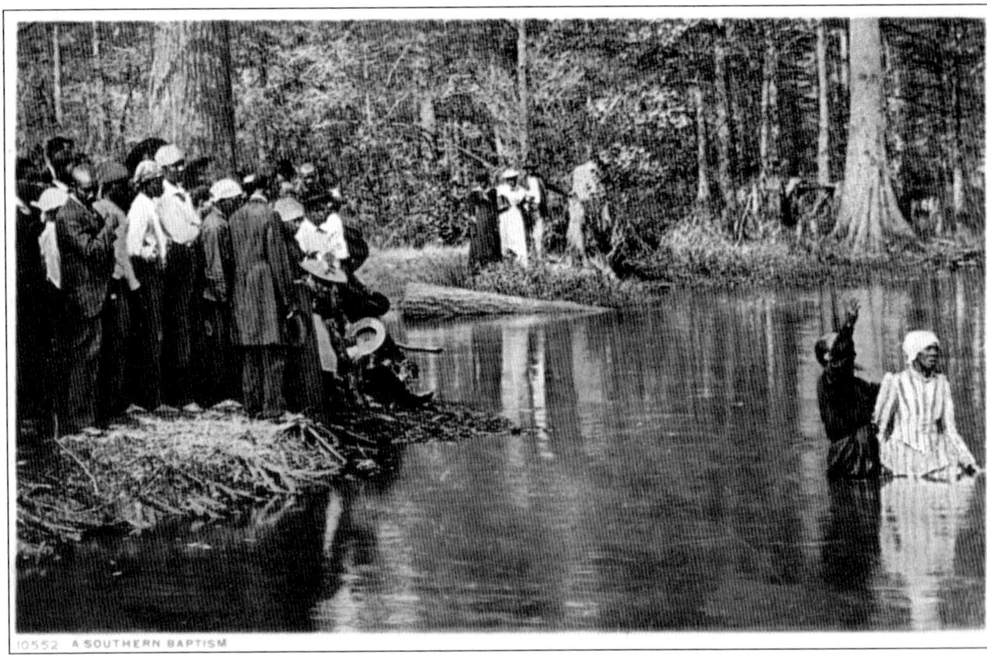

An early example of a Southern baptism shows an African American congregation standing on the creek bank as an unidentified person is baptized by the preacher. This scene is said to be in the Deep Creek borough of Norfolk County. Another location for baptizing that was often used by members of Grove Baptist Church in the Churchland Borough of the county was Bruce Station.

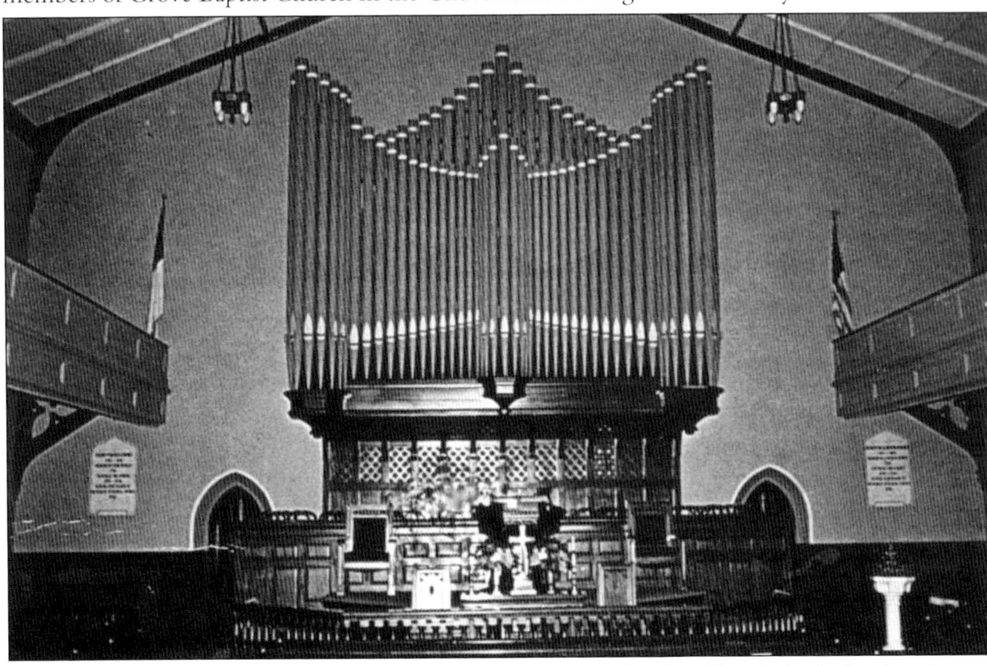

A view from the early 1950s taken inside Monumental Methodist Church includes the chancel and the Austin Opus 446 Pipe Organ. Arthur J. Lancaster was the director of music from 1911 until his death in 1961. During his tenure, he was recognized for his excellent performances on the organ and his contributions and dedication to music within the church and community.

Four

Hungry and Tired?

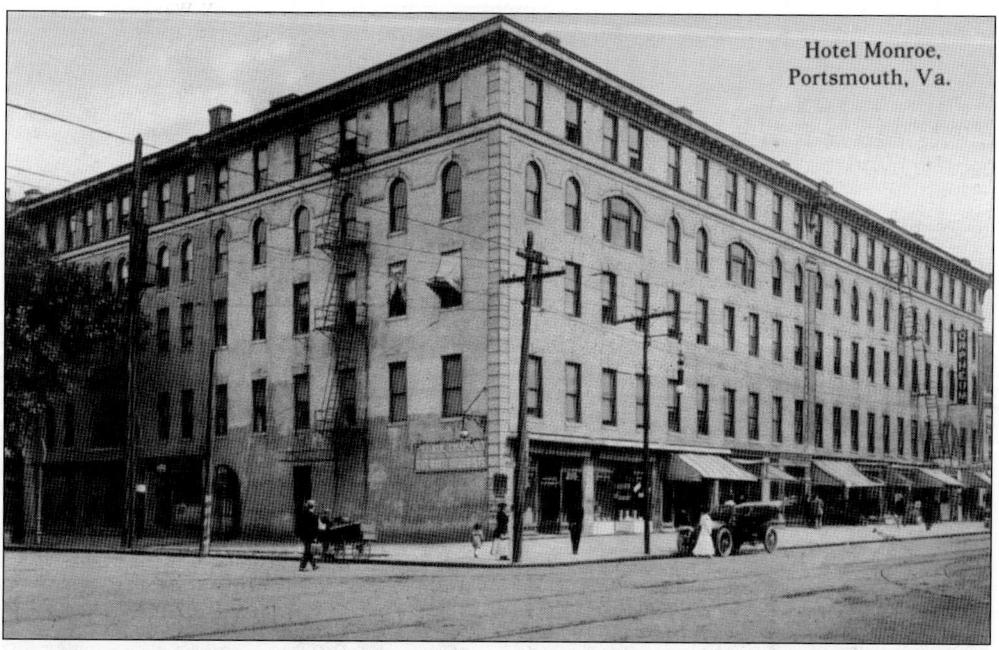

The Hotel Monroe (in earlier days the Ocean House Hotel) was built in the 1850s and remained a city landmark until 1957, when it was lost in a major fire. During the Civil War, after Union forces reoccupied the city, the hotel was converted to the Balfour US General Hospital and used for the treatment of African American troops who had been wounded in skirmishes around Petersburg.

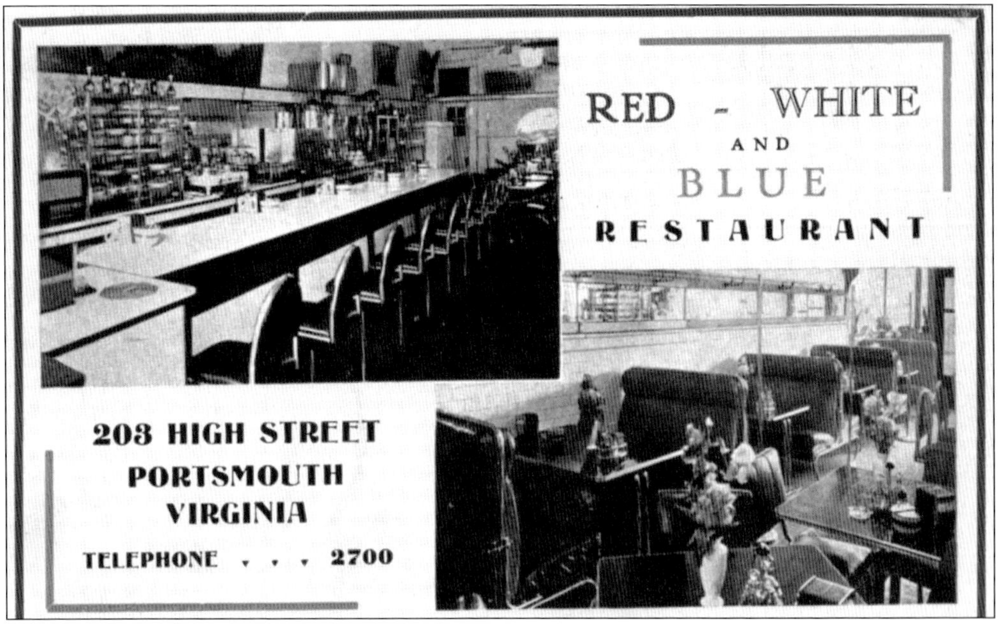

The Red, White, and Blue was located in the 200 block of High Street, next to the Greyhound Bus Station. A popular eatery for locals and servicemen passing through on leave or reporting to duty, it was hailed as a first-class restaurant for "ladies and gentlemen" with its "Royal Chrome booths and counter." Home-cooked meals and blue plate specials were always on the menu.

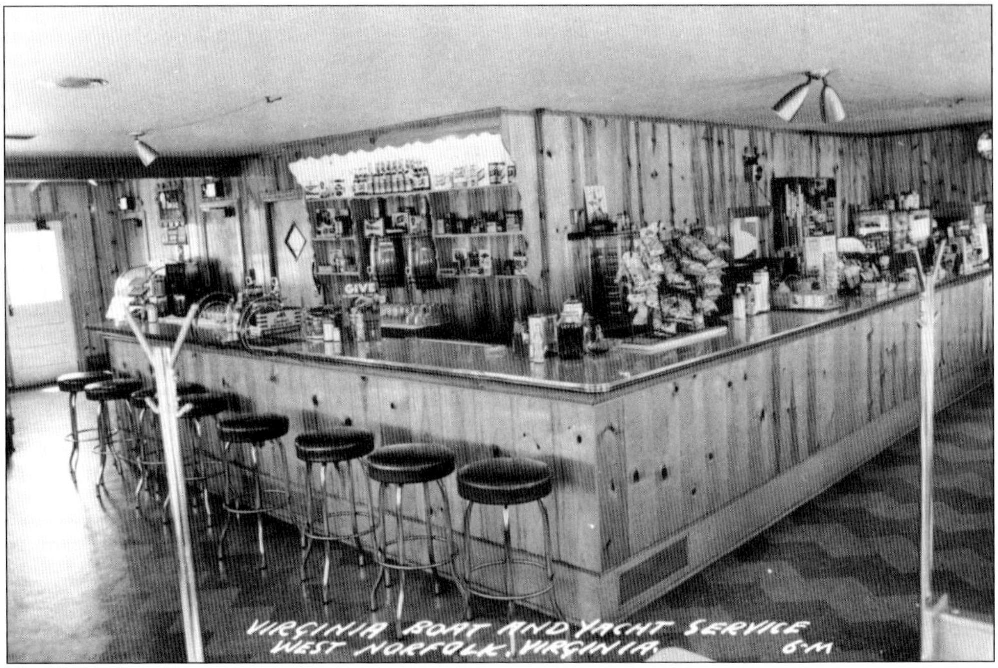

This 1950s view shows the restaurant at the end of the pier that offered boaters passing through to the Intracoastal Waterway an opportunity to eat and pick up needed supplies. Workers at the Curtis-Dunn Marine Shipyard could stop in for lunch or a cold beverage after work. In later years, it was remodeled and became a popular seafood restaurant, the Scale O' De Whale.

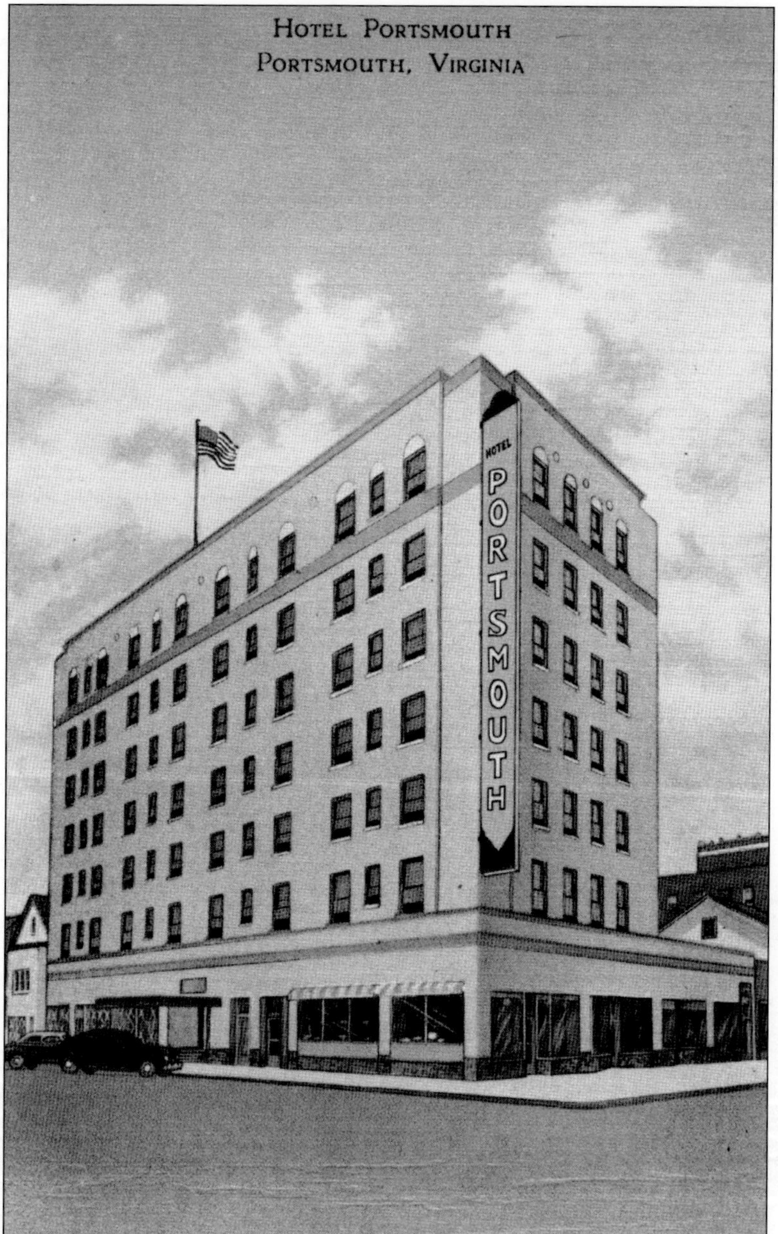

The Hotel Portsmouth, located on the corner of High and Dinwiddie Streets, was completed and opened for business in 1945. Built as a joint public and private venture, the hotel literature read that it was a "fireproof hotel, [with] 100 rooms all with private bath, [a] dining room, coffee shoppe, service of the highest quality and completely air-conditioned." During the 1950s, the name was changed to the Hotel Governor Dinwiddie in honor of the Colonial governor of Virginia. After years of neglect, the hotel underwent extensive remodeling and restoration work, returning it to its original design. Reopening in 2005, it was placed on the register of Historic Hotels of America and recognized by the National Trust for Historic Preservation. Claims have been made that Pres. Harry S. Truman stayed here during his visit to the Norfolk Naval Shipyard in 1949.

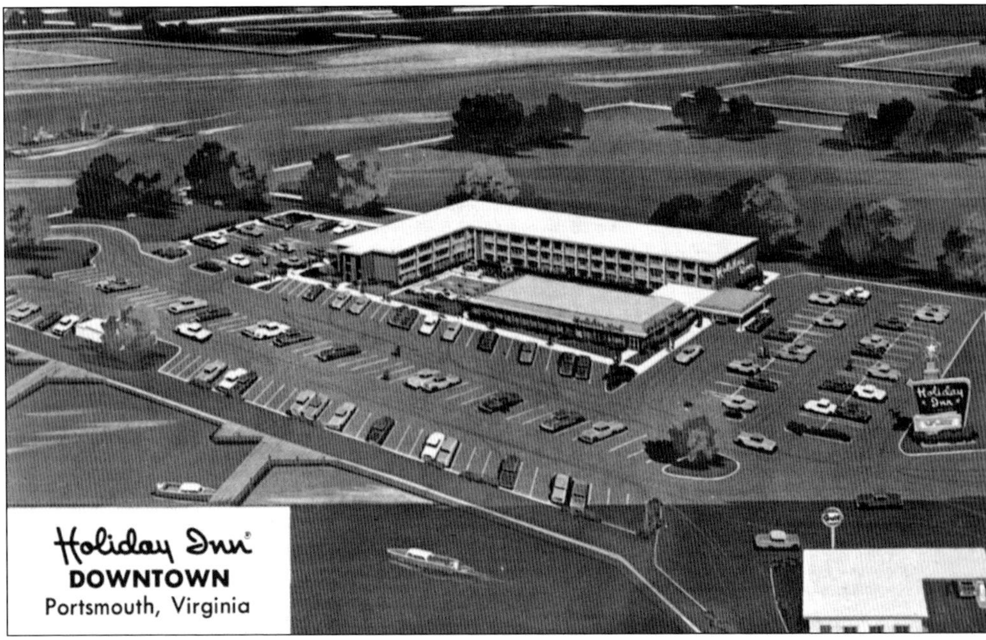

An artist's rendering depicts the Holiday Inn that was located on Crawford Street at the Elizabeth River. In earlier days, this had been the site for the warehouses and docks of the Seaboard Airline Railroad. Locals and visitors alike enjoyed many nights in the lounge on the waterfront, shag dancing and watching the fireworks.

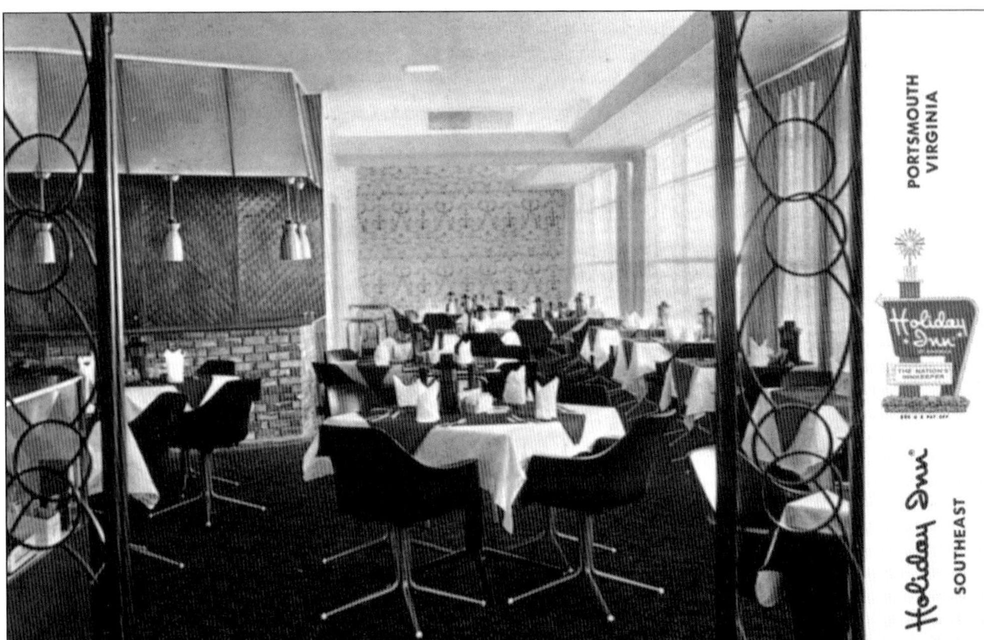

The Holiday Inn Southeast was located on US Routes 13 and 460 in Norfolk County. Travelers and local residents enjoyed eating at the Red Coals Restaurant, where they could have thick-cut, sizzling steaks from the open-hearth broiler. As usual for those traveling through the Southeast, hospitality is always assured.

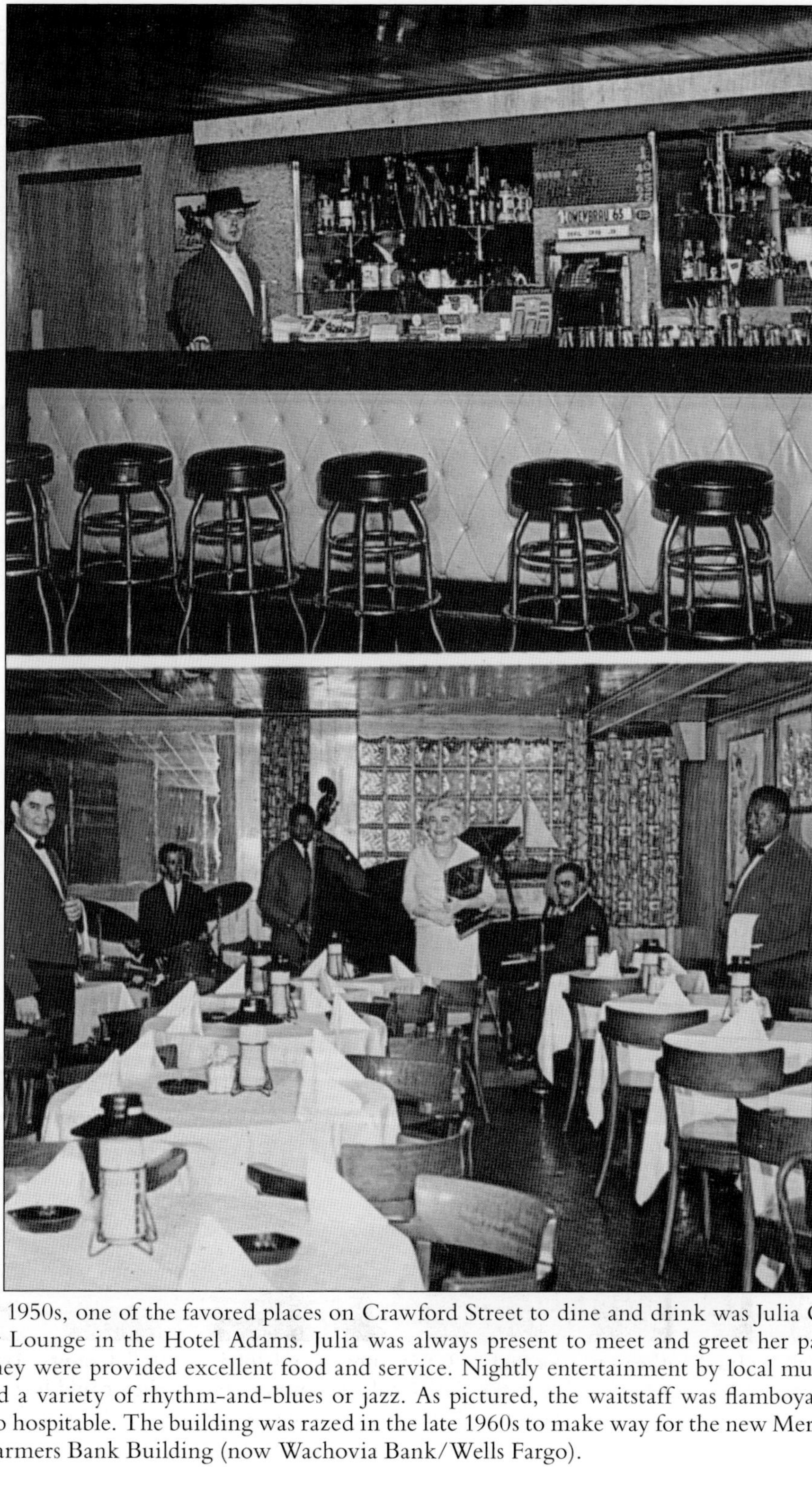

In the 1950s, one of the favored places on Crawford Street to dine and drink was Julia Cook's Cellar Lounge in the Hotel Adams. Julia was always present to meet and greet her patrons, and they were provided excellent food and service. Nightly entertainment by local musicians offered a variety of rhythm-and-blues or jazz. As pictured, the waitstaff was flamboyant but ever so hospitable. The building was razed in the late 1960s to make way for the new Merchants and Farmers Bank Building (now Wachovia Bank/Wells Fargo).

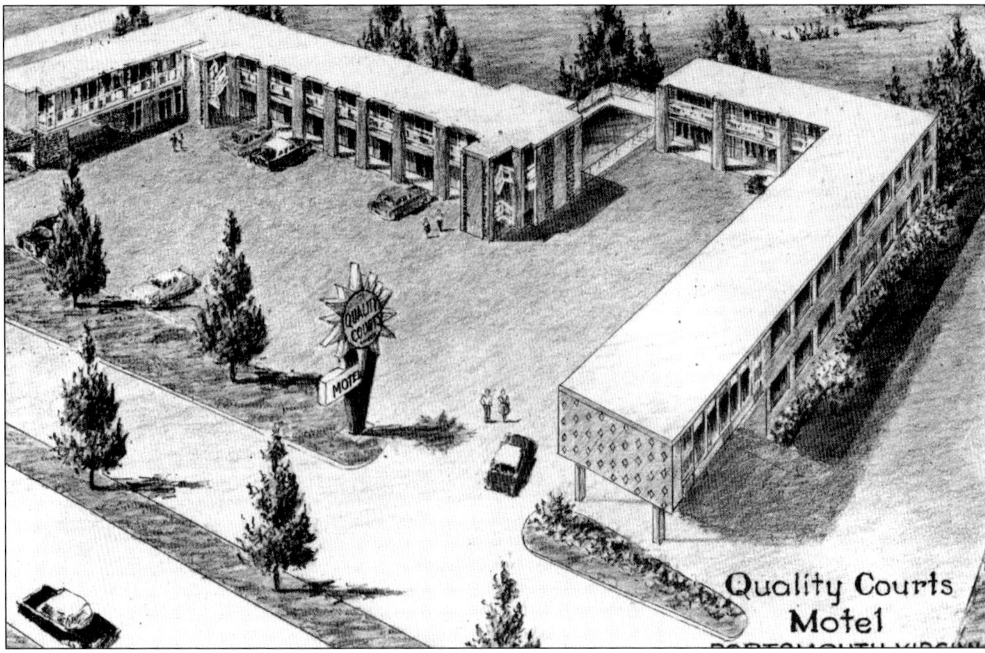

The Quality Court Motel was located at the corner of Frederick and Airline Boulevards in the Midcity District. A popular stop on Routes 17 and 58, it offered a swimming pool, television, and everything to make one's visit pleasant. What was even more popular was Flip Boyette's Pancake House at the entrance to the motel's office. Many late-night revelers would stop in for an "early" breakfast before heading home.

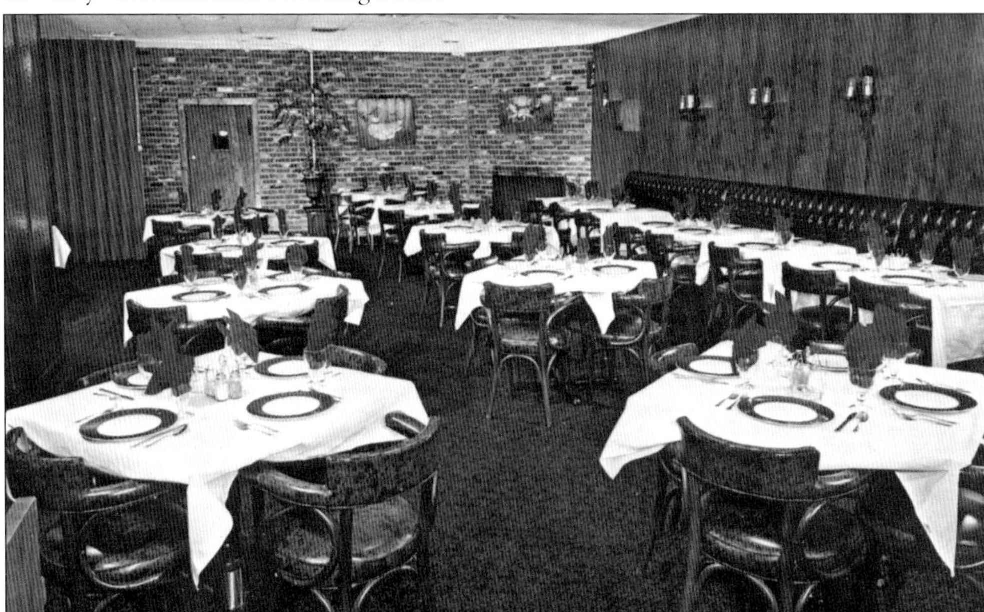

Specializing in steaks and seafood, the beautiful Embers was located on County Street next to the Quality Court Motel. The restaurant offered candlelit dining, and every meal was a delightful experience. On weekends during the disco era, patrons could enjoy dancing to tunes provided by a disc jockey or local musicians.

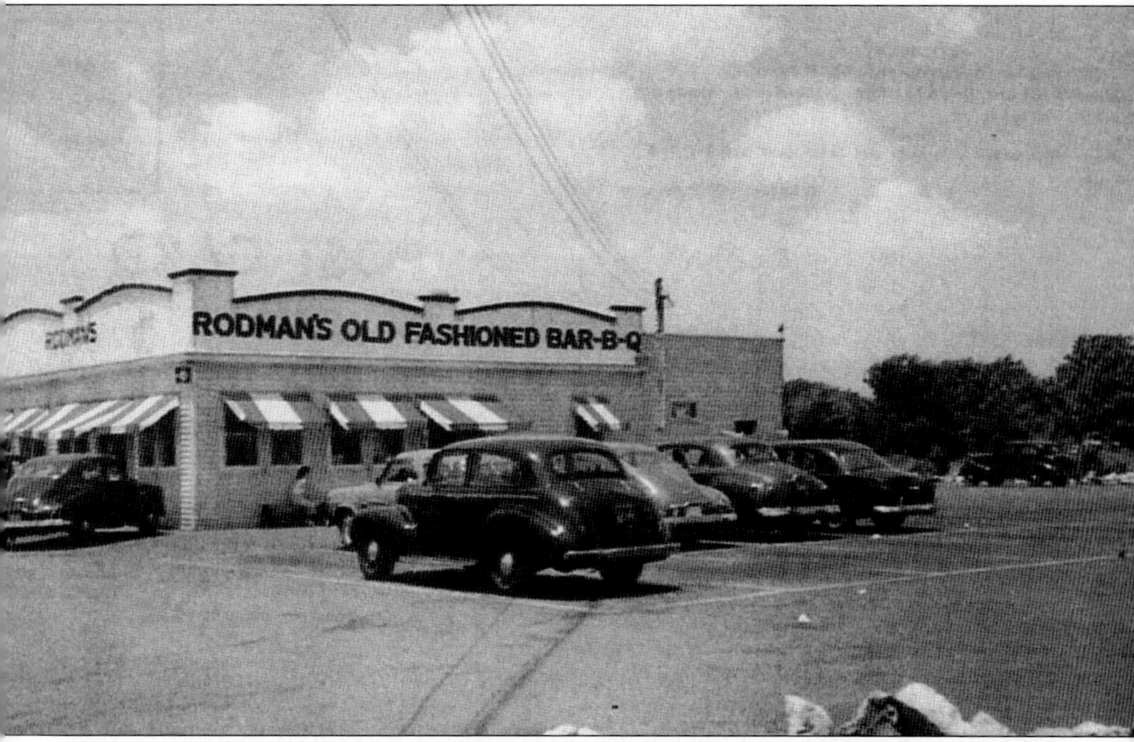

Founded in 1929 by Howard P. Rodman, a blacksmith by trade, Rodman's Old Fashioned Bar-B-Q came into being with his recipe for barbecued pig. He would slow roast the pork at the local smithy for civic and political gatherings. The public demand for his barbecue grew to such an extent that in 1929 he decided to rent a vacant Texaco gas station at High and Cumberland Streets and open his own restaurant. Business prospered, and a larger restaurant with drive-in curb service was constructed in the 1930s a few blocks east at the corner of High and Hamilton Streets (pictured). During the 1950s, the building was enlarged, and a brick-veneer facade was added to give it a modern appearance. The restaurant then offered banquet facilities and catering services for private parties and civic functions. The building is gone, but just a few blocks down the street, Rodman's barbecued pig is still available today.

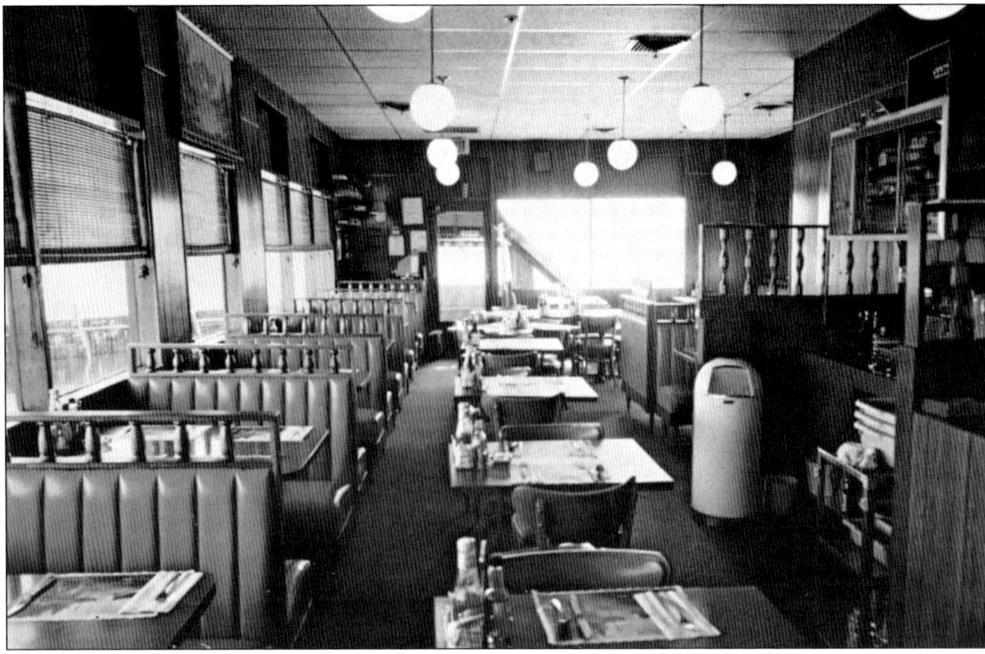

In this view from the early 1960s is the interior of the Deck Restaurant, located on the end of the pier at Holiday Marinas International. Famous for its seafood dishes and cocktails, the restaurant has been a favorite among locals and boaters traveling on the Elizabeth River. Despite a name and ownership change (Armory's Seafood Restaurant), as well as the occasional hurricane, it has been enlarged and has returned to the original name.

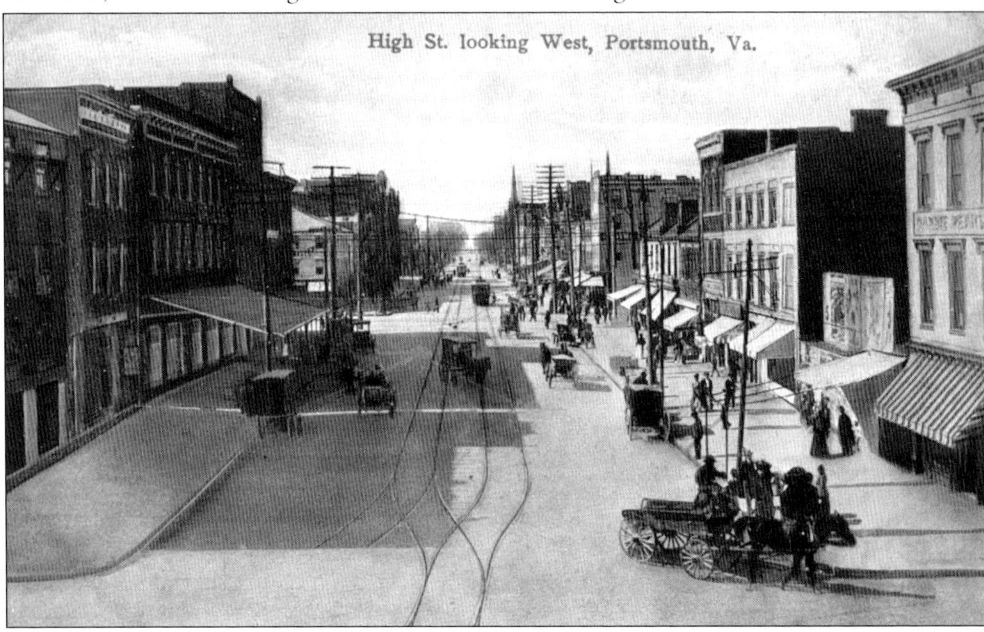

During the early 1900s, along the 100 block of High Street, no one had a problem locating somewhere to eat or drink. Sustenance could be found at Harrie Pearson's Saloon on the corner or a few doors down at Charlton's Saloon. If there were crowds at these establishments, a walk across the street to Dolan's Saloon would most likely prove fruitful.

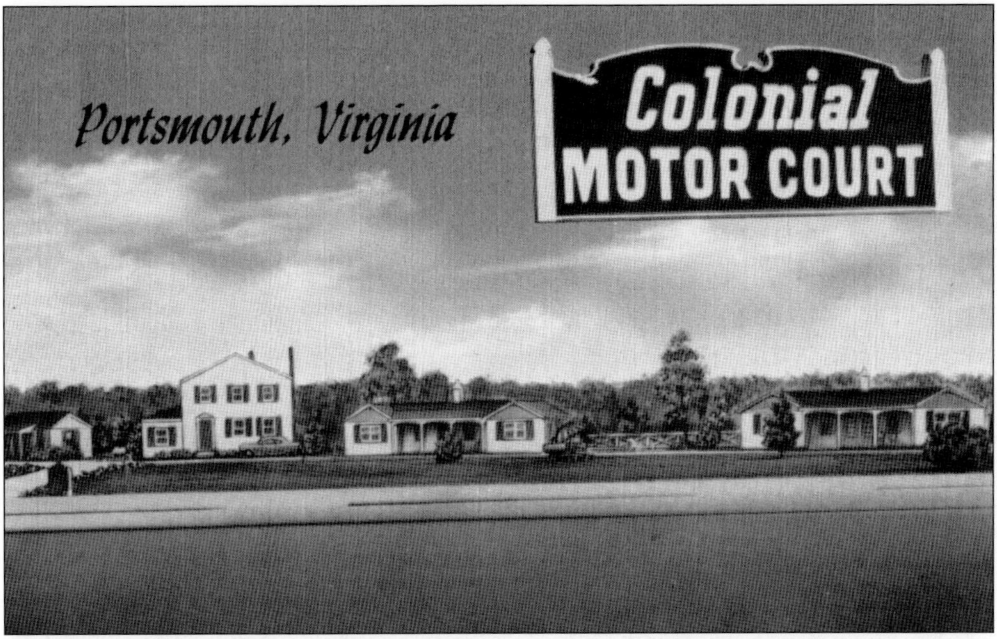

The Colonial Motor Court was located on Route 17 in Norfolk County at the junction of Route 13. Accommodations included tile baths, air conditioning, and free radios in every room. Route 17 was frequently used by travelers heading south to Florida for a summer vacation or to spend the winter in a warmer climate. The sender of this card writes, "first nite [*sic*] going down to Florida."

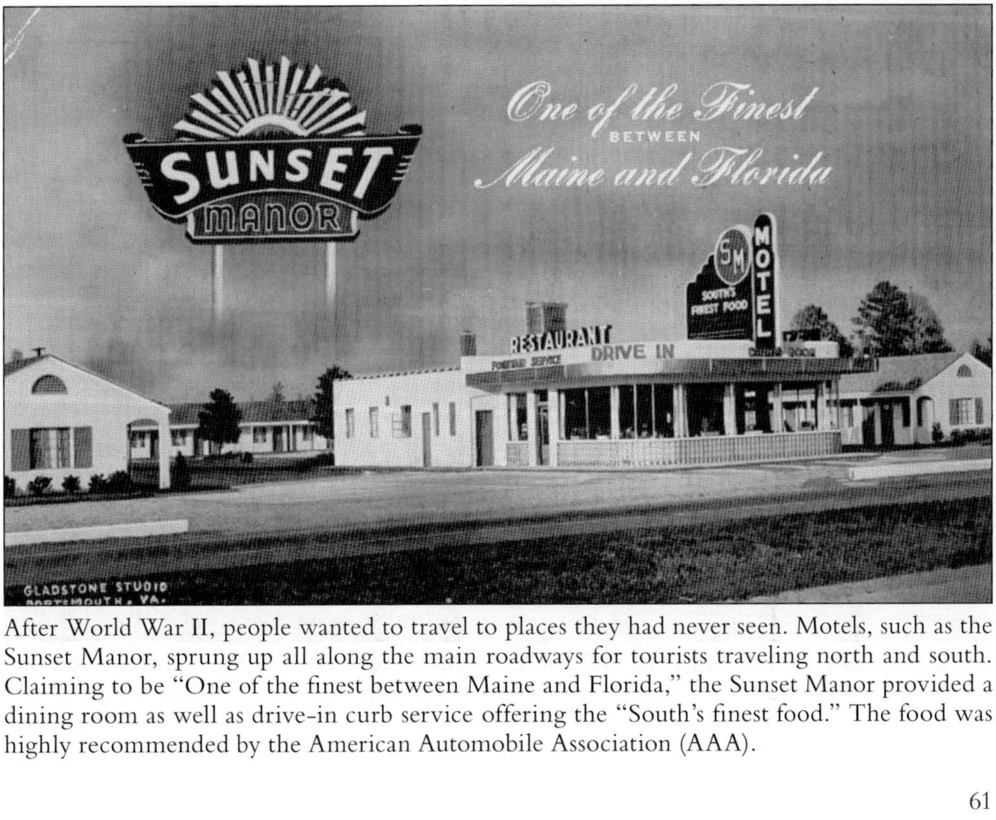

After World War II, people wanted to travel to places they had never seen. Motels, such as the Sunset Manor, sprung up all along the main roadways for tourists traveling north and south. Claiming to be "One of the finest between Maine and Florida," the Sunset Manor provided a dining room as well as drive-in curb service offering the "South's finest food." The food was highly recommended by the American Automobile Association (AAA).

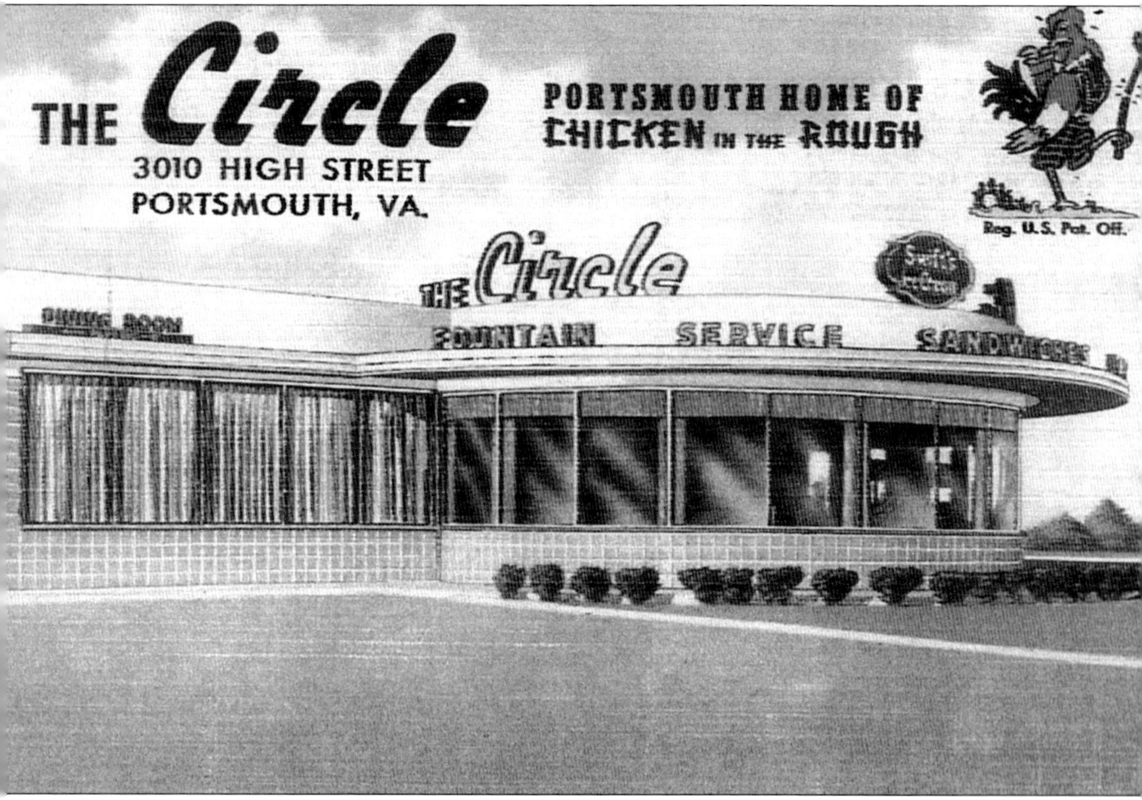

The Circle Restaurant, designed in a modern postwar style by Dorothy Morgan, was opened by Stewart Mathews in 1947. The facade was built in a circular shape, incorporating square glass blocks, stainless steel trim, and neon lighting, giving it the ambiance of a fine-dining establishment. "Chicken in the Rough," local seafood, and home-style cooking were offered, and one could eat in the dining room or outside at the drive-in, where the waitresses would deliver the food on a specially designed metal tray that hung from the car windows. A newspaper wrote that the restaurant had "Virginia's most beautiful drive-in," and it was also mentioned in the *Duncan Hines Vacation Guide*. During the 1960s, the drive-in closed, but the restaurant continued to flourish. The interior was revitalized in 1961, when a large mural in the caricature style was painted at the counter bar. Some of the celebrities depicted were Marilyn Monroe, Lucille Ball, Louie Armstrong, and the Marx Brothers. The restaurant is on the Virginia Landmarks Register.

Five

Getting There

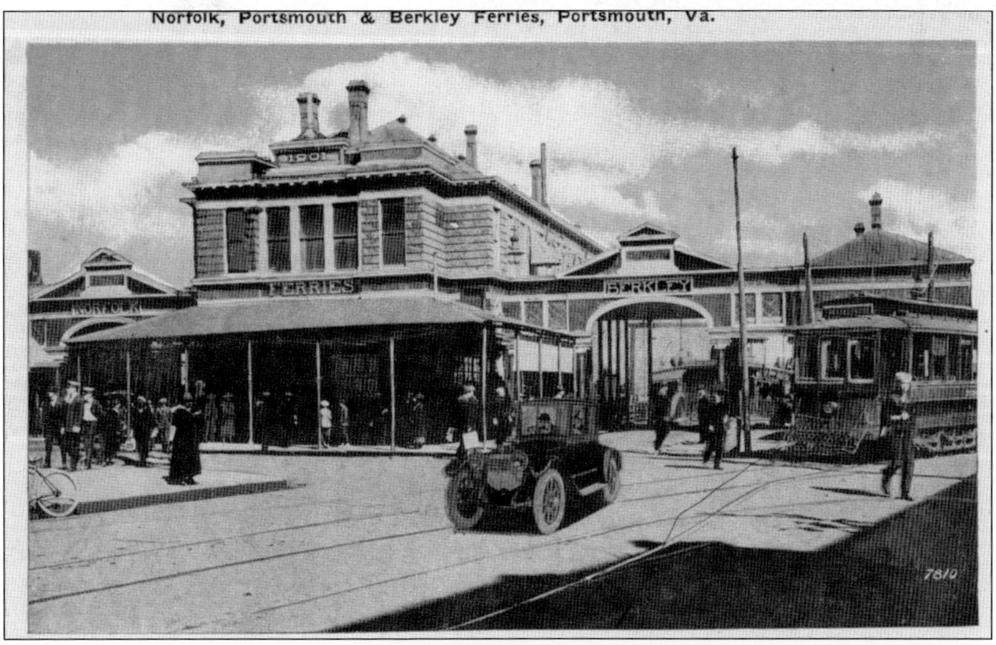

Ferries crossed the Elizabeth River between Portsmouth and Norfolk as early as 1637. The first steam ferry, the *Gosport*, was put into service in 1832, and over time, the fleet of ferries grew. The original ferry landing was at the foot of North Street; however, in 1839, it was moved to the foot of High Street, as seen in this view from the early 1900s. The car was added to the picture by the photographer.

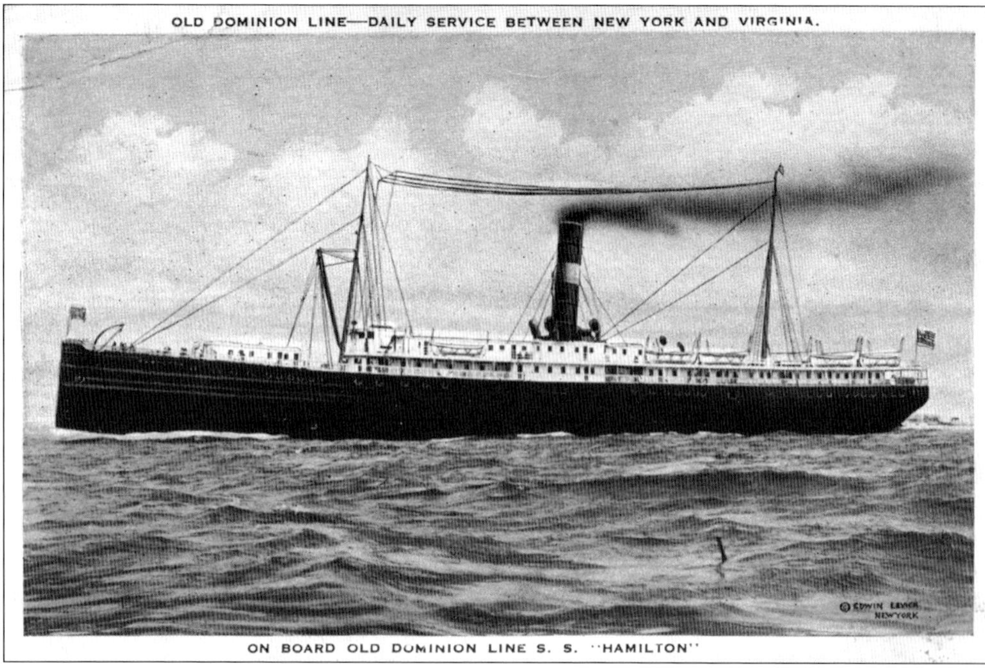

The SS *Hamilton* of the Old Dominion Line was one of the many passenger steamers that docked in Portsmouth and offered daily service between Virginia and New York. Travelers heading south could easily disembark from the ship and walk over to the Seaboard Airline Railway Depot to purchase tickets to their next destination or stay and visit the many attractions in the city.

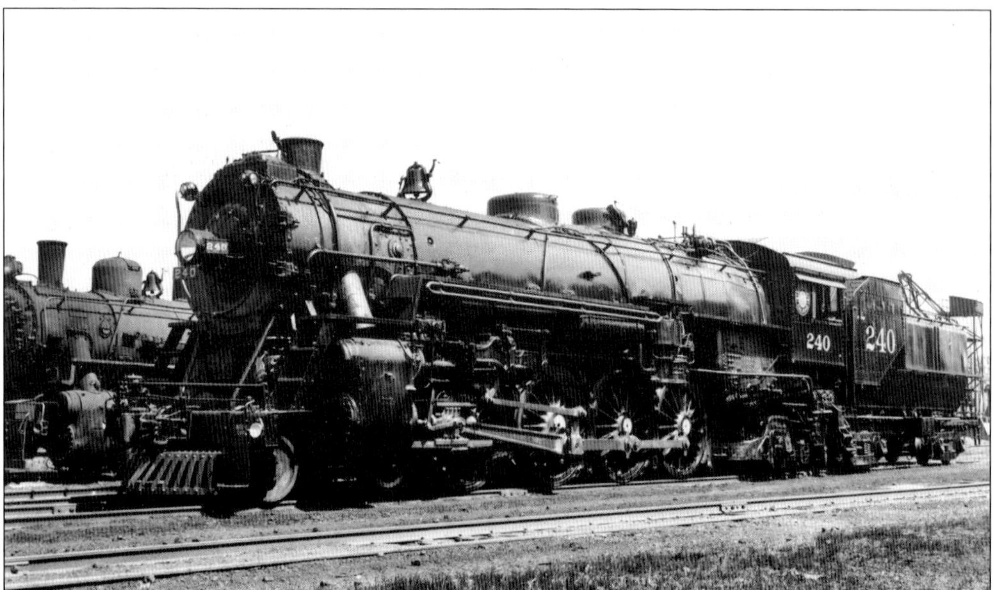

A sight often seen on the waterfront was steam locomotives of the Seaboard Airline Railway pulling in and out at the loading platform behind the Seaboard Building. The headquarters for the rail line and the repair shops were located in Portsmouth until the late 1950s. This real photo postcard was taken near the repair shop in 1951 of a type 4-8-2 locomotive.

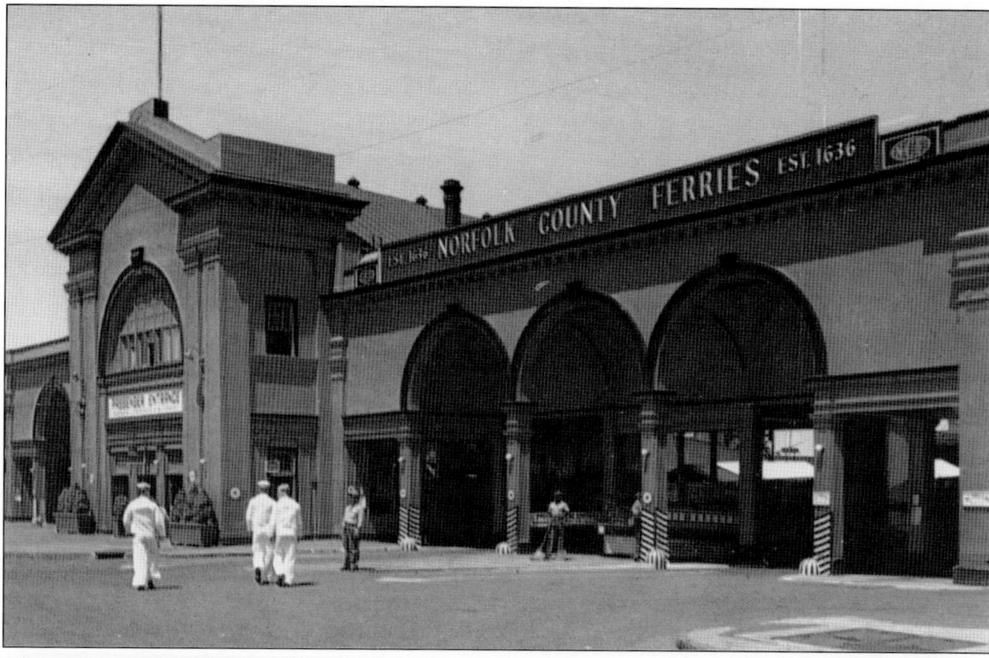

This view of the Norfolk County Ferries Terminal from the early 1950s pictures a group of sailors on shore leave walking towards the passenger entrance. Annually, thousands of foot passengers would ride the ferry back and forth across the Elizabeth River, either for business or pleasure. The parade float parked under the vehicle passageway was used in the Portsmouth Bicentennial Celebration of 1952.

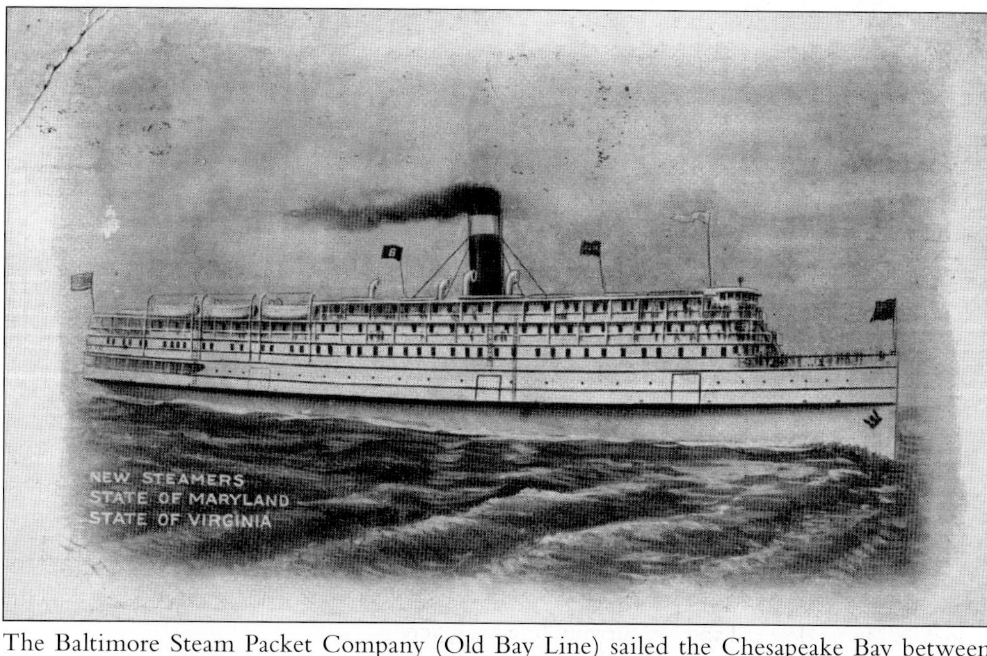

The Baltimore Steam Packet Company (Old Bay Line) sailed the Chesapeake Bay between Portsmouth and Baltimore on a daily schedule. With a steady flow of goods and passengers arriving and leaving each day by steamship or railway, today, as then, the city's motto accurately remains "where rail meets sail."

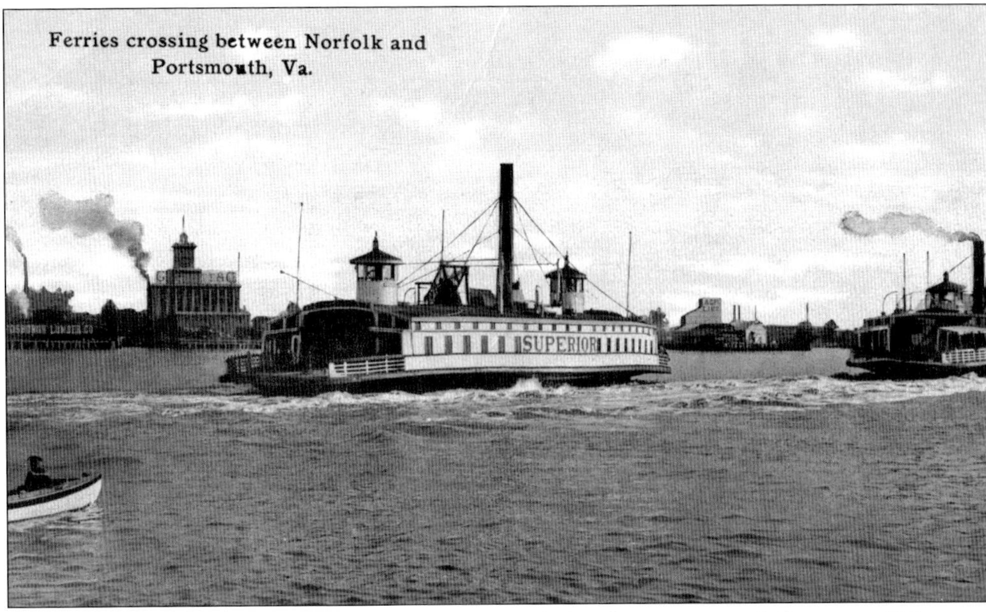

This view of the steam-powered ferry *Superior* includes the Garrett and Company Winery of Berkley in the distance. A sailor in a small boat is maneuvering to get out of the ship's way and possibly downriver to the Norfolk Navy Yard. In earlier days, when the circus would leave Norfolk and come to Portsmouth, the elephants would not board the ferries because of the waves rocking the vessel; the trainers would have to swim with them across the river.

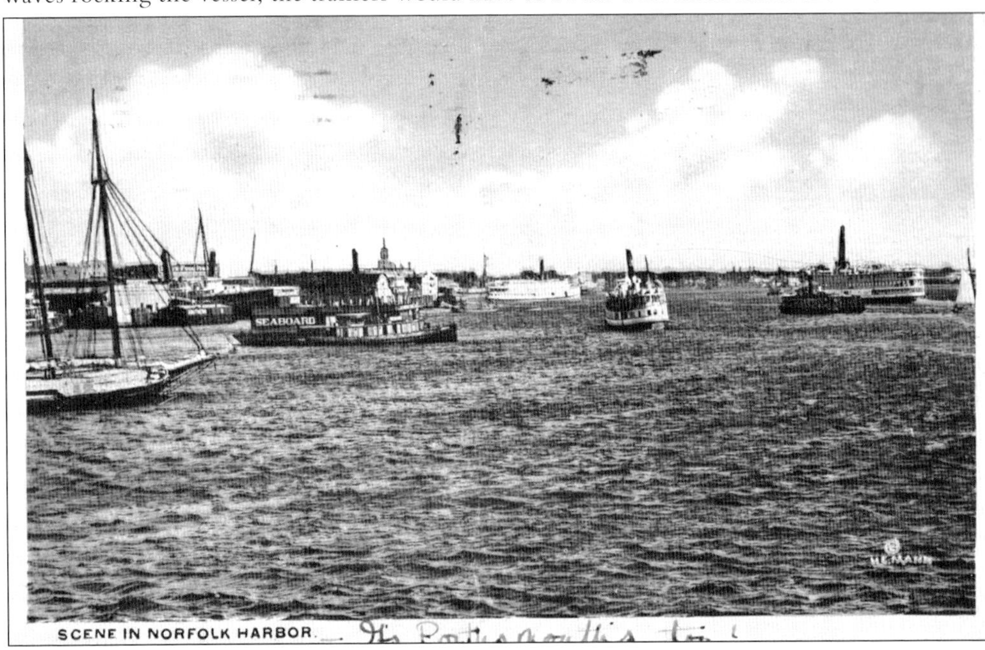

Navigating around the harbor was crazy at times, with steamships, ferries, sailboats, tugs, and schooners trying to avoid each other. Travelers and sailors just arriving found that they could be confused by the name designation by the federal government of the Naval hospital and shipyard located in the city. The sender of this card in 1929 decided to clarify the issue by writing next to the printed caption, "Its Portsmouth's, too!"

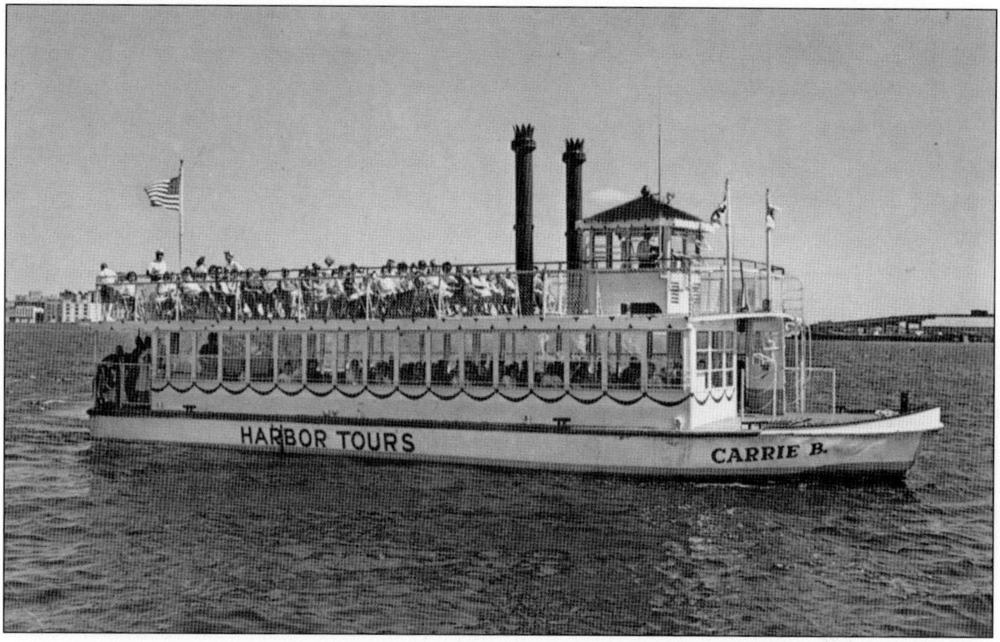

The *Carrie B.*, a replica of a 19th-century paddlewheel riverboat, has been an attraction on the Elizabeth River since 1959. Family owned and operated, the boat and crew have provided memorable cruises of the "world's finest harbor" to over one million patrons since they went into operation. There have been numerous high school class reunions, political rallies, and private events hosted onboard, as well as special cruises during the Seawall Festival and the Parade of Ships at the start of Harborfest. The tours depart and return to the North Landing on the city's waterfront.

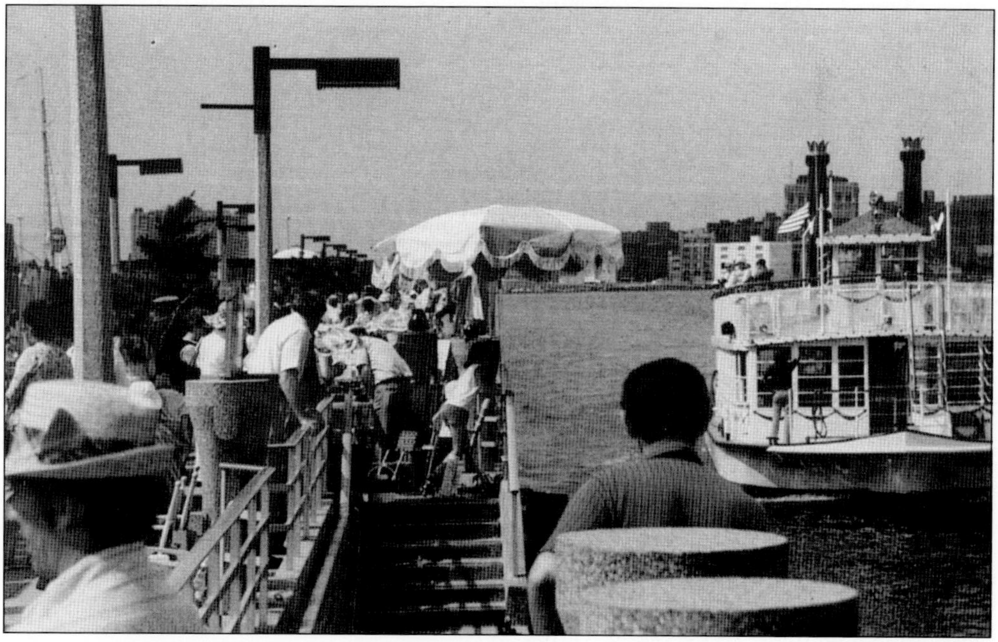

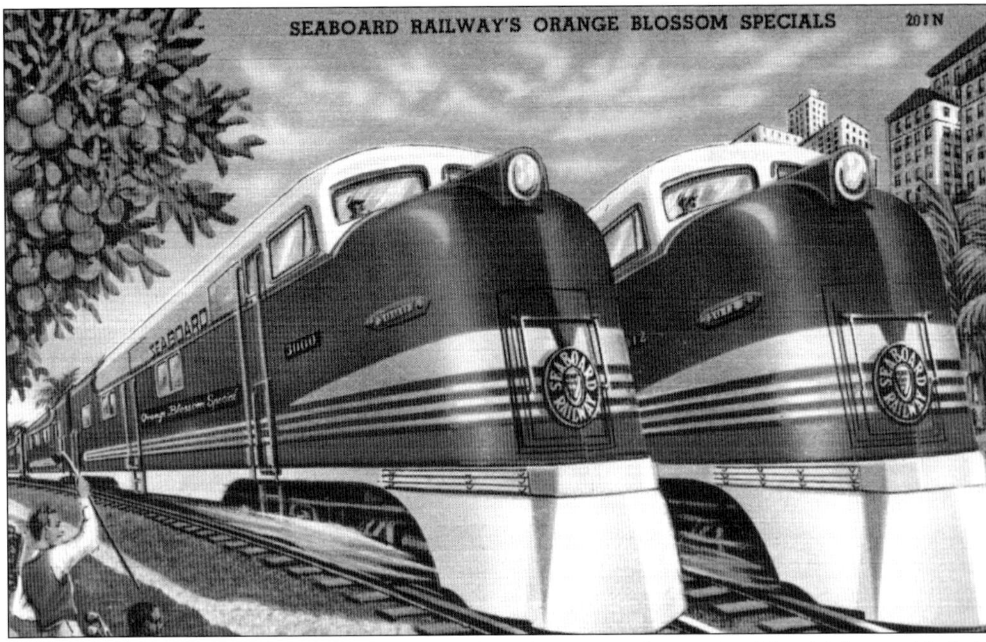

A souvenir postcard shows the Seaboard Railway's *Orange Blossom Special*, which provided the only diesel and electric Pullman service between points along the Eastern Seaboard to Florida. The colorful trains, often seen at the loading platform behind the Seaboard Building, set a festive atmosphere, with passengers returning from their vacation and those boarding the train to leave for sunny beaches further south.

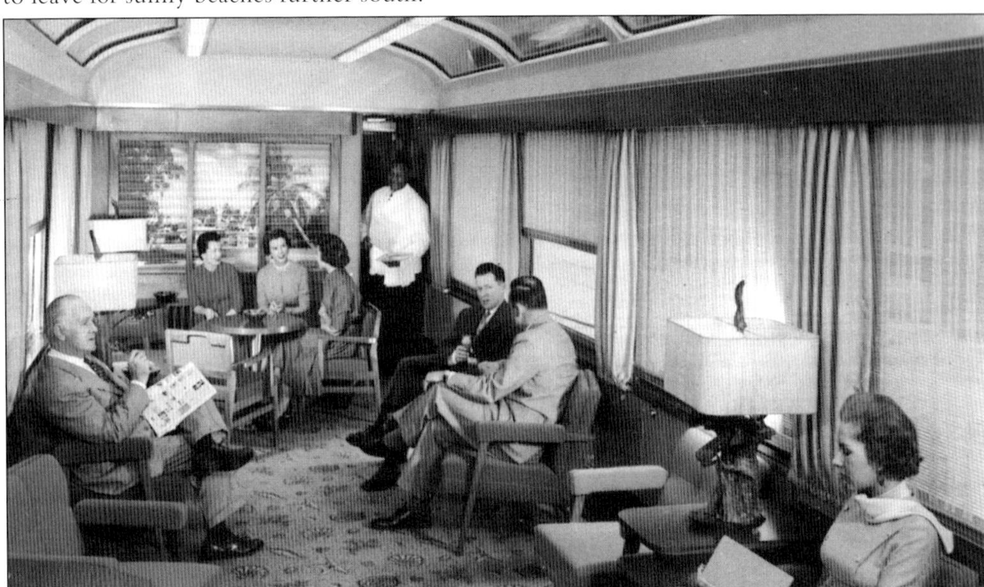

The Sun Lounge on Seaboard Railway's *Silver Meteor* provided passengers with all of the amenities of home. This type of streamlined Pullman car was constructed of a shiny stainless-steel exterior, and the interior was decorated with modern furnishings and lamps made with coastal driftwood. With its main offices located here, Seaboard Railway honored the city by naming one of the new railcars *Portsmouth*.

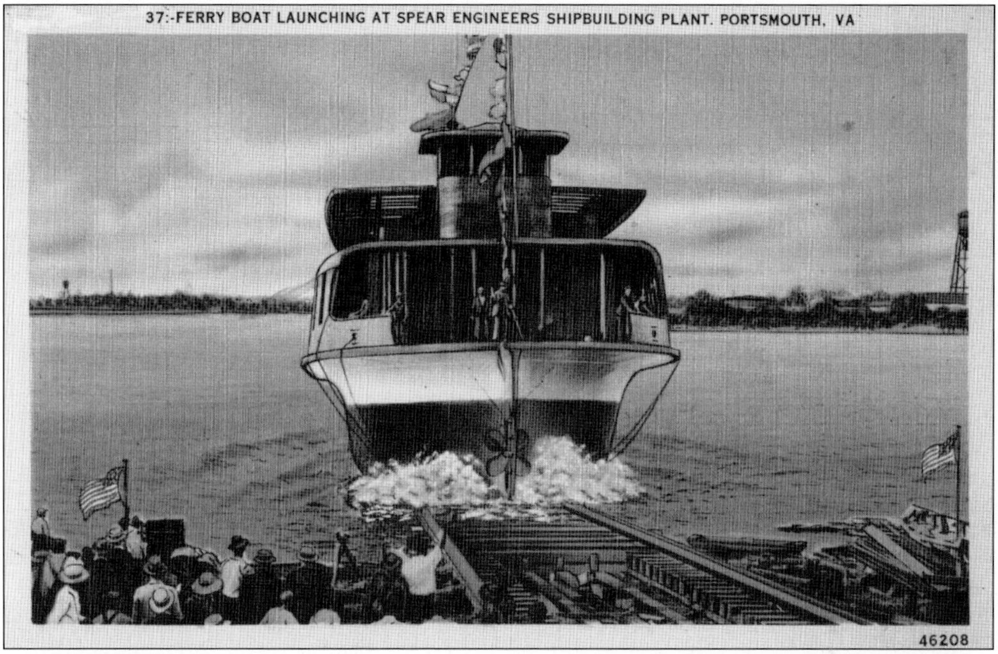

Throughout the years, along the shore of the Elizabeth River in West Norfolk, Port Norfolk, Pinners Point, and Scott's Creek, the one industry that has always thrived is the ship and boat repair facilities. Whether it is a marine railway at the Spear Engineers Shipbuilding Plant launching a ferry in the 1930s or hull work on a cabin cruiser at Virginia Boat and Yacht Service in the 1950s, boats of all sizes are an everyday sight in Portsmouth. Since the city's early days, the harbor and waterways have provided generations of skilled tradesmen a continuous flow of commercial and recreational vessels in need of service and repairs.

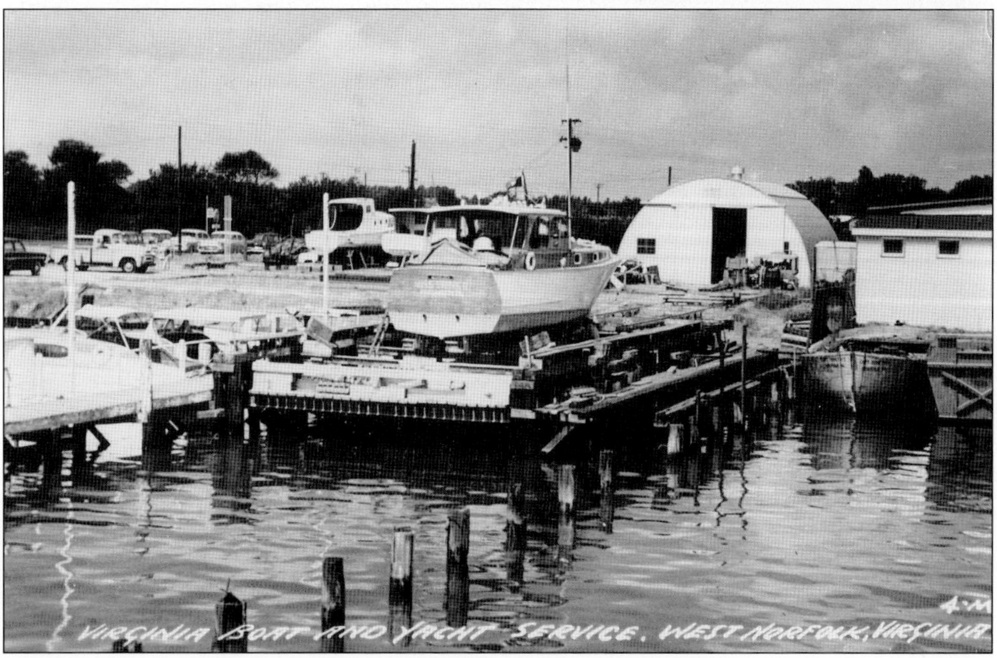

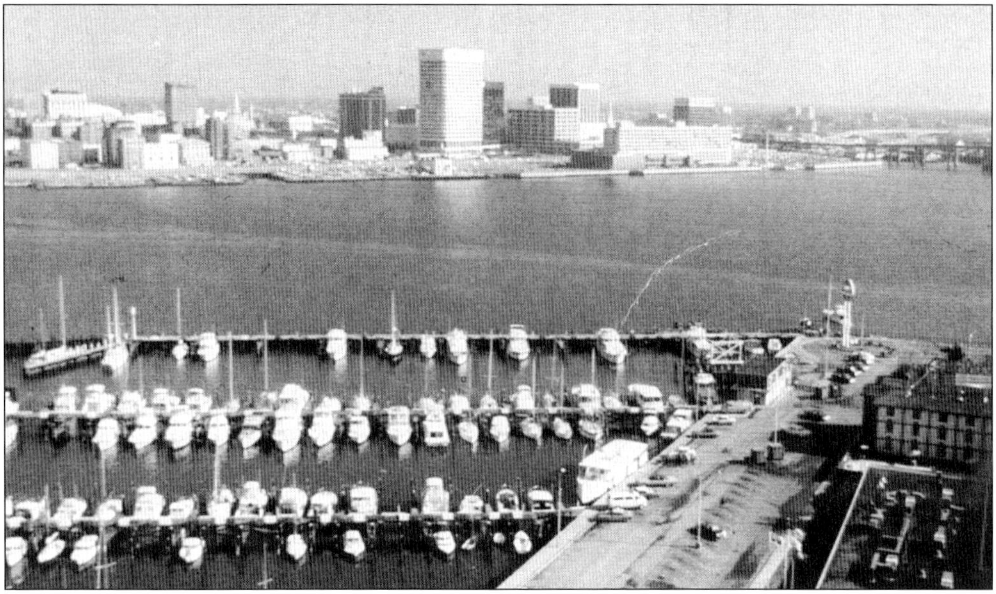

This aerial view of the Tidewater Yacht Agency and Marina at Crawford Bay on the Elizabeth River is near the Zero Mile Marker for the Intracoastal Waterway. The marina is home to numerous local boating enthusiasts and is a favorite stopover for those plying the waterway. In 1989, a resident's houseboat, tied up at "A" dock, brought momentary fame to the marina during the filming of the movie *Navy Seals*.

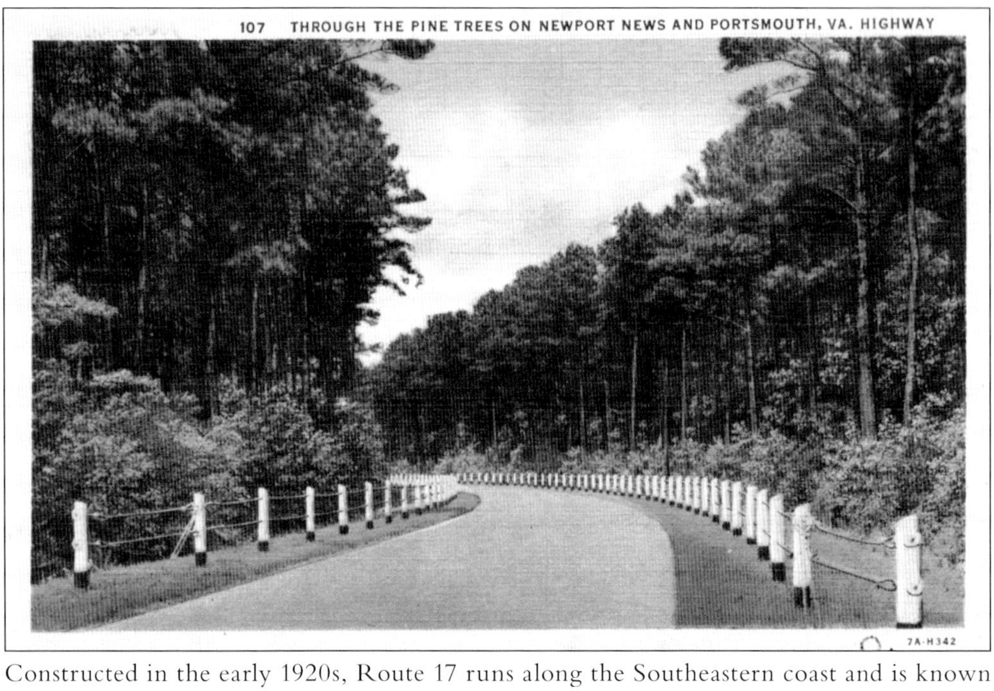

Constructed in the early 1920s, Route 17 runs along the Southeastern coast and is known as the Coastal Highway. This view is reminiscent of passing through the pine trees in Churchland when traveling towards Portsmouth. In 1938, the writer of this card noted that they were on a Greyhound bus going on a tour from the Peninsula over the James River Bridge to Portsmouth.

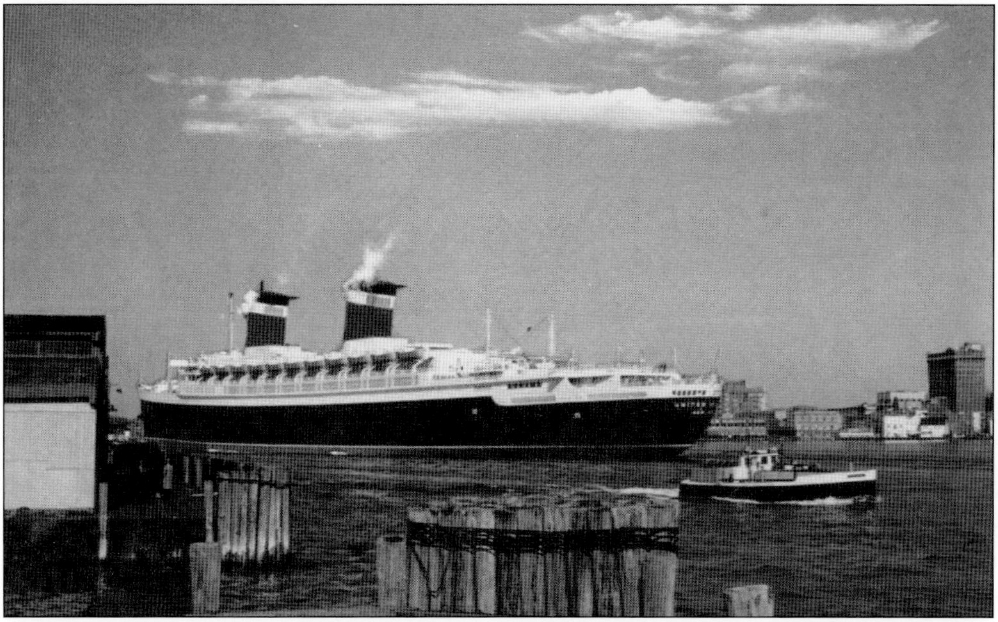

A colorful view of the SS *United States* shows the ship sailing past the Seaboard wharves on the Portsmouth waterfront, leaving the Norfolk Naval Shipyard in December 1952. After completing its 10th voyage, the ship was dry-docked for a survey of the hull, as scheduled by the federal government, which had underwritten $50 million towards the cost of building this vessel that could be converted into a troop transport.

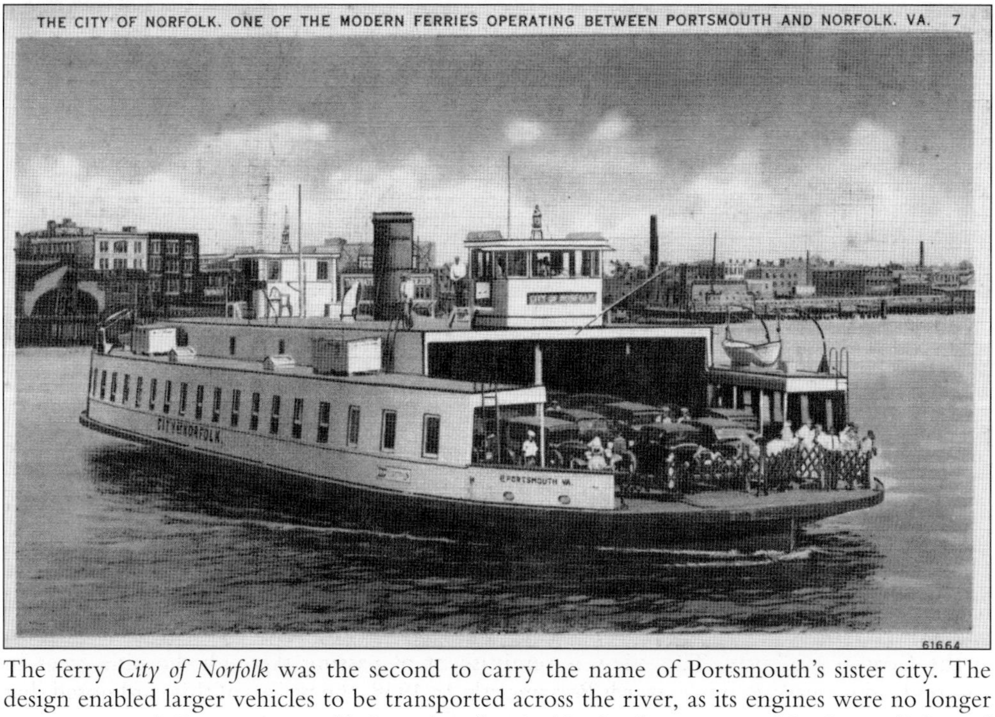

The ferry *City of Norfolk* was the second to carry the name of Portsmouth's sister city. The design enabled larger vehicles to be transported across the river, as its engines were no longer steam powered. Passengers could sit on benches inside the ferry or stand in the sunlight and enjoy the breeze off the river.

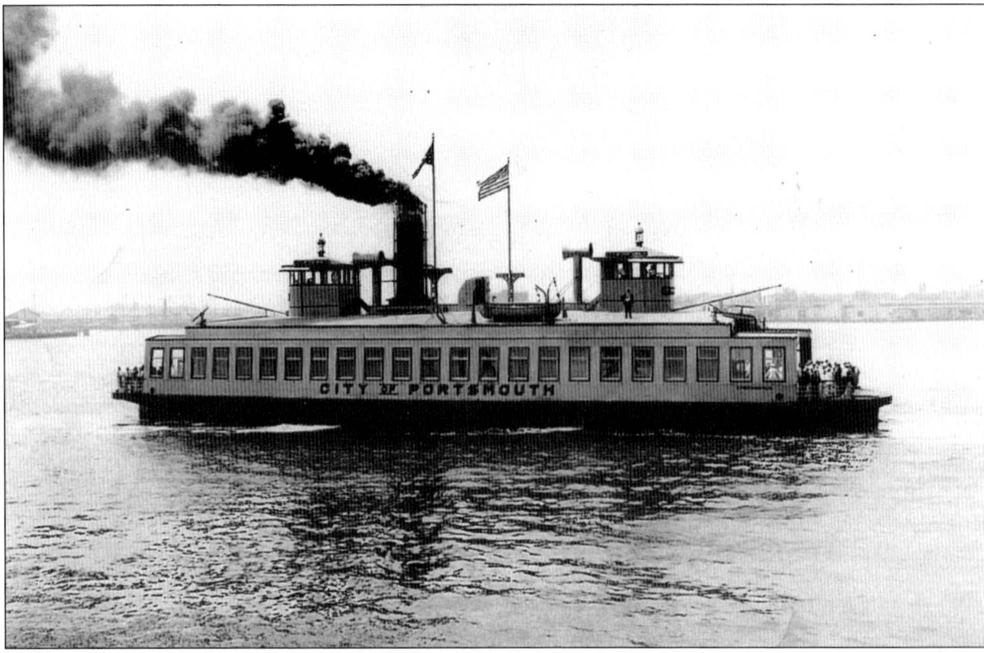

A real photo postcard from the 1930s shows the ferry *City of Portsmouth* crossing the Elizabeth River towards its namesake. This was the second ferry to be christened the *City of Portsmouth* and was in service from 1935 until 1949. On August 25, 1955, the last ferry made the final run between the two cities, but in 1983, passenger ferry service was restored to the river onboard replica paddlewheel steamboats.

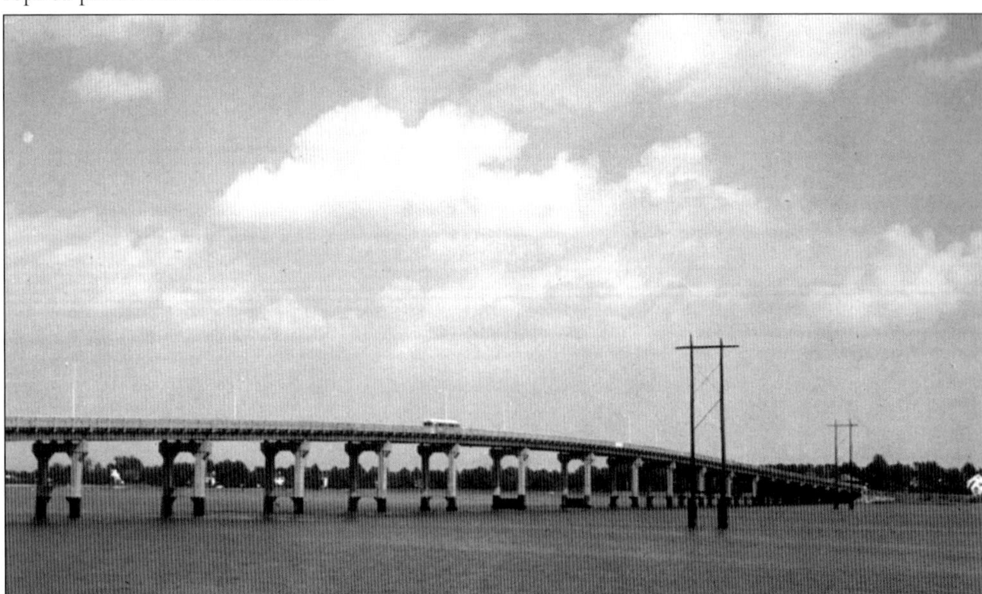

The Churchland Bridge was built across the western branch of the Elizabeth River in 1952 to connect the city of Portsmouth to the suburbs in Norfolk County. The original bridge was constructed as a two-lane bridge, but as the population grew, the bridge was expanded to four lanes. A Community Motor bus can be seen crossing at the top of the span.

Six

Where Do You Want to Go Today?

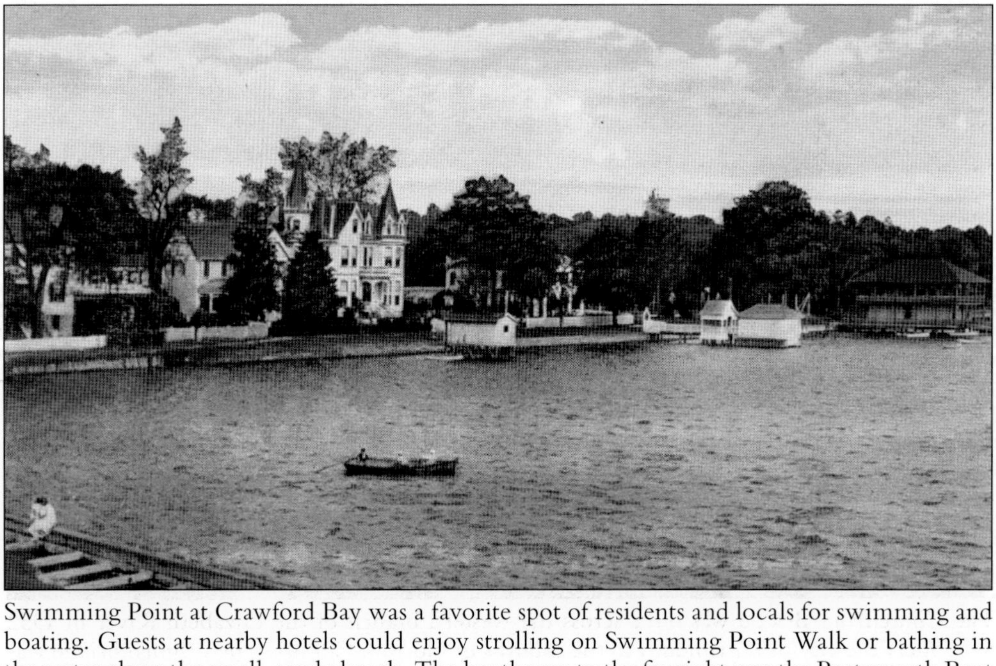

Swimming Point at Crawford Bay was a favorite spot of residents and locals for swimming and boating. Guests at nearby hotels could enjoy strolling on Swimming Point Walk or bathing in the water along the small, sandy beach. The boathouse to the far right was the Portsmouth Boat Club, established in 1905.

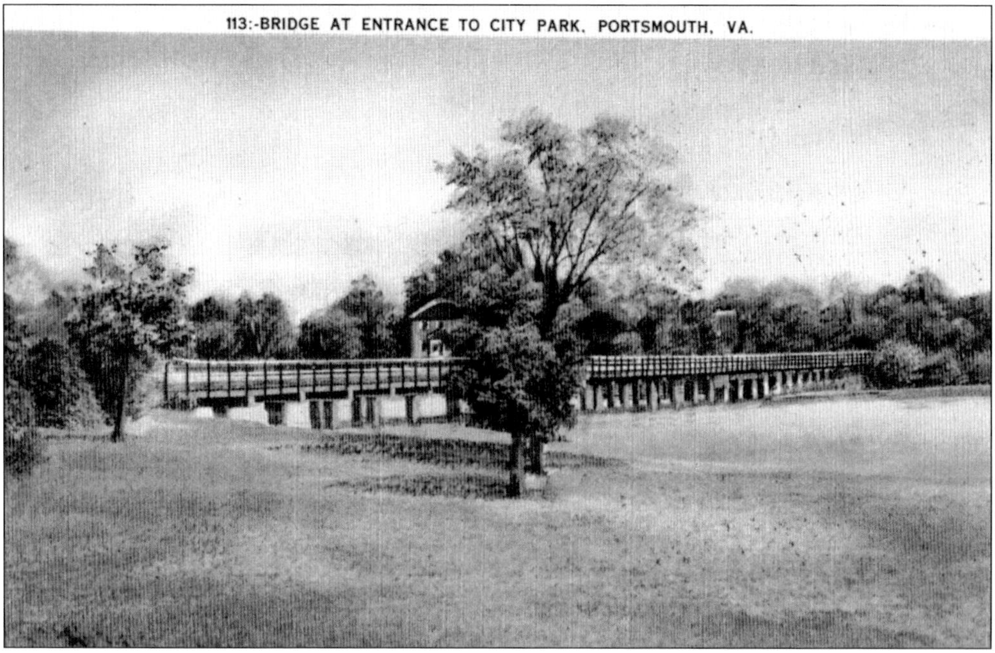

The City Park Bridge at King Street crossed Baines Creek onto Park Drive and was used by vehicles and pedestrians traveling to the park. The park opened in the early 1900s, with Olive Branch Cemetery the larger section of the park. Over time, a boat ramp, playgrounds, and miniature steam train were added to the park. On patriotic holidays, the city would have brilliant firework displays over the river.

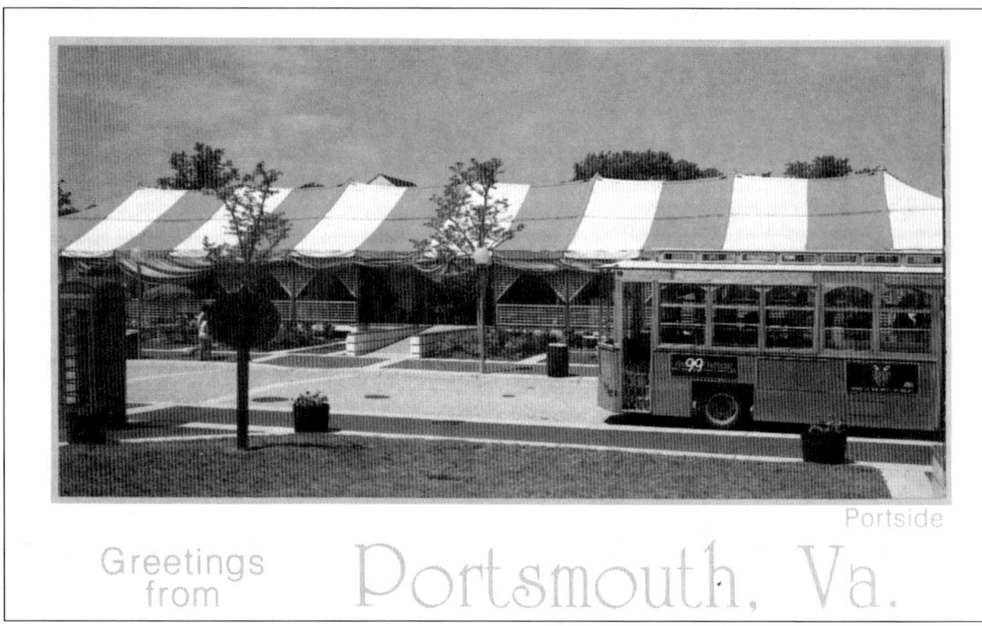

Portside was a festive market at North Landing that consisted of specialty shops and small eateries offering locals and tourists a place to meet and eat. During the Seawall Festival and on other special occasions, live entertainment was provided by hometown favorite Bill Deal and the Rhondels, and there would be dancing in the streets.

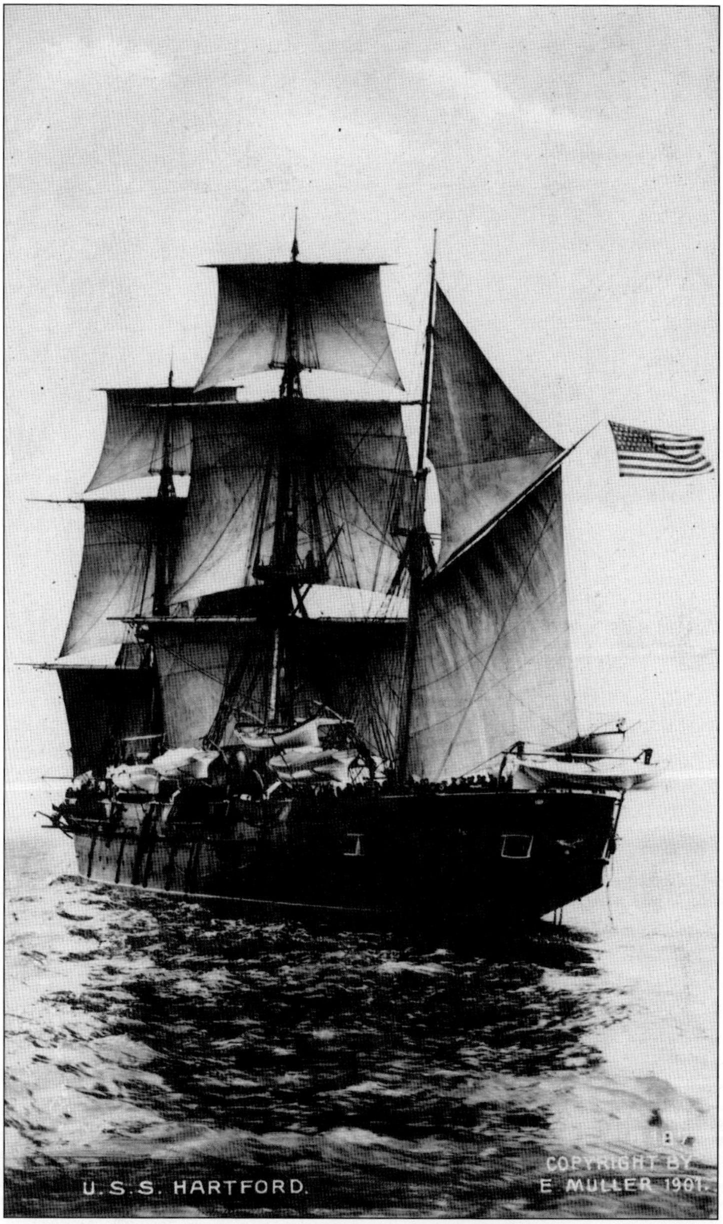

Commissioned in 1859, the USS *Hartford* would be remembered as the flagship for Adm. David G. Farragut during the Civil War. During the early years of his career, Farragut was stationed in Portsmouth, where he met his future wife while attending a dinner at the shipyard commandant's home. Rising to the rank of admiral, he would be remembered for his order given at the Battle of Mobile Bay: "Damn the torpedoes, full steam ahead." During the late 1800s, the *Hartford* served as a training ship for the Navy before it was decommissioned. On October 19, 1945, the ship was towed to the St. Helena Annex at Norfolk Naval Shipyard, where it was berthed and classified a relic. After years of neglect, the *Hartford* sank on November 20, 1956. Lacking the funds to raise and restore the ship, various artifacts were removed from the vessel and placed in museums; some of them are displayed at the Portsmouth Naval Shipyard Museum. The remaining derelict was towed to a point off Craney Island and sent to a fiery grave.

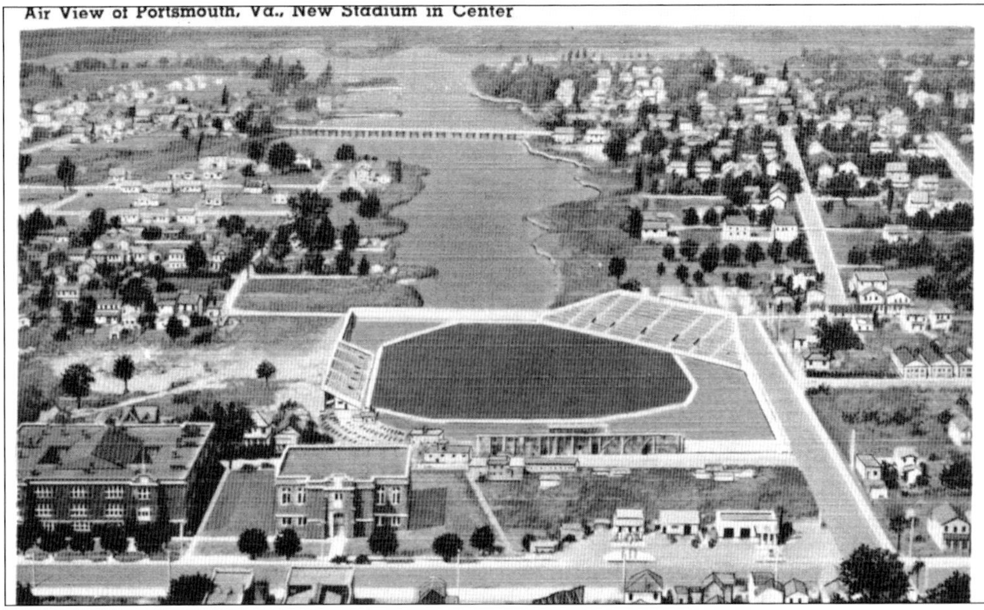

An aerial view of the Portsmouth Stadium in 1940 shows the structure under construction, with the concrete foundations for the grandstands being formed. The stadium was built on the low, marshy end of Scott's Creek, which had been used for dumping large rubbish and scrap automobiles in earlier years. The bridge in the distance is the old, wooden Leckie Street Bridge, which connected the neighborhoods of West Park View and Shea Terrace.

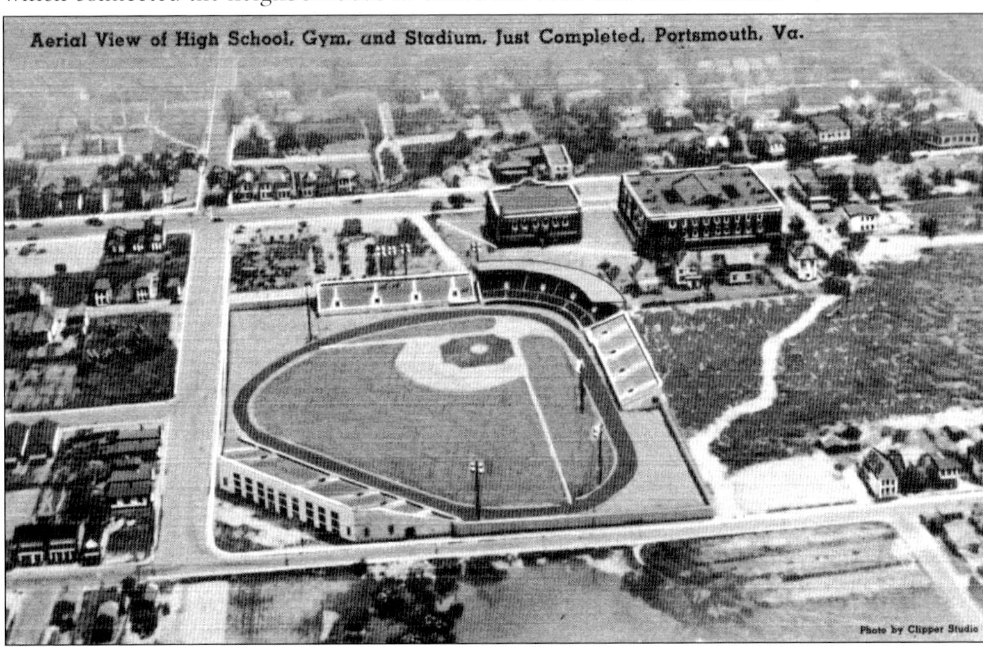

Portsmouth Stadium, as it appeared after completion in 1941, was a state-of-the-art facility, complete with covered grandstands and stadium lighting for night games. Home field for the Portsmouth Cubs baseball team, it was also used for the Woodrow Wilson Presidents' football games. In 1964, the city recognized Frank D. Lawrence, the owner of the Tidewater Tides, by renaming the ballpark in his honor.

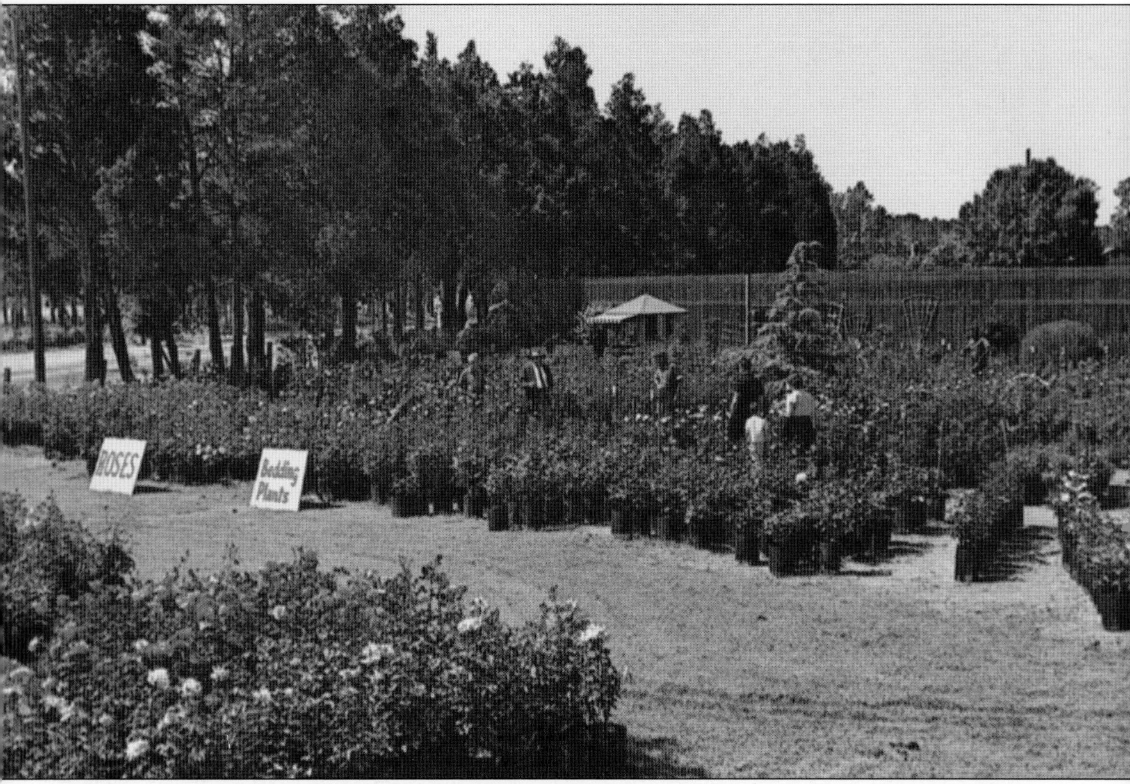

This is a colorful view from the early 1960s showing the many varieties of roses that were part of the rose garden at Coleman's Nursery. The nursery was located at the corner of Route 17 and Cedar Lane for more than 40 years and provided new homeowners in Churchland an array of plants and flowers with which to landscape their new yards. In 1966, during the Christmas holidays, the owners added to the garden center a new attraction for children—animated figures. "Coleman's Winter Wonderland," as it was named, grew larger each year, with the addition of new animated figures and scenes throughout the buildings. In 1996, a carousel and other rides were added to the area in front of the nursery. Coleman's Nursery remained in business for another eight years until the property was sold. The city wanted to keep the Coleman's Winter Wonderland collection intact and in the city. The Portsmouth Department of Museums negotiated a contract with the nursery owners, and Winter Wonderland is now displayed at the 1846 Courthouse Gallery and other locations in Olde Towne.

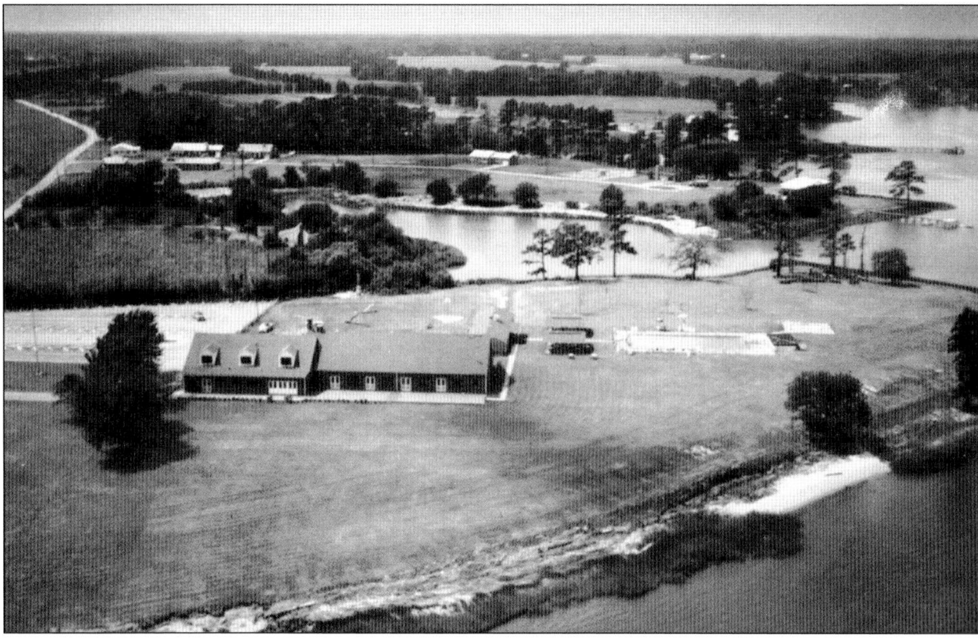

The Suburban Country Club was founded in 1948 as a private Jewish social club that offered a large bar, a dining room, a ballroom, and a swimming pool to its members. Formal balls and cocktail parties would be held here as fundraisers for various civic organizations, as were high school proms. The upper rooms were for playing cards, and it is been said that for a brief time it also housed slot machines.

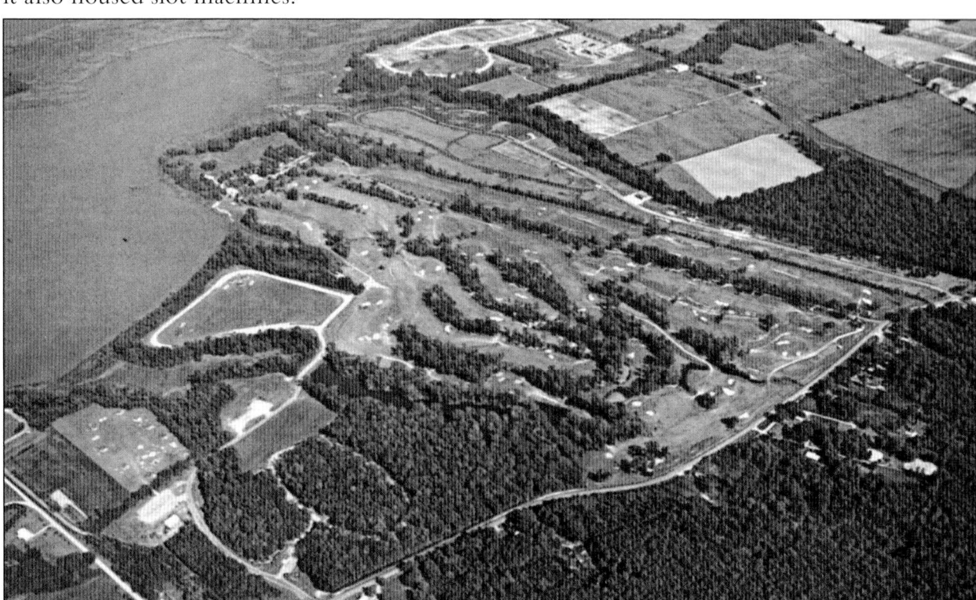

Sleepy Hole Park was laid out in the 1960s and included an 18-hole golf course, nature trails, camping and picnic facilities, and canoe and paddleboat rides. The focal point of the park is the beautiful mansion that was home to Amadeo and Louise Obici, which is undergoing restoration. Located in Suffolk, Portsmouth owned the park until it was deeded back to Suffolk in a trade agreement.

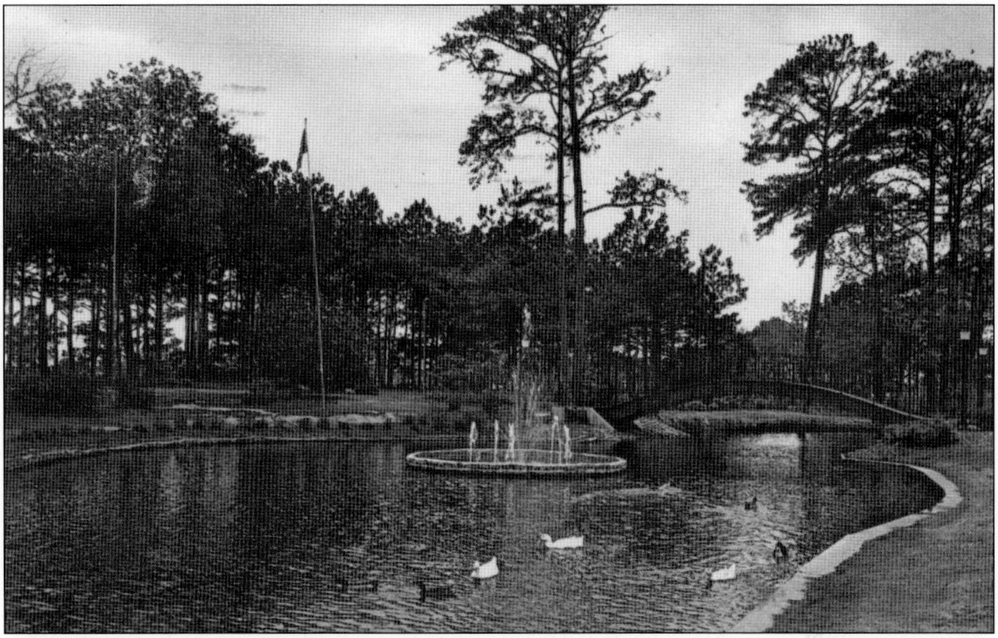

This is a picturesque image of the Friendship Garden, which was established in City Park in 1963 by the Portsmouth Area Council of Garden Clubs. The garden was beautifully landscaped with ornamental shrubs along paths that wound through the trees and across a footbridge over the pond. Portsmouth dedicated this section of the park as a tribute to New Zealand sister city Dunedin.

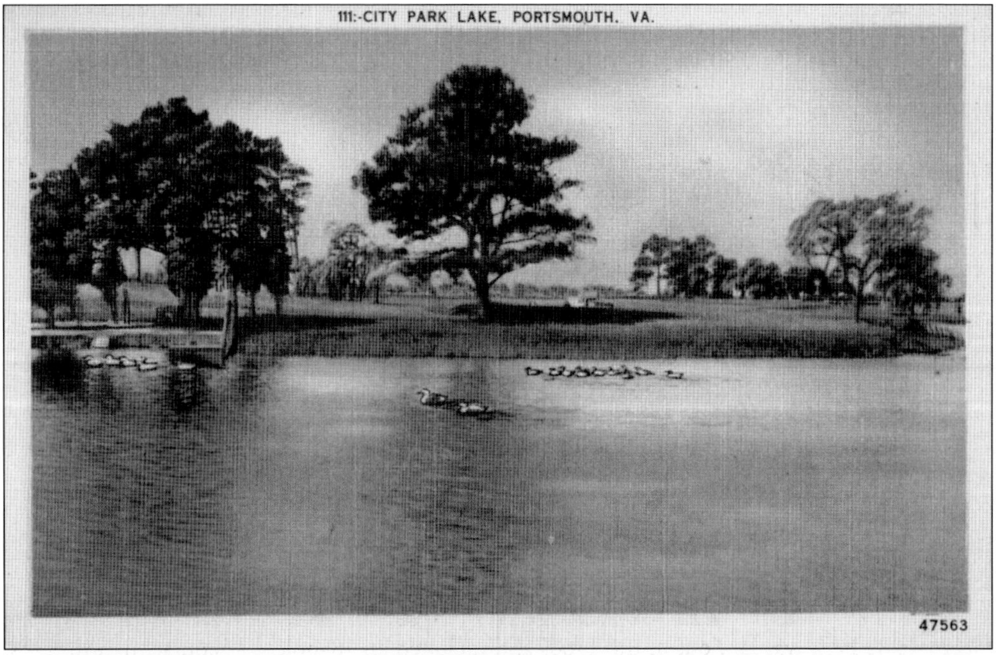

In the early 1920s, City Park was designed and built overlooking the western branch of the Elizabeth River. The landscaping included picnic grounds on the riverfront and a golf course that wove around the lakes. When the clubhouse and golf course first opened, there were only six holes of golf; the other three were added in later years.

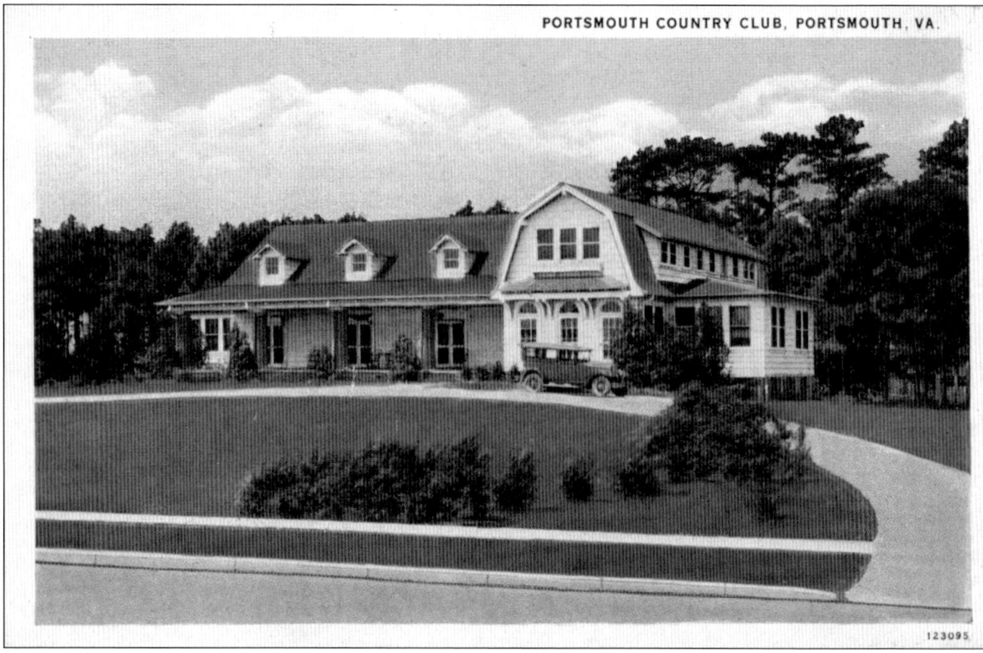

The Portsmouth Country Club, as it appeared in the 1920s, offered golfers a difficult but sporting golf course where for 25¢ they could play nine holes of golf. The golf course was sold in the early 1950s to make way for residential development, but the clubhouse was purchased by the Portsmouth Women's Club and is still in use today for private and public functions.

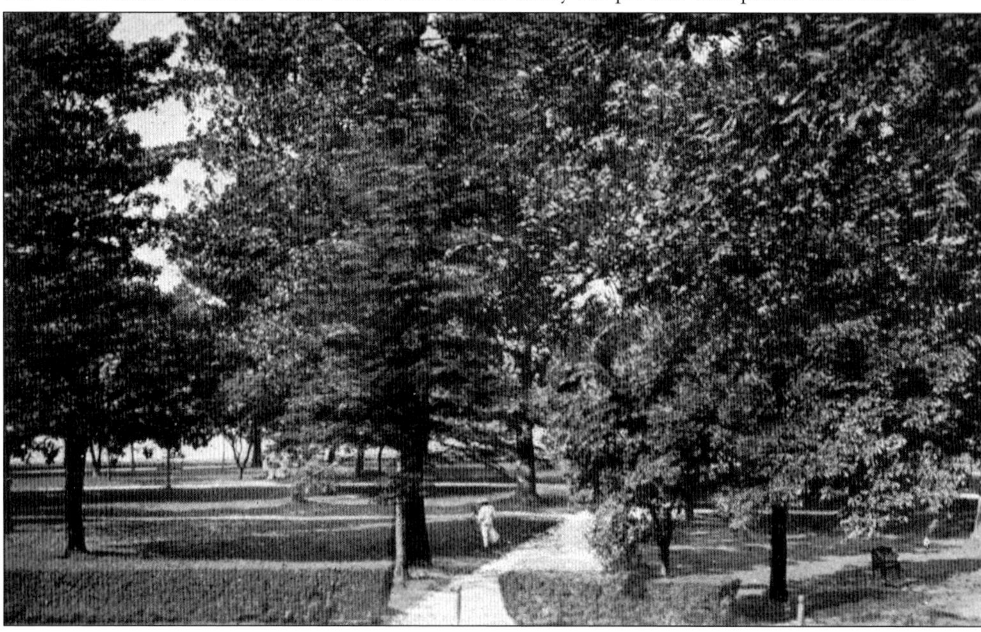

The park at the Norfolk Naval Hospital was a popular place where members of the military and residents of the city could enjoy quiet strolls or afternoon picnics amongst the trees. Park View, the neighborhood adjacent to the hospital, was named for the view across the acreage of park grounds. The park is no longer open to the public due to Department of Homeland Security restrictions.

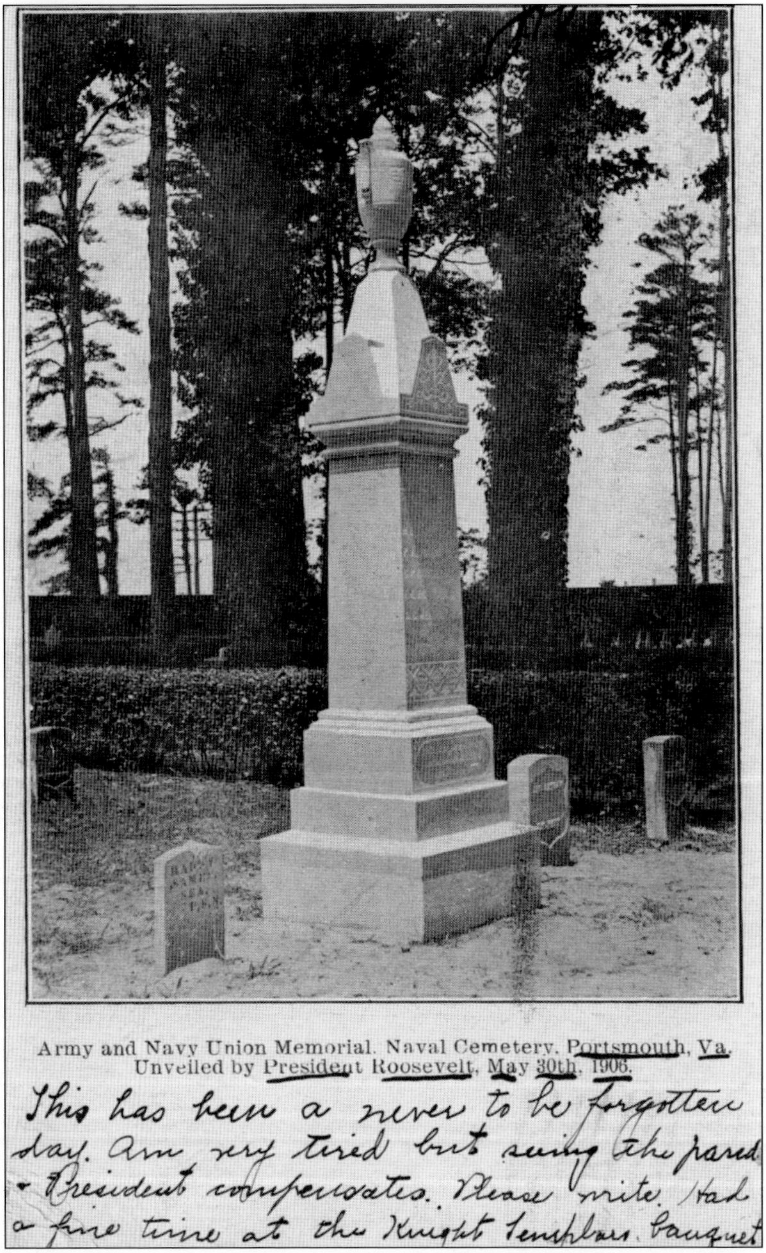

The Army and Navy Union Memorial, located at the Naval Cemetery on the grounds of Norfolk Naval Hospital in Portsmouth, was dedicated and unveiled on May 30, 1906, by Pres. Theodore Roosevelt. The monument was erected by Spanish-American War veterans in memory of their fallen comrades. Prior to the dedication ceremonies, a parade honoring Memorial Day and the president's visit proceeded down Court Street, where the homes and light poles were decorated with red, white, and blue bunting. The streets were lined with residents and visitors, and as the parade passed, they followed along to the hospital grounds. With a jubilant and patriotic crowd listening, the president delivered his speech from the hospital's portico. The sender of this card wrote, "this has been a never to be forgotten day, am very tired, but seeing the parade and President compensates."

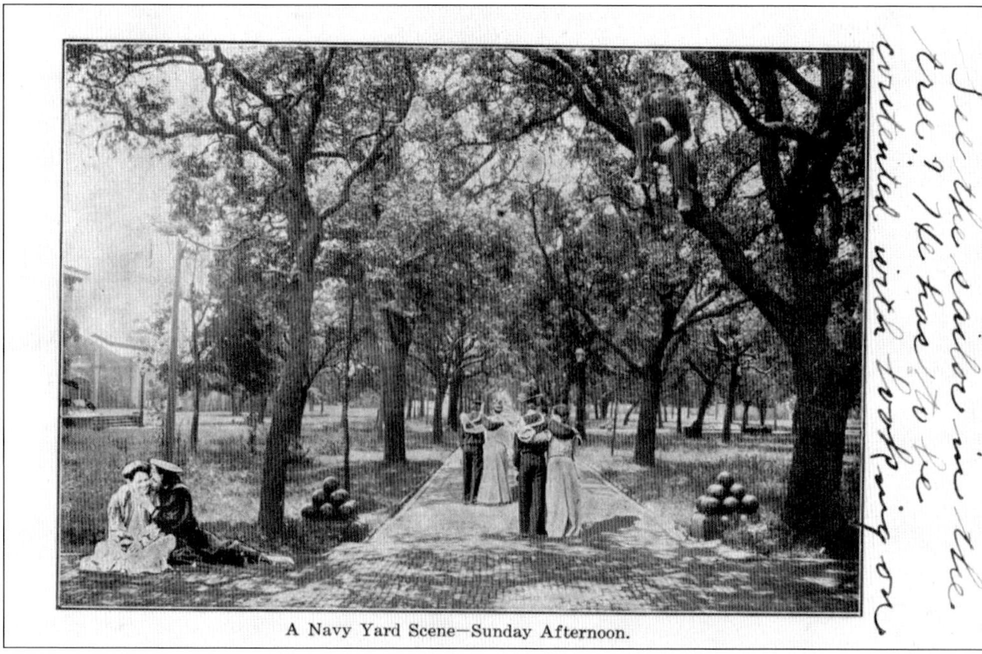

This card from the early 1900s is of a Norfolk Navy Yard scene in Trophy Park on a Sunday afternoon. The park was created around 1870 as a place to display war artifacts and to offer a quiet setting for strolls and picnics by members of the military and the residents of the city. The sender writes, "See the sailor in the tree? He has to be contented with looking on."

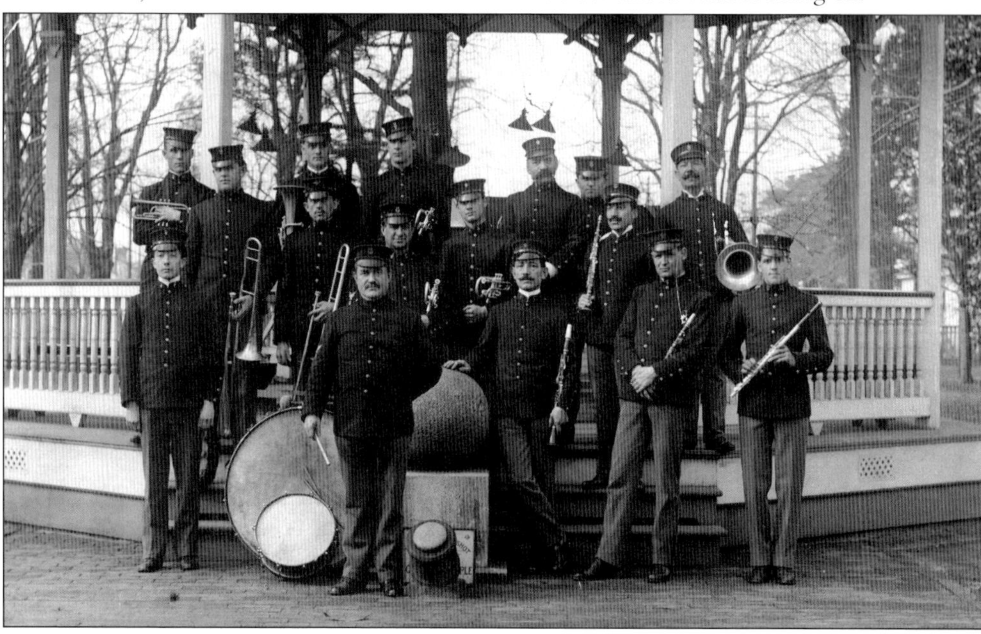

The gazebo at Trophy Park was used as a bandstand and ceremonial platform for military and civic events. On holidays and weekends, there would be free concerts that were open to the public with performances by one of the ships' bands stationed at the Norfolk Navy Yard. The gazebo and park are now closed except on special occasions due to Department of Homeland Security restrictions.

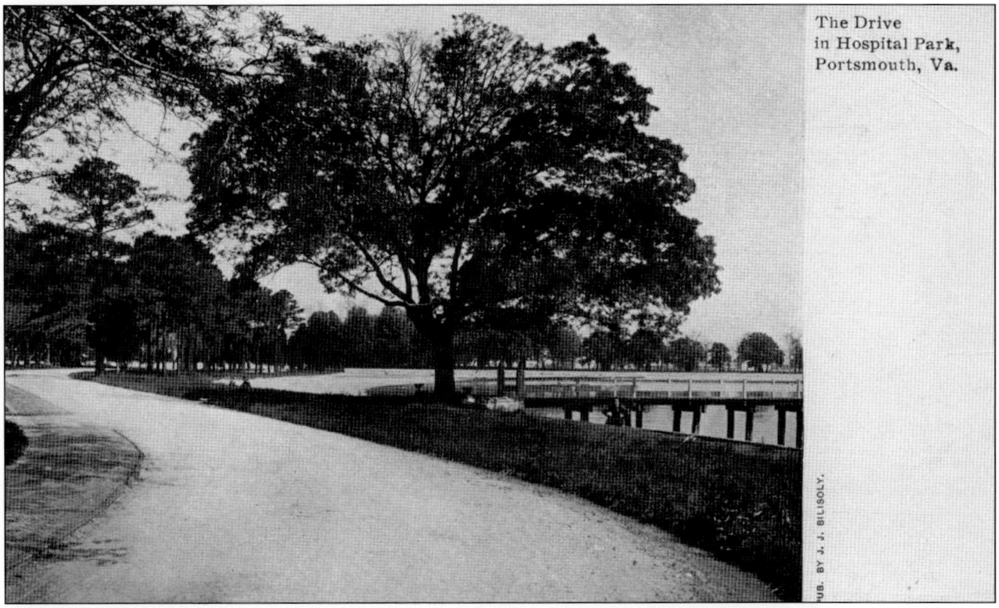

This postcard from the early 1900s shows the drive along the waterfront in Hospital Park. The drive is made of oyster shells, which when crushed and packed down provided a suitable hard surface for wagons and motor-driven vehicles. Access to the hospital could only be gained by crossing over a narrow bridge at the foot of Dinwiddie Street and another that spanned Island Creek on the hospital grounds.

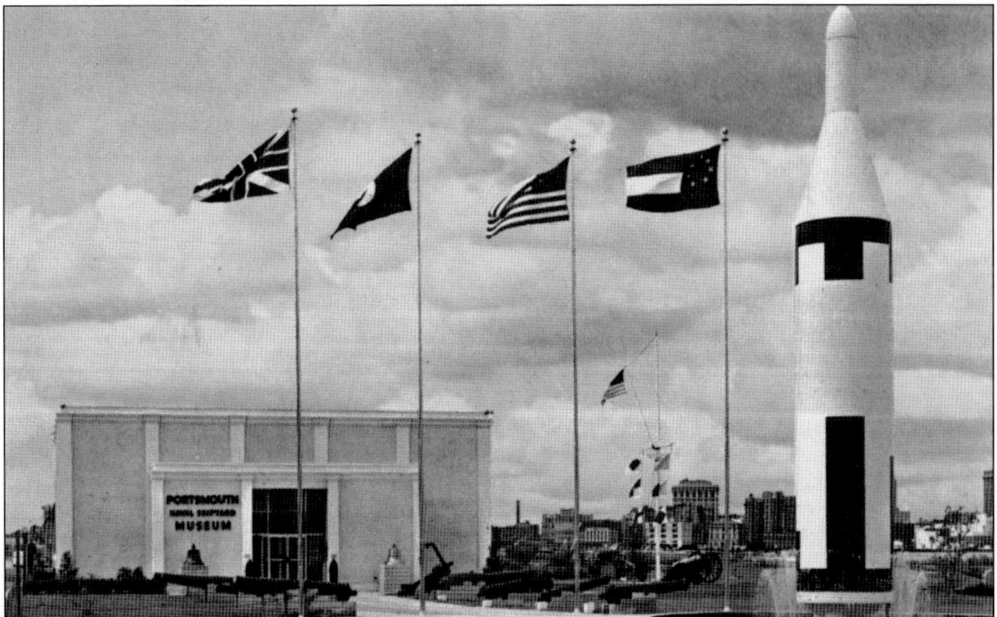

Once a part of the Norfolk County Ferry Terminal, this building was renovated and in 1963 became the home of the Portsmouth Naval Shipyard Museum. The museum houses an extensive collection of nautical and historical artifacts relating to the Norfolk Naval Shipyard and the city. In the late 1960s, the fountain was tempting to pranksters, who poured laundry detergent into it, causing a large bubble bath at the foot of High Street.

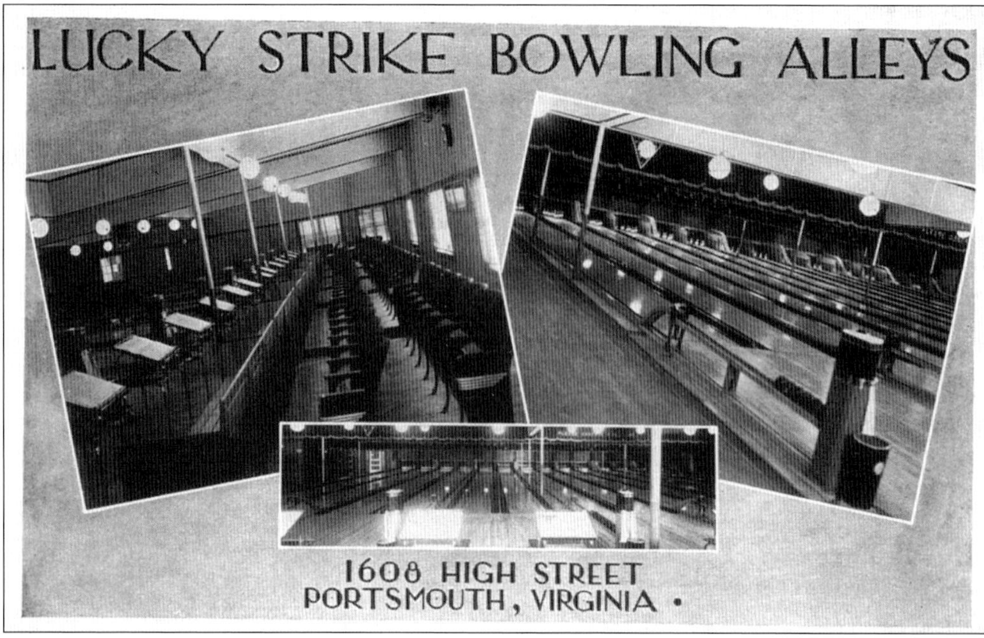

Having 14 streamlined Brunswick 20th-century alleys and boasting "Tidewater's finest equipment," the Lucky Strike Bowling Alleys opened in 1939. Located on the second floor above the A&P Grocery Store, on warm days when the windows were open, people passing by could hear the rumble and crashing of the bowling balls and pins.

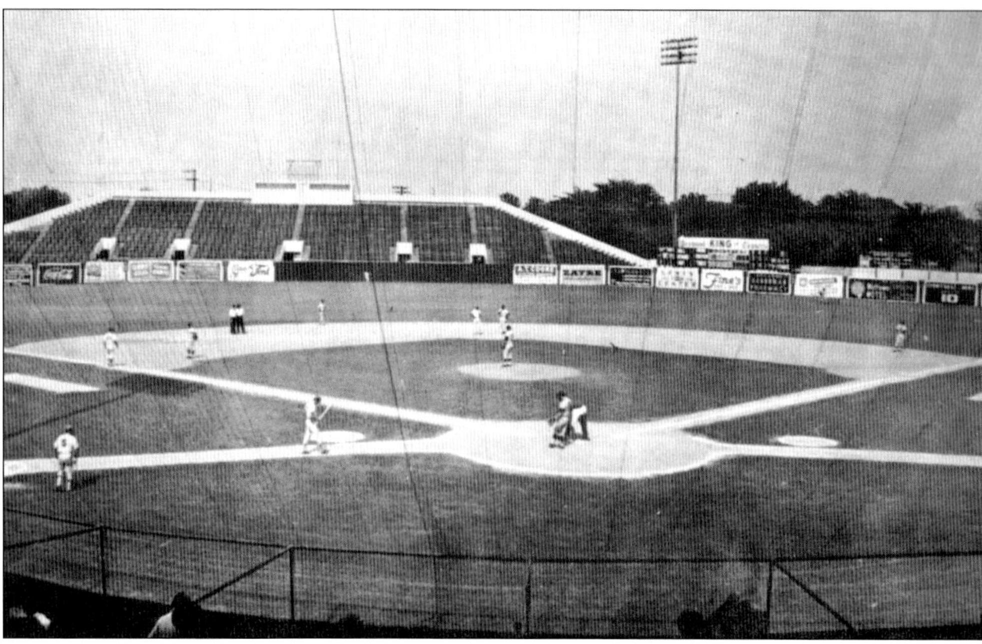

This postcard is of an unobstructed view from behind home plate during a home game of the Tidewater Tides, held at Frank D. Lawrence Stadium. The umpire is sweeping off home plate, and a runner is on second, possibly a runner scored. The year of this real photo postcard was 1969, when the Tides cinched the International League pennant.

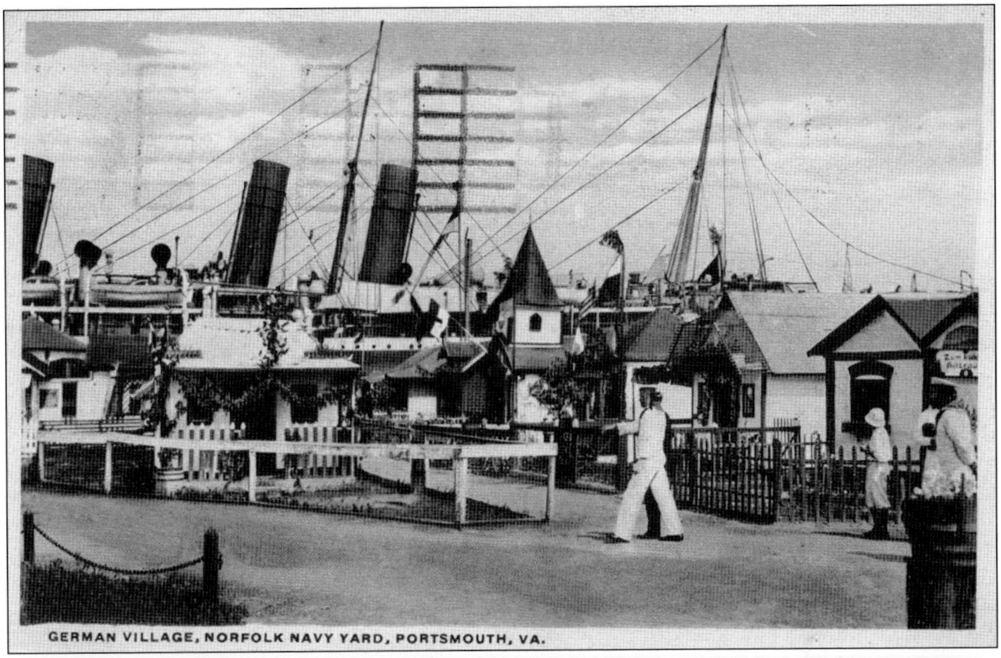

In 1915, the two captured German cruisers, *Kronprinz Wilhelm* and *Prince Eitel Frederick*, were interned at the Norfolk Navy Yard. The combined crews of both vessels totaled 600 or more men, but they were not considered prisoners of war, as the United States had not yet entered into the conflict. The sender of this card, postmarked October 1916, complains, "The state goes dry November 1st." Prohibition in Virginia begins.

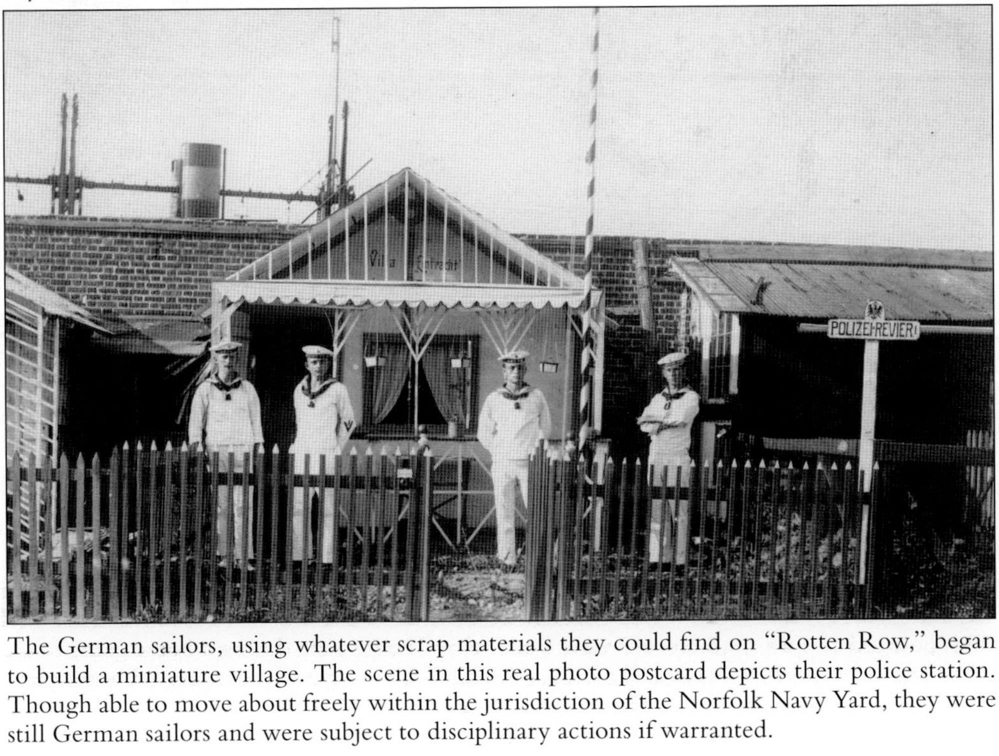

The German sailors, using whatever scrap materials they could find on "Rotten Row," began to build a miniature village. The scene in this real photo postcard depicts their police station. Though able to move about freely within the jurisdiction of the Norfolk Navy Yard, they were still German sailors and were subject to disciplinary actions if warranted.

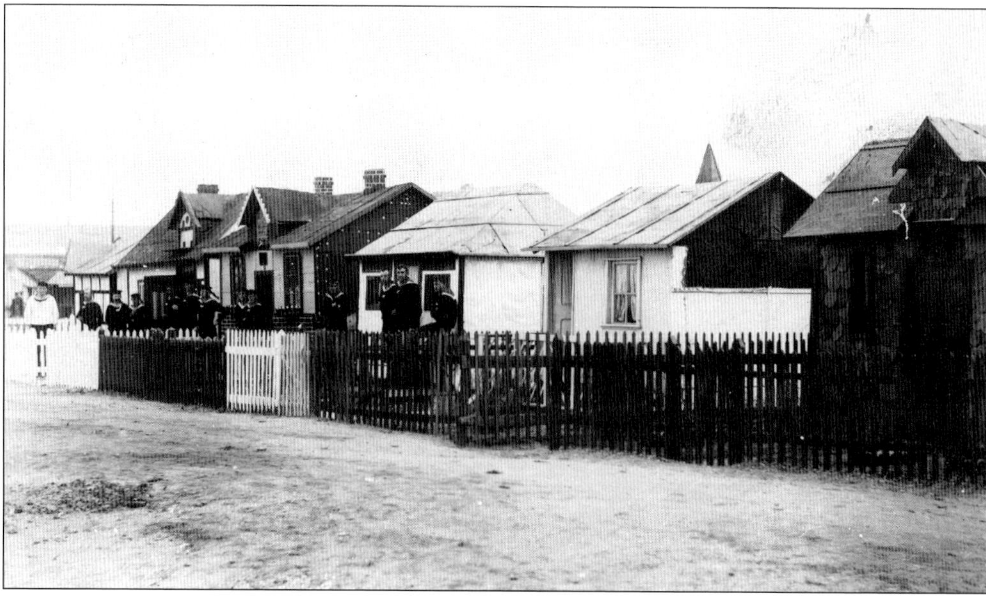

The village, with more than 50 miniature buildings, was named "Eitel Wilhelm" and became quite a tourist attraction. For a 10¢ donation, visitors could tour the village and marvel at the colorful replicas of buildings while conversing with the sailors. The bakery sold authentic German cakes and pastries, and visitors could board the *Eitel Frederick* to enjoy a "cold one" in the rathskeller.

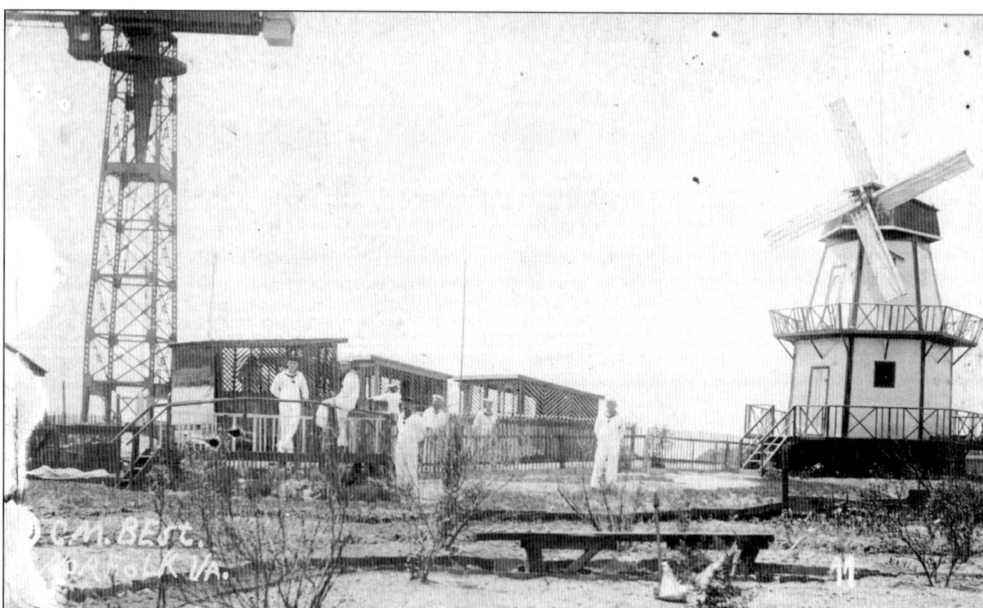

After having thousands of visitors, the sailors disassembled their village and loaded what they could onboard their ships. Congress had appropriated the funds for additional dry docks and expansion of the Norfolk Navy Yard. On September 29, 1916, the *Kronprinz Wilhelm* and *Eitel Frederick*, along with the village Eitel Wilhelm, departed Portsmouth under the escort of US Navy warships bound for the Philadelphia Navy Yard.

Seven

Look at All of the People in Uniform

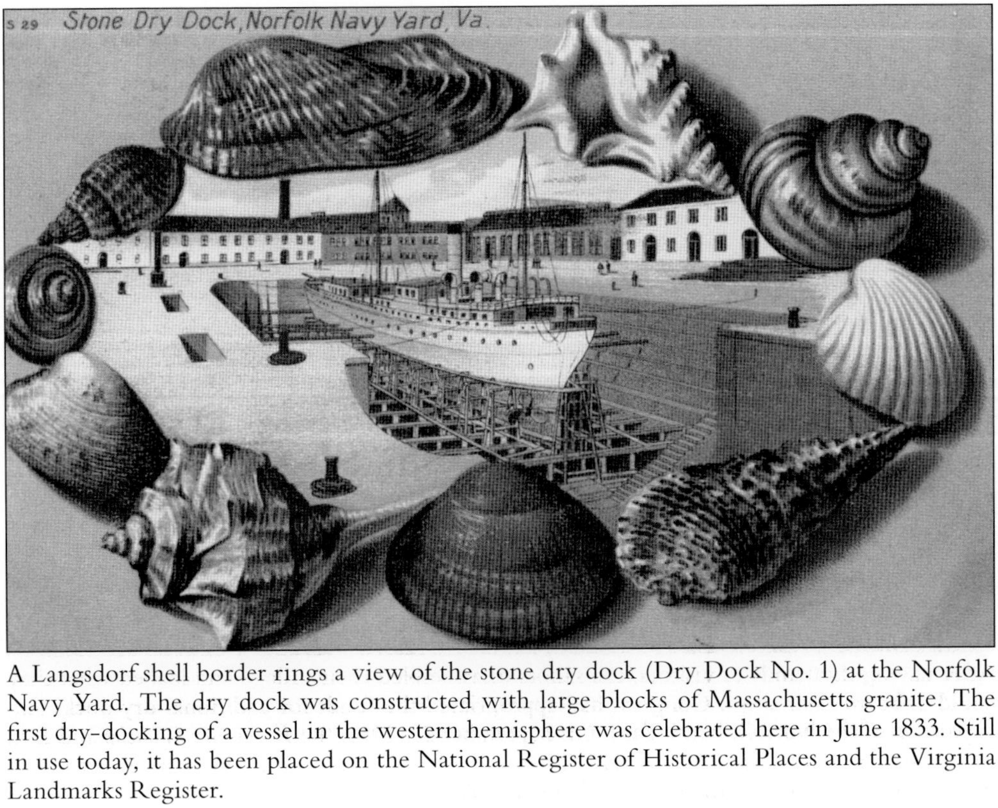

A Langsdorf shell border rings a view of the stone dry dock (Dry Dock No. 1) at the Norfolk Navy Yard. The dry dock was constructed with large blocks of Massachusetts granite. The first dry-docking of a vessel in the western hemisphere was celebrated here in June 1833. Still in use today, it has been placed on the National Register of Historical Places and the Virginia Landmarks Register.

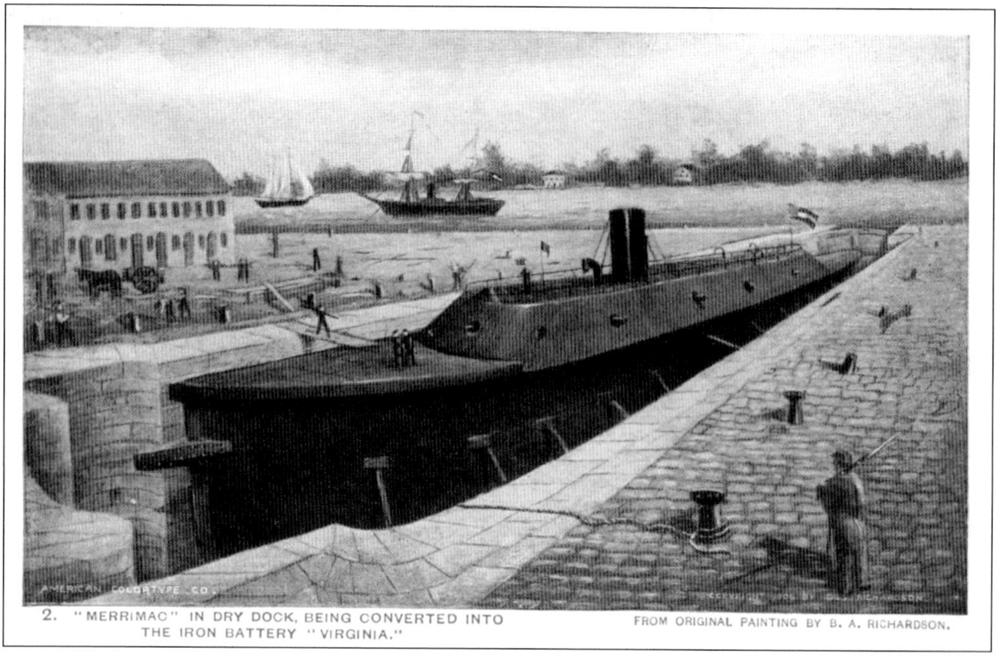

A souvenir postcard from the Jamestown Exposition, published by the Merrimac & Monitor Post Card Company, offers an artist's rendering of the USS *Merrimac* being converted into America's first ironclad vessel, the CSS *Virginia*. John L. Porter, a Portsmouth native and naval constructor, was instrumental in the design and conversion of the burned frigate that would change naval warfare.

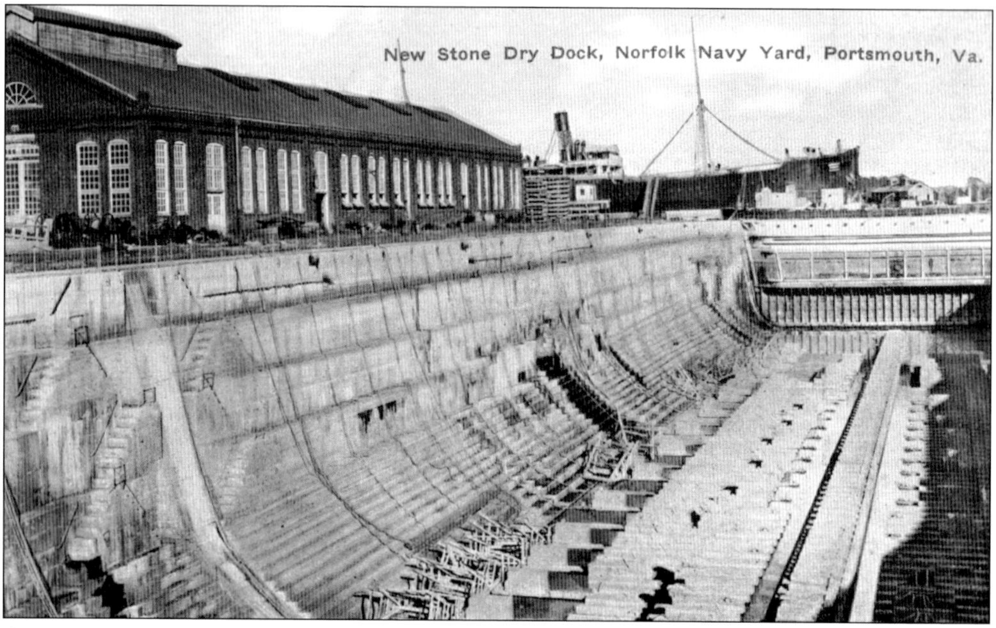

Construction on Dry Dock No. 3 began in November 1903 and was completed in December 1908, with the armored cruiser USS *North Carolina* being the first ship to be docked there. In the coming years, the Norfolk Navy Yard and Portsmouth would witness the construction of three additional dry docks and an increase in population due to World War I.

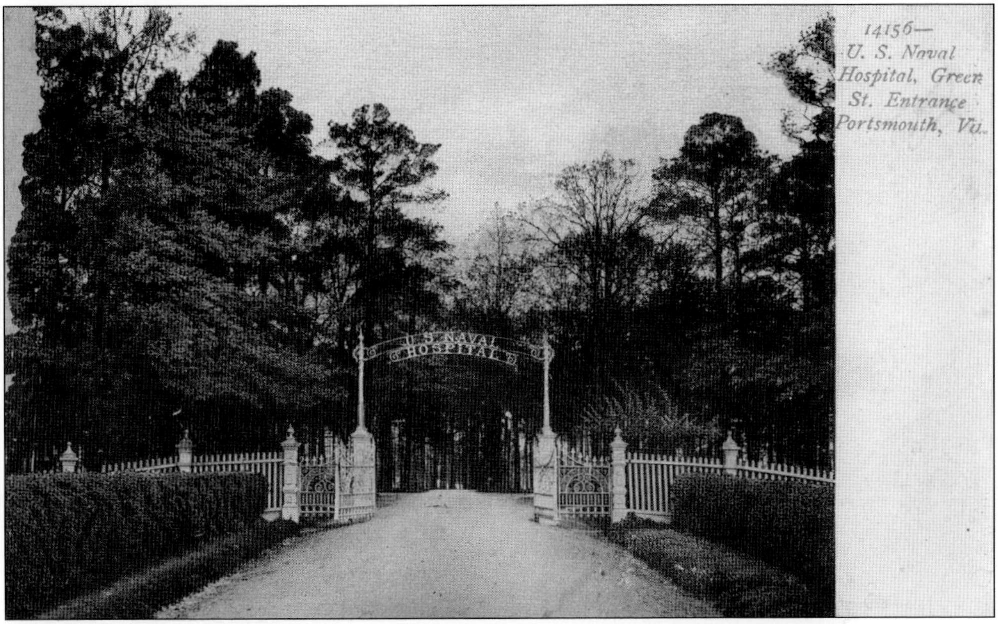

The view of the main entrance to the Norfolk Naval Hospital on Green Street from the early 1900s offered a tranquil setting. During the 1860s, Congress appropriated funds for improvements and the beautification of the grounds surrounding the hospital. The design included meandering roads through the pines and along the waterfront as well as an ornate cast-iron fence and gates.

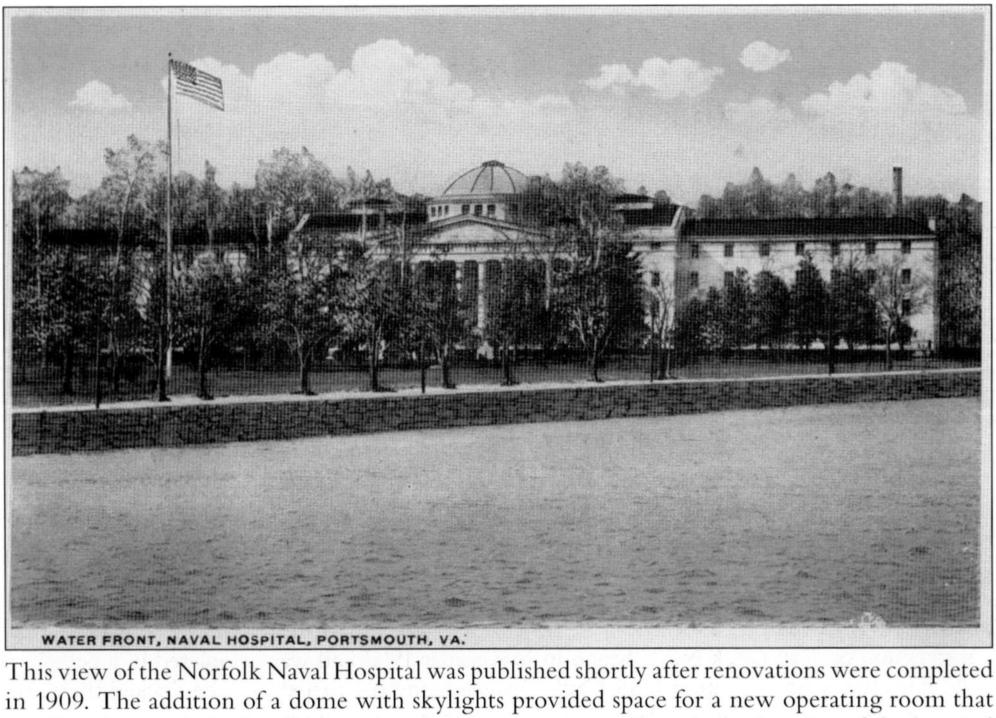

This view of the Norfolk Naval Hospital was published shortly after renovations were completed in 1909. The addition of a dome with skylights provided space for a new operating room that could utilize sunlight for illumination during operations. Though the interior of the hospital was demolished, the neoclassical design of the exterior walls remained.

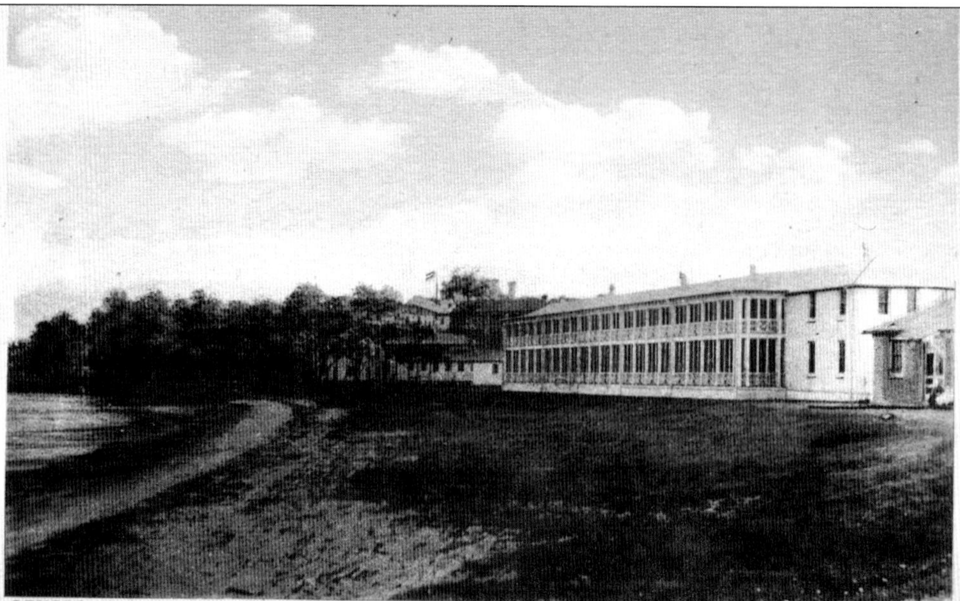

GENERAL VIEW ON HOSPITAL GROUNDS, NAVAL HOSPITAL, PORTSMOUTH, VA.

During World War I, the hospital experienced an increase in staff officers and enlisted personnel due to the number of wounded and sick being treated at the facility. By September 1917, eight temporary wards, four barracks for the Hospital Corps, and 26 bungalows had been constructed on the western grounds of the hospital. The wards in this view were part of the contagious camp for those infected with the measles, mumps, or scarlet fever.

PASSED BY CENSOR.

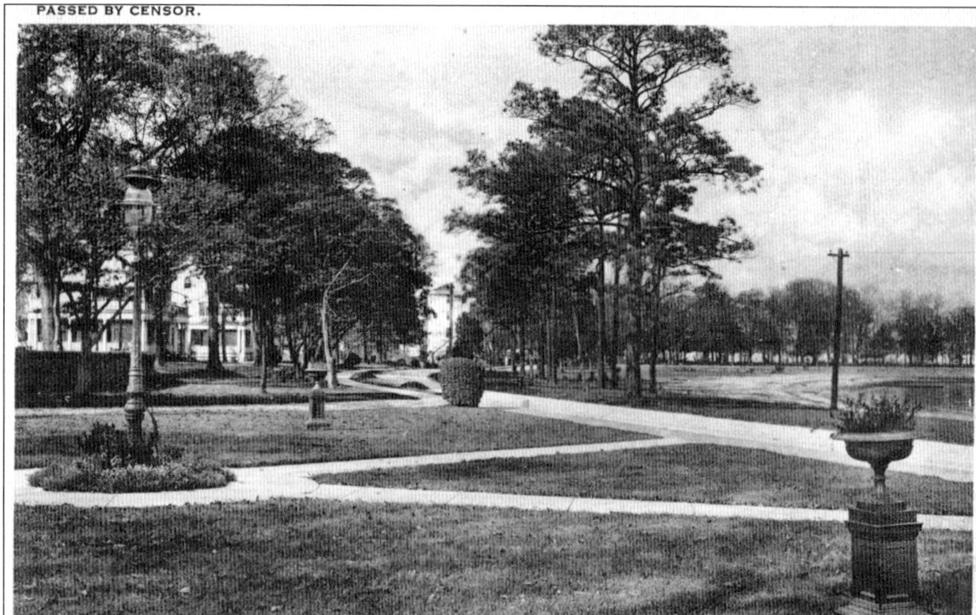

GROUNDS OF U. S. NAVAL HOSPITAL. PORTSMOUTH, VA.

The officers' quarters along River Road were well-maintained homes with immaculate lawns and a spectacular view of the river. Residents could stroll through the elaborate parks or walk along the sandy beach during the daylight hours or at night under the moonlight. Due to the growth of the medical center, most of this is now nothing more than memories.

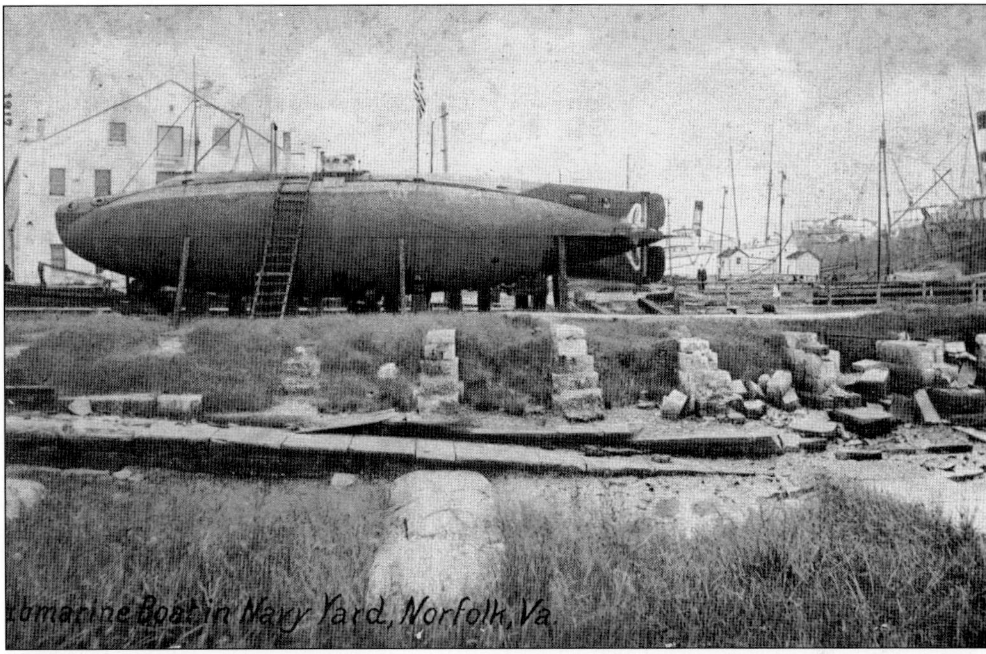

In December 1903, the Wright brothers were preparing for their first powered flight at Kitty Hawk, while the USS *Yantic* was dispatched from the Norfolk Navy Yard to assist two submarines that had broken loose from their towlines. The rescue of the USS *Adder* and USS *Moccasin* drew attention away from the first flight. The *Adder* and the *Moccasin* were eventually towed to the Norfolk Navy Yard to undergo repairs.

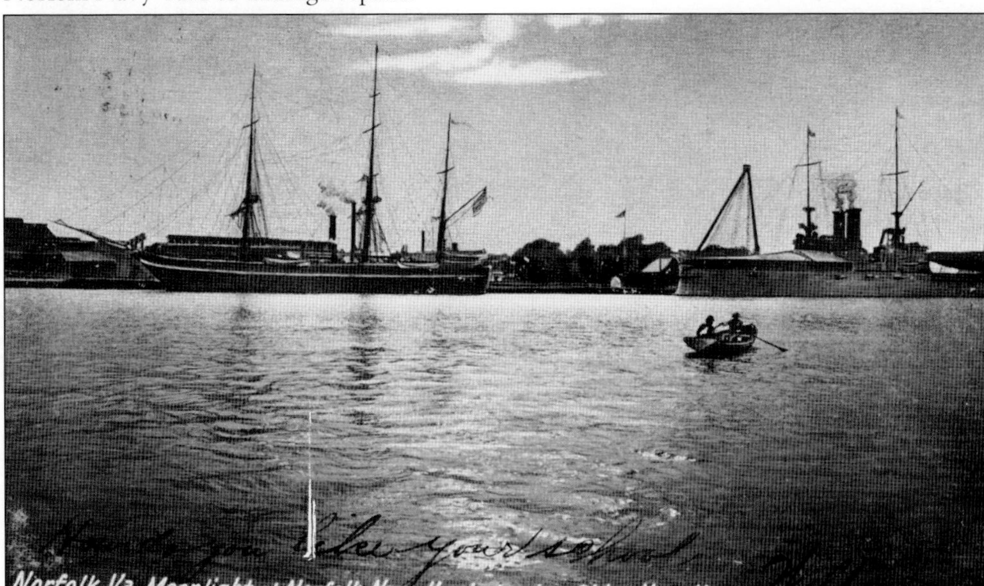

On a moonlit night in the early 1900s, the old Navy (USS *Constellation*) and the new Navy (USS *Texas*) were moored at the Norfolk Navy Yard. The USS *Constellation* was no stranger to Portsmouth, having fought in the 1813 Battle of Craney Island as well as having been rebuilt at the shipyard in 1855. The USS *Texas*, built in the late 1800s at the shipyard, was the first steel-hulled battleship.

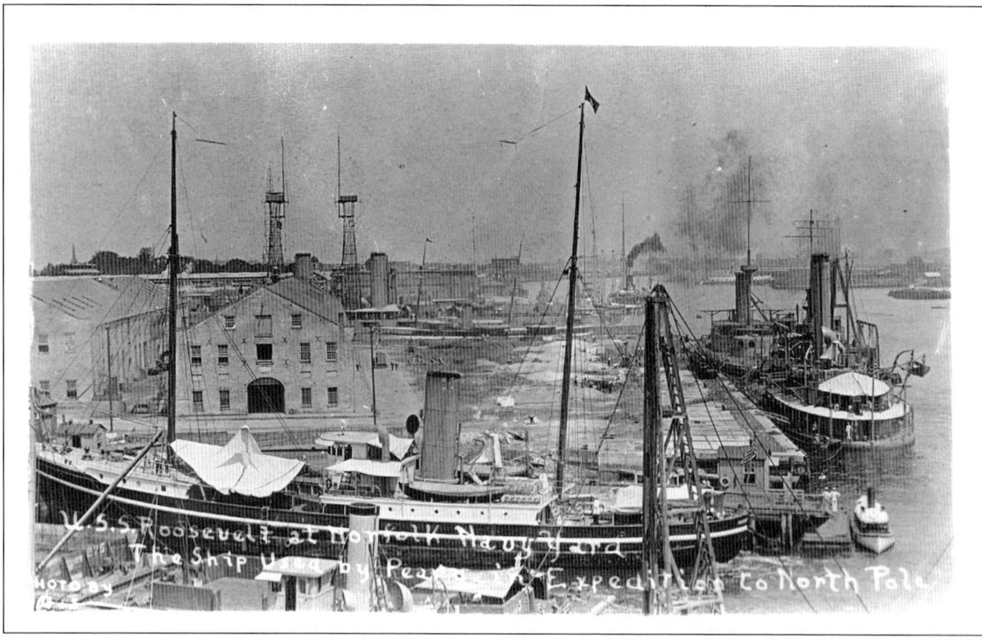

A real photo postcard from the early 1900s shows the USS *Roosevelt* berthed at Norfolk Navy Yard. The image was taken after Robert E. Peary, American explorer and Naval officer, had completed his expeditions to the North Pole, according to the handwritten note on the card. To the right in this view are two Monitor-class warships, possibly the USS *Amphitrite* and USS *Puritan*.

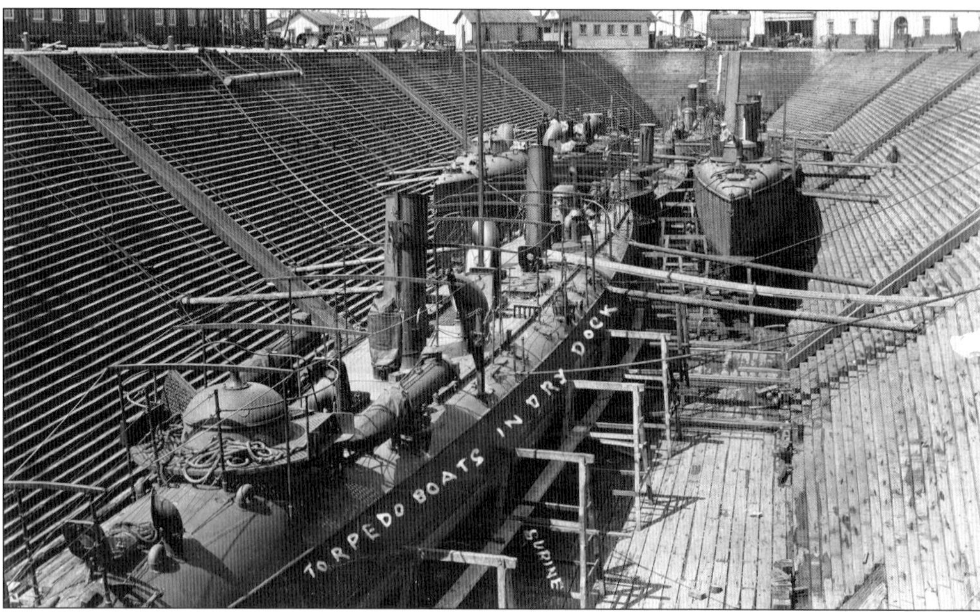

On April 26, 1907, the day this real photo postcard was postmarked, Pres. Theodore Roosevelt made his announcement that the entire fleet of battleships in the US Navy would come in December 1907 to Hampton Roads to begin a world cruise. Repairs on torpedo boats, as shown, would be a small task compared to the larger one of painting 16 battleships white (the Great White Fleet).

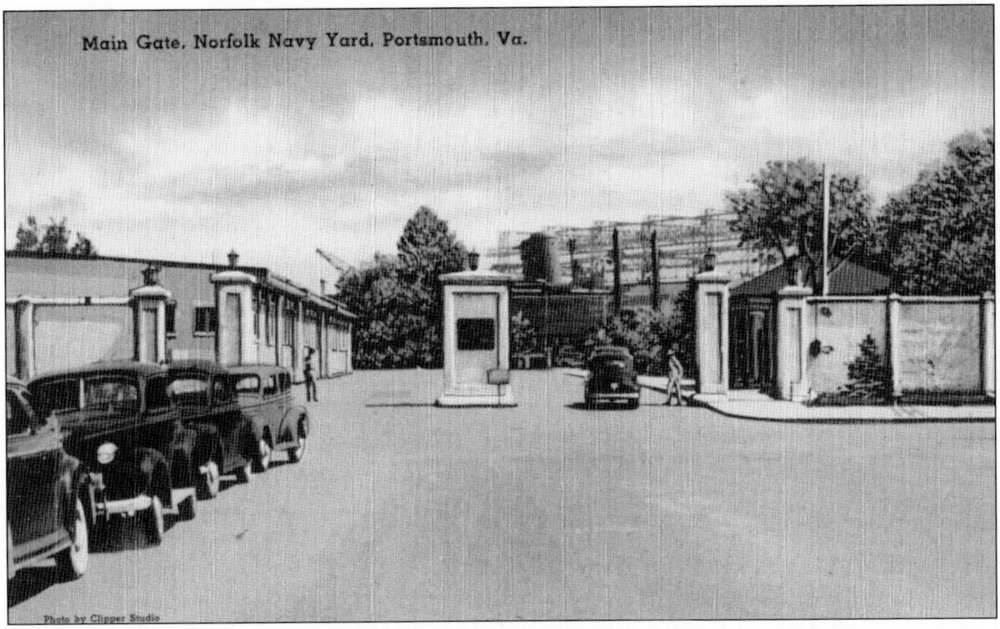

This is the main gate, or the Fourth Street Gate, as it was commonly called by the shipyard workers who passed through it every day. During World War II, the sidewalks were lined 24 hours a day with workers and sailors. Slim's Restaurant and the Southern Lunch Room were just a couple of the eateries located outside the gate where workers could grab a quick bite anytime of the day.

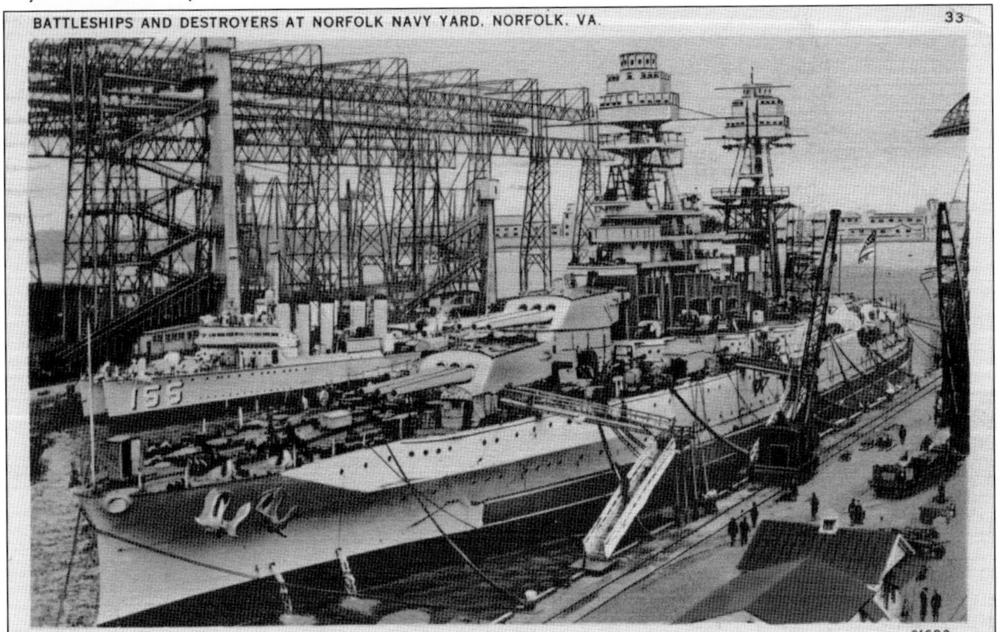

The Navy began a modernization program in 1925 that included six battleships to be overhauled at the Norfolk Navy Yard. The battleship shown in this view was the USS *Arizona*, which upon completion of its modernization departed on August 1, 1931, to join the Pacific Fleet. Americans would see the images of it sinking on December 7, 1941, at Pearl Harbor.

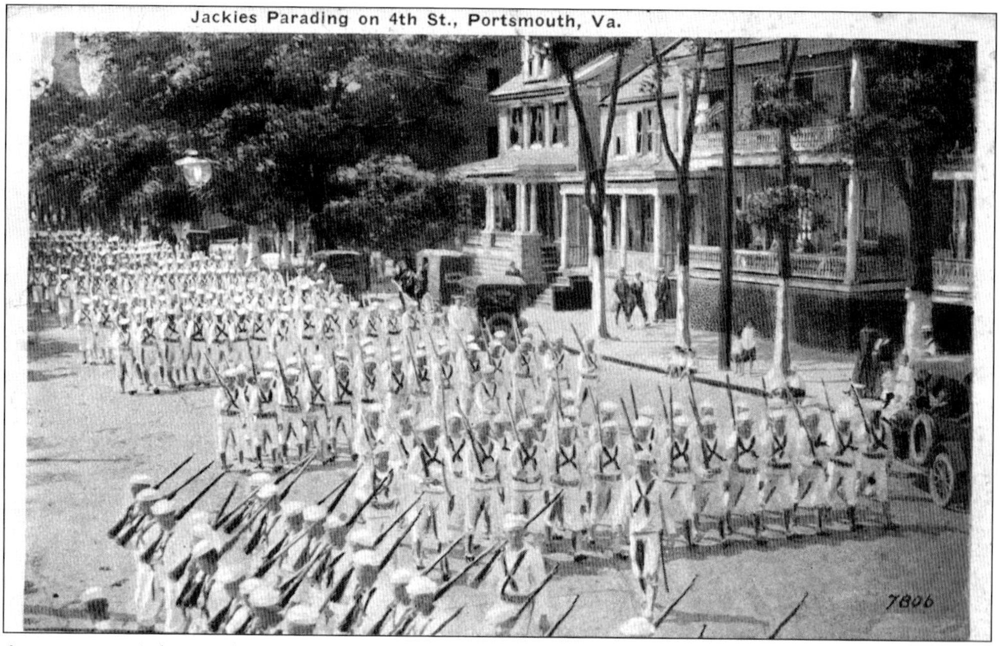

A common sight on the Southside (Newtown), in the neighborhood near the Norfolk Navy Yard, would be "jackies" (sailors) drilling and parading along the streets. The residents, a number of who were employed at the shipyard, were accustomed to the sailors and their bands marching through their streets towards downtown for special occasions.

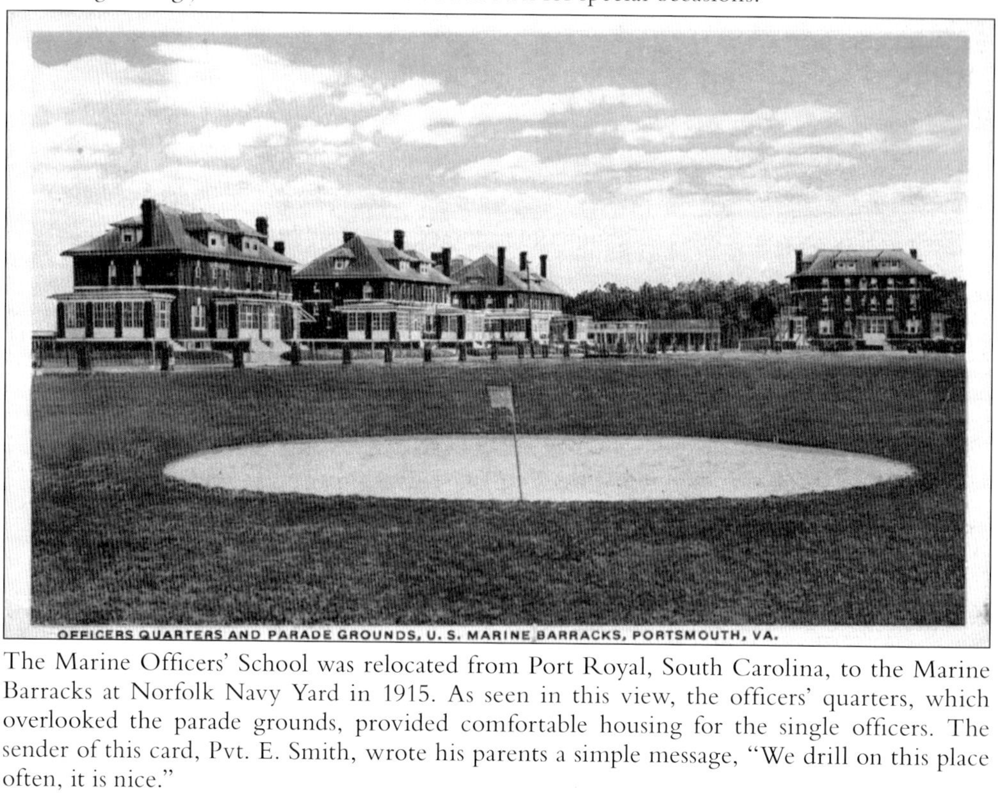

The Marine Officers' School was relocated from Port Royal, South Carolina, to the Marine Barracks at Norfolk Navy Yard in 1915. As seen in this view, the officers' quarters, which overlooked the parade grounds, provided comfortable housing for the single officers. The sender of this card, Pvt. E. Smith, wrote his parents a simple message, "We drill on this place often, it is nice."

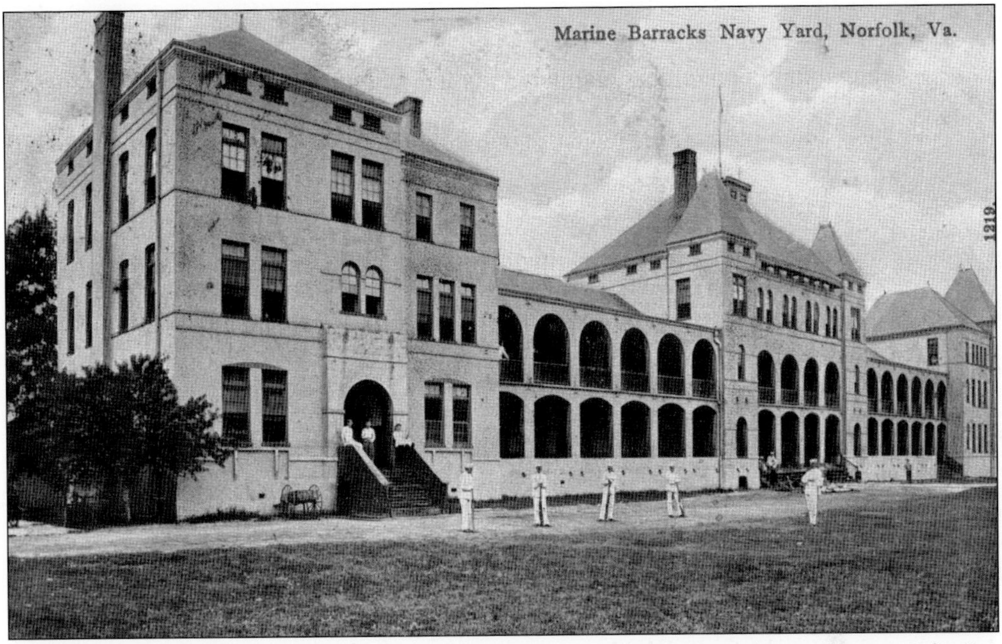

The Marine barracks, pictured, were completed in the early 1900s and were home to the Sea School Detachments stationed at the Norfolk Navy Yard. The Marines standing out front may have been members of 7th Drill Company G, one of the rifle companies quartered at the barracks.

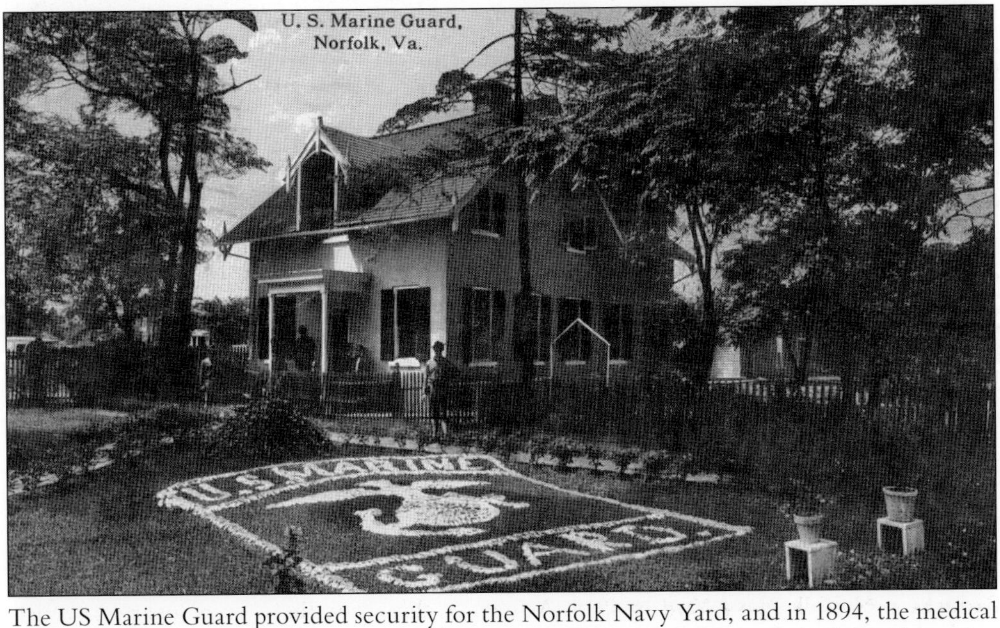

The US Marine Guard provided security for the Norfolk Navy Yard, and in 1894, the medical officer in command at the Norfolk Naval Hospital requested a Marine guard detachment to secure and patrol the hospital grounds. This view of the guardhouse in 1913 was described as resembling a park in arrangement and appearance.

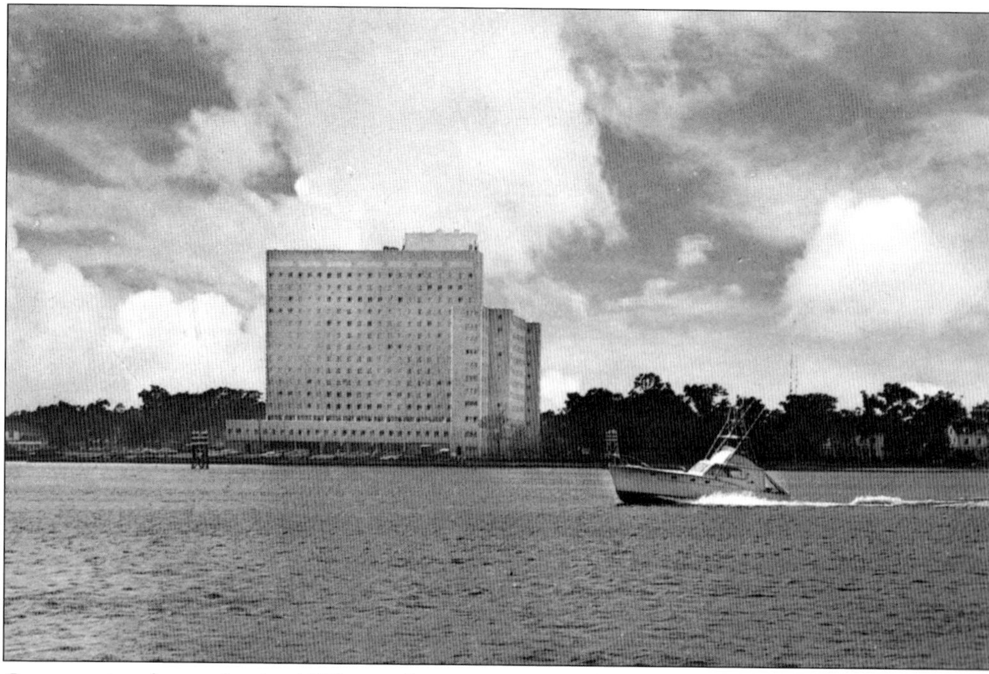

Construction began in the 1950s on the new US Naval Hospital (Building 215), and it was dedicated in 1960. The 18-story, ultramodern building was completed at a cost of $15 million and became the nation's largest military hospital. To accommodate the construction of the new building, several of the older buildings and quarters had to be moved from the waterfront.

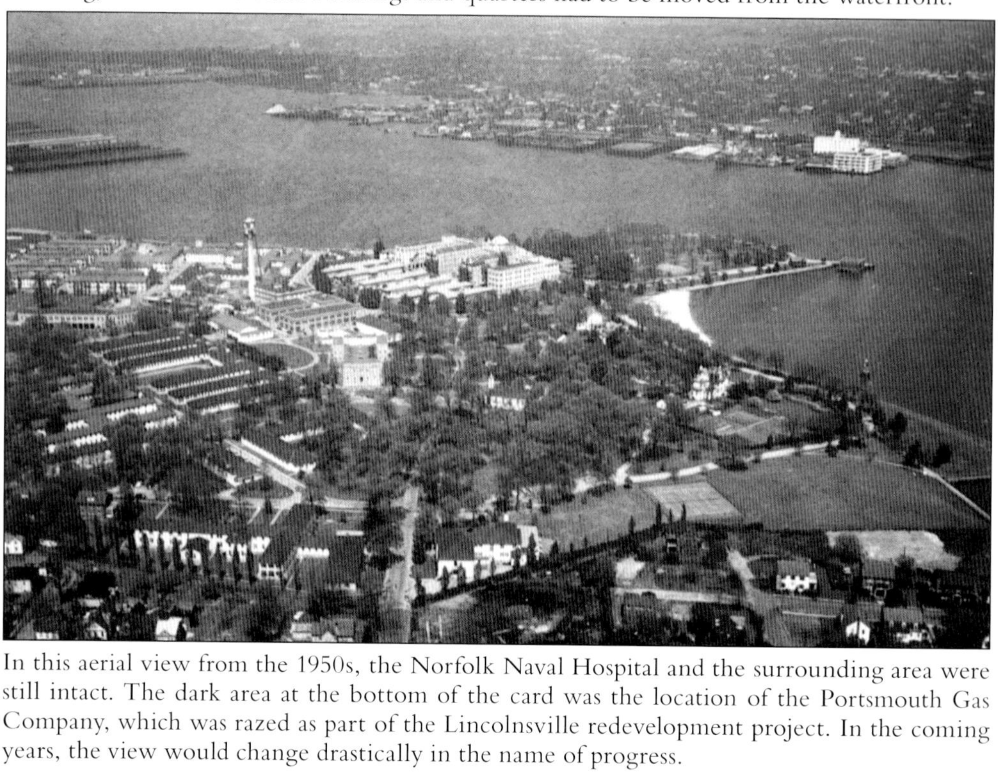

In this aerial view from the 1950s, the Norfolk Naval Hospital and the surrounding area were still intact. The dark area at the bottom of the card was the location of the Portsmouth Gas Company, which was razed as part of the Lincolnsville redevelopment project. In the coming years, the view would change drastically in the name of progress.

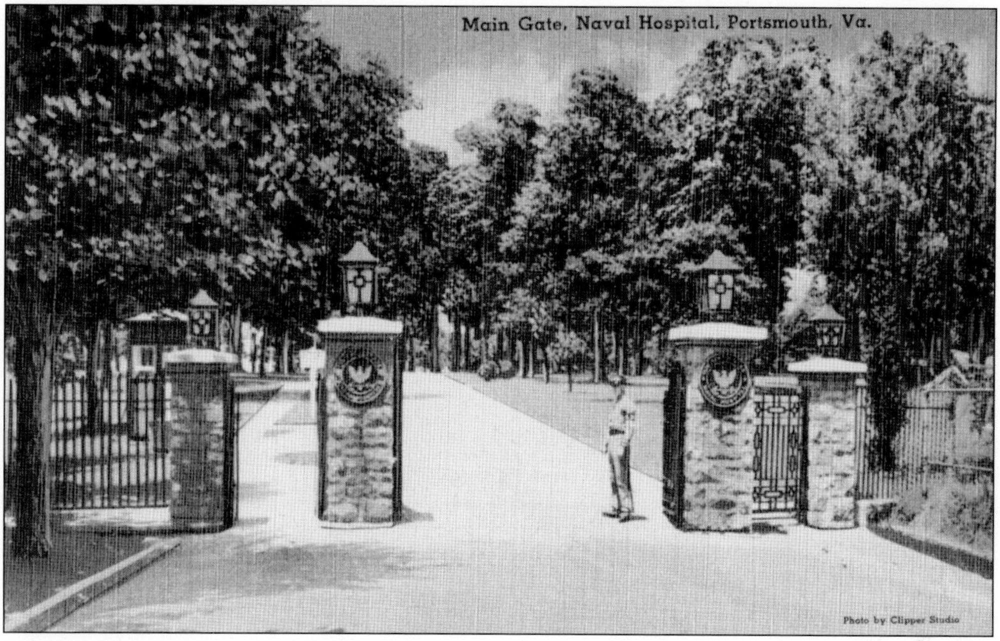

Entering the main gate at the Norfolk Naval Hospital back in the 1930s, as shown in this view, was simpler than it is today. The stone columns and ornate lamps are gone, as well as the elaborate gates and fencing. Marines provided security at the gates, and during the 1960s, Effingham Street replaced Green Street as the main entrance to the medical center.

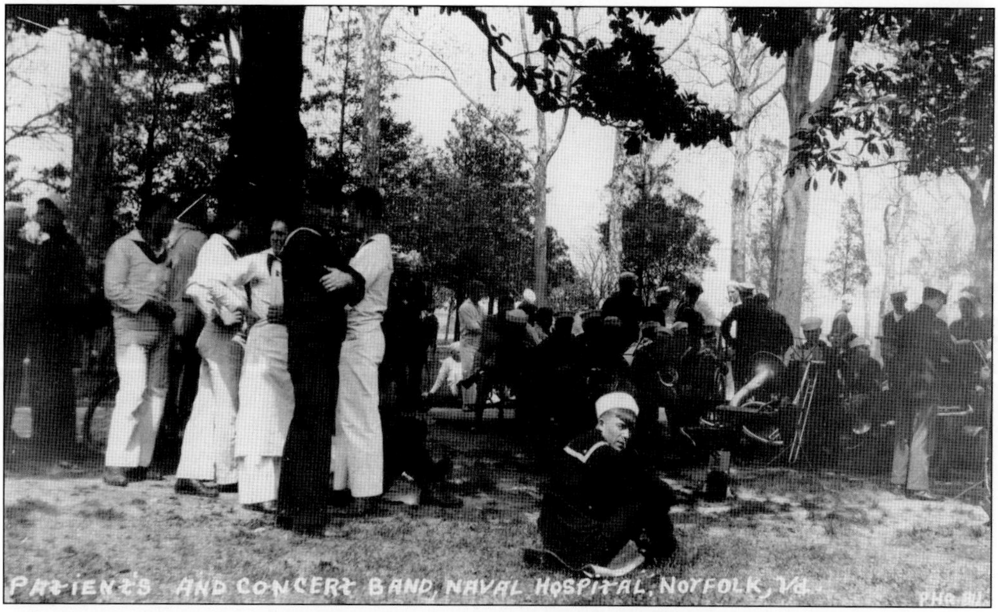

Concerts and picnics were a common scene amongst the trees in the waterfront park, located at the front of the hospital. Patients and hospital staff would be entertained by a band from a ship that was in port, and food would be provided by the culinary department. The medical officer in command saw this as a morale booster for the patients and the medical corps.

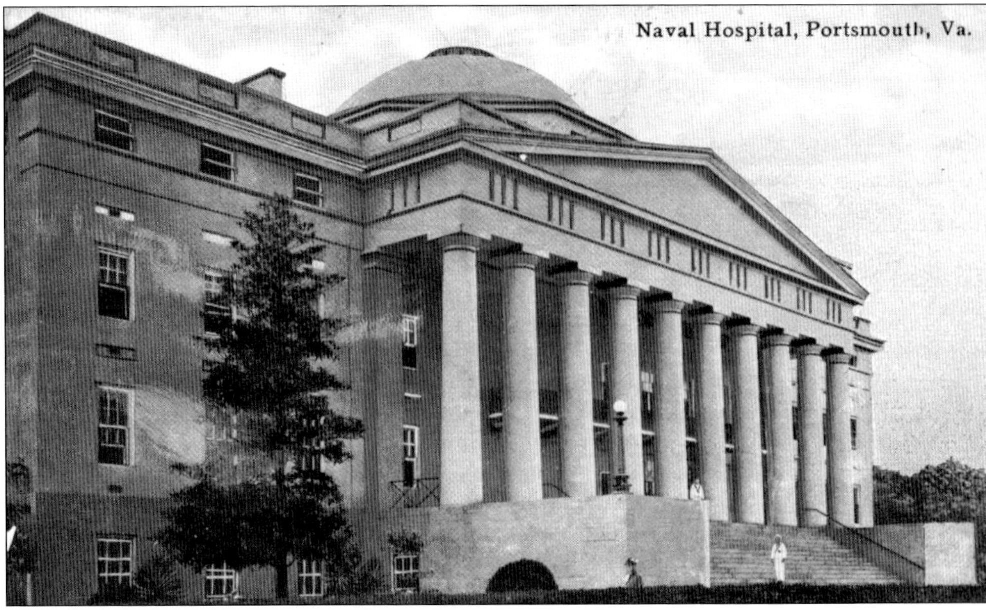

The construction of the Portsmouth Naval Hospital began in 1827, and the first patients were treated at the facility in 1830. Designed by John Haviland of Philadelphia, the foundation incorporated bricks taken from the demolition of Fort Nelson. In 1972, the Portsmouth Naval Hospital was placed on the National Register of Historic Places, and it has also been placed on the Virginia Landmarks Register.

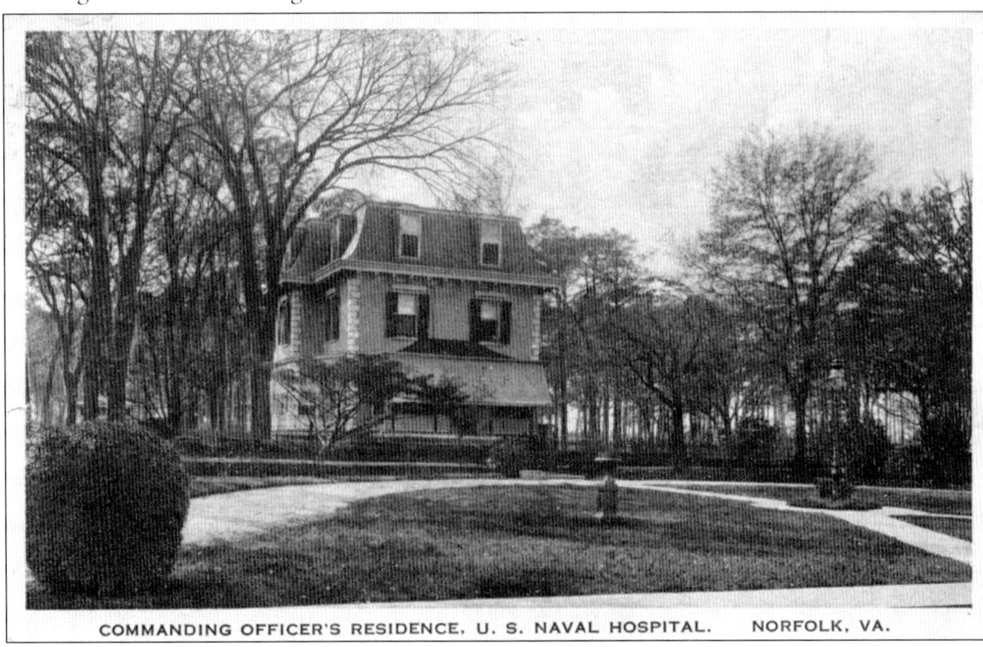

A view from 1936 shows the commanding officer's residence, called "the Myrtles," which was built in 1857. The residence was renovated in the early 1900s, with the third floor added to the structure providing a panoramic view of the beach along the Elizabeth River. During the 1950s and again in the 1990s, most of the beauty and charm of the officers' quarters and the surrounding parks was bulldozed to make way for newer facilities.

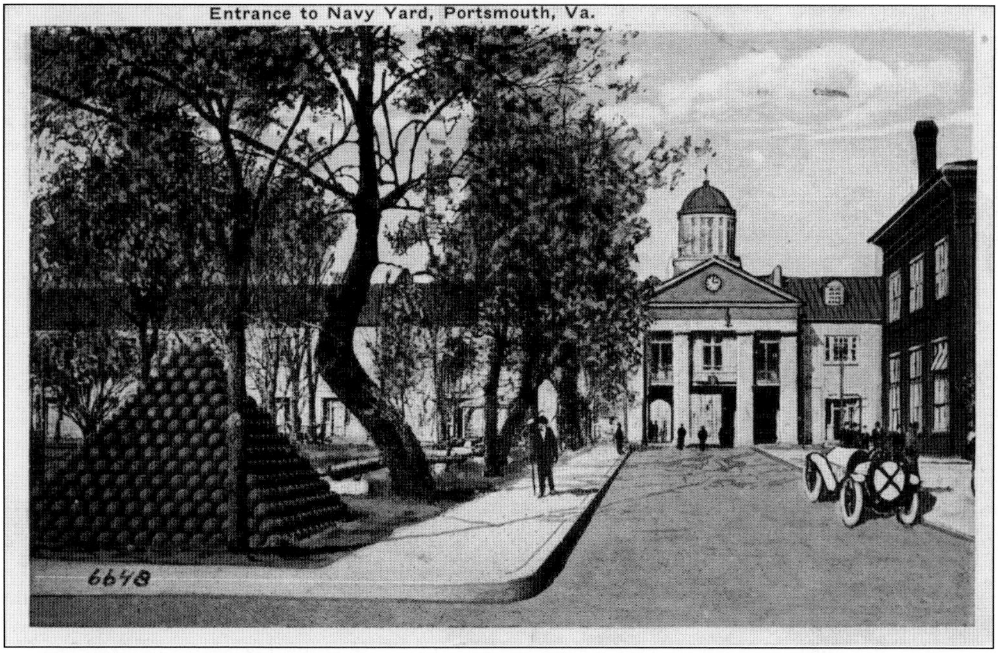

A postcard view displays the entrance to the Norfolk Navy Yard and Trophy Park, located on First Street. The two buildings pictured here were constructed in 1852, and the one with the cupola housed the Marine guard stationed at the shipyard. To the left is Trophy Park. Amazingly, the bent gumball tree, as seen during the early 1900s, has survived the past 100 years.

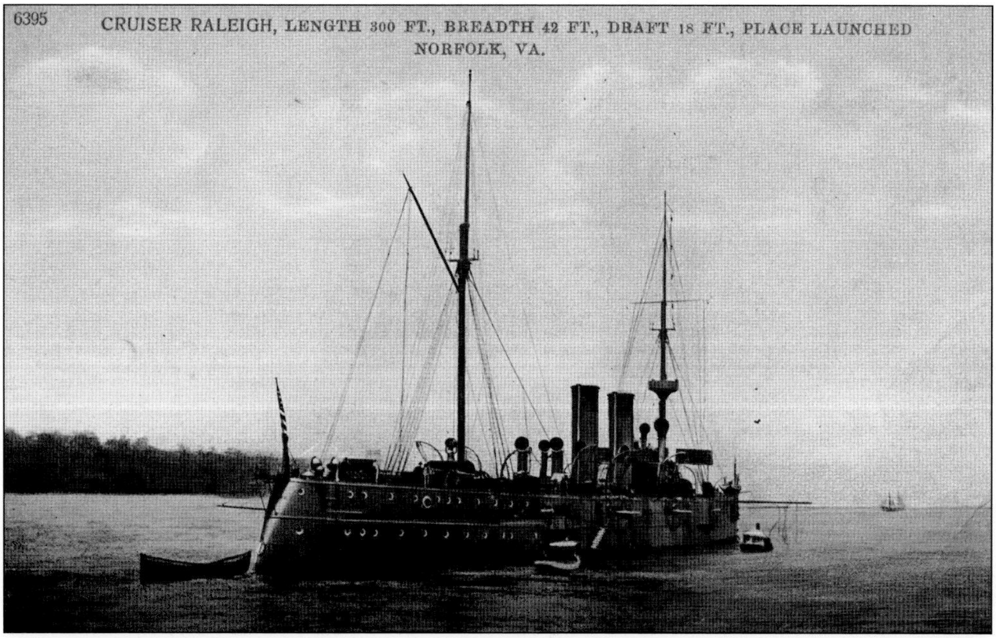

The keel laying for the USS *Raleigh* was in December 1889, and it was launched in March 1892 at the Norfolk Navy Yard. Commissioned in 1894, the ship saw action during the Spanish-American War in the Philippines and during World War I off the coast of Virginia, guarding commercial ships from German U-boat attacks.

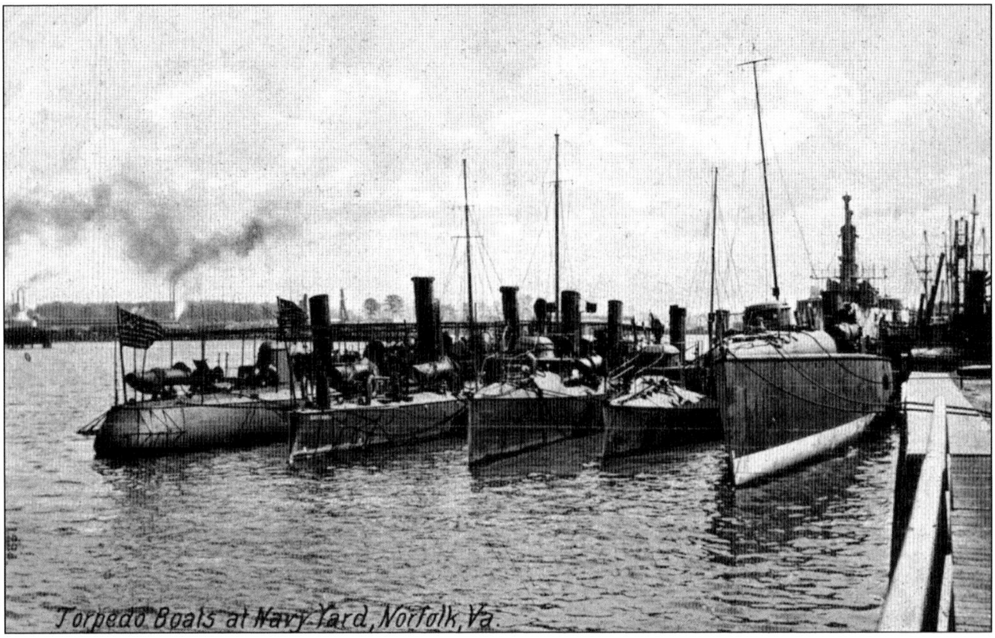

A scene on the Elizabeth River in the autumn of 1907 that was characteristic of the Naval presence was that of the torpedo boats USS *Hull*, USS *Hopkins*, USS *Lawrence*, USS *Whipple*, and USS *Truxtun* at the Norfolk Navy Yard. One of the maneuvers practiced on the river, the laying of a smokescreen, would cause concerns of fire in the residents on the opposite shores, depending on which way the wind was blowing.

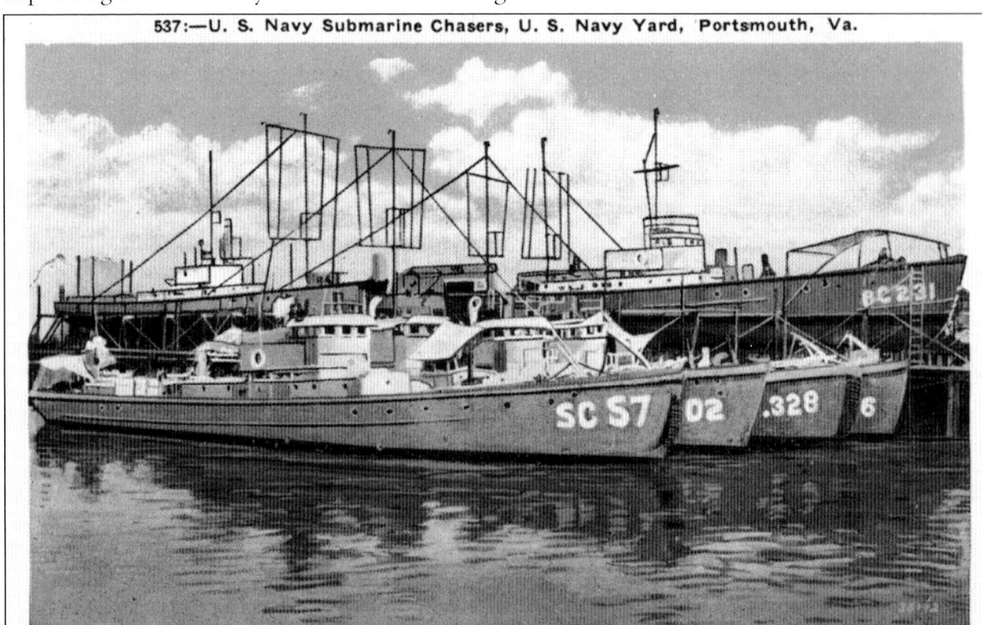

The Norfolk Navy Yard built 21 wooden-hulled submarine chasers during World War I to aid in the fight against the German U-boats that were causing havoc to ships along the East Coast. This view, at the southern end of the shipyard, was taken prior to these ships being reactivated with Coast Guard and Navy Reserve crews during World War II.

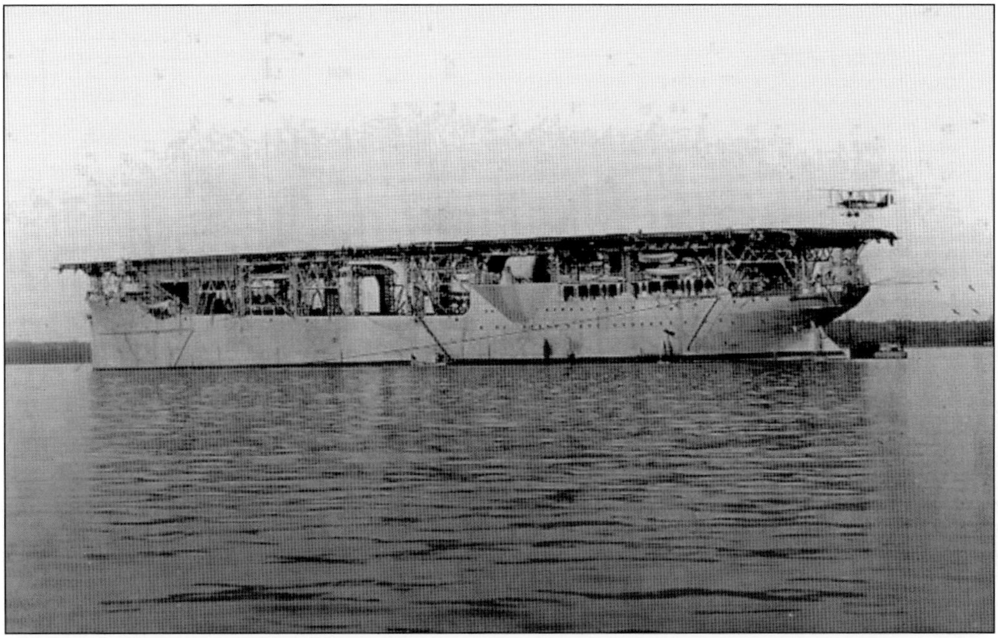

The first aircraft carrier, the USS *Langley*, was commissioned on March 22, 1922, at Norfolk Navy Yard. Transformed from the collier USS *Jupiter*, the odd-looking vessel awed the residents who had gathered along the banks of the Elizabeth River on October 17, 1922, when the first airplane flew from its deck. A new era in US Naval history had been written in Portsmouth.

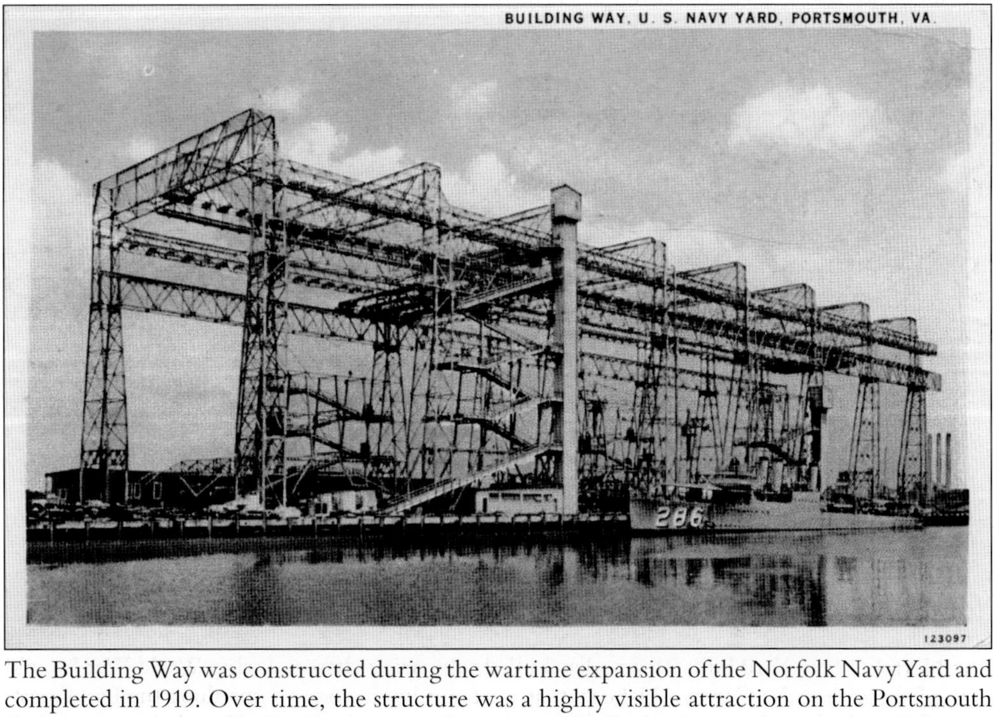

The Building Way was constructed during the wartime expansion of the Norfolk Navy Yard and completed in 1919. Over time, the structure was a highly visible attraction on the Portsmouth skyline. During World War II, the aircraft carrier USS *Shangri-La* was launched on February 24, 1944, from the Building Way. In 1974, the structure was dismantled and sold for scrap.

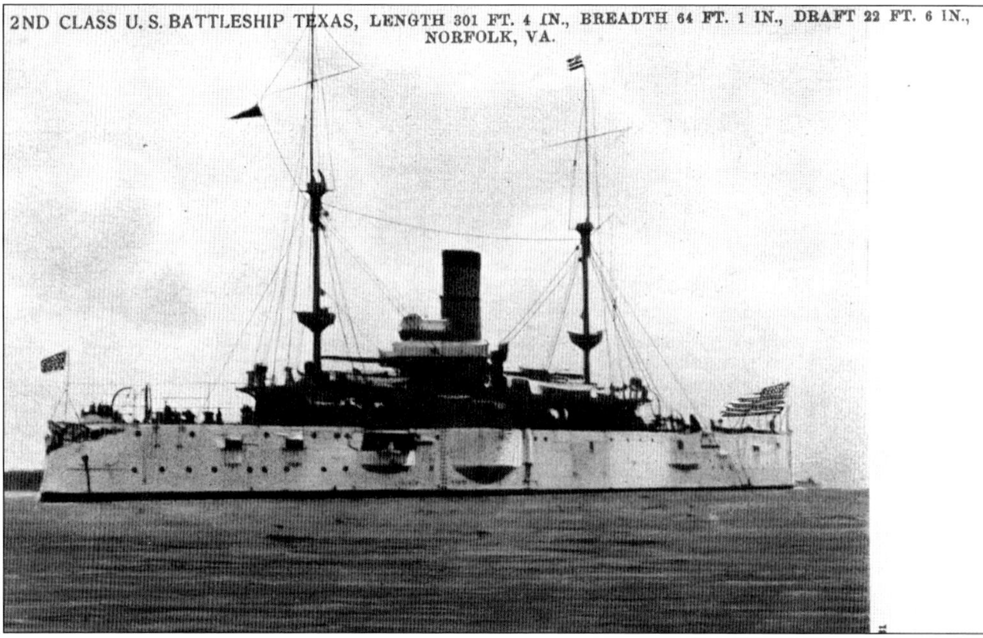

The first steel-hulled battleship, the USS *Texas*, was launched on June 28, 1892, and was commissioned in August 1895. A true piece of Virginia craftsmanship, it was built at the Norfolk Navy Yard in Portsmouth, and its machinery was manufactured at the Richmond Locomotive Works. During the Spanish-American War, this battleship played an integral role in the defeat of Spain's Atlantic Squadron at Santiago Harbor. Between the years of 1902 and 1905, the ship served as the flagship for the Atlantic Coast Squadron. Sadly, after being renamed the USS *San Marcos*, the ship was stricken from the Navy rolls in the fall of 1911 and towed to Tangier Island to be used for target practice until sinking. In the 1950s, the sunken hull was blasted until it was no longer a danger to ships on the Chesapeake Bay.

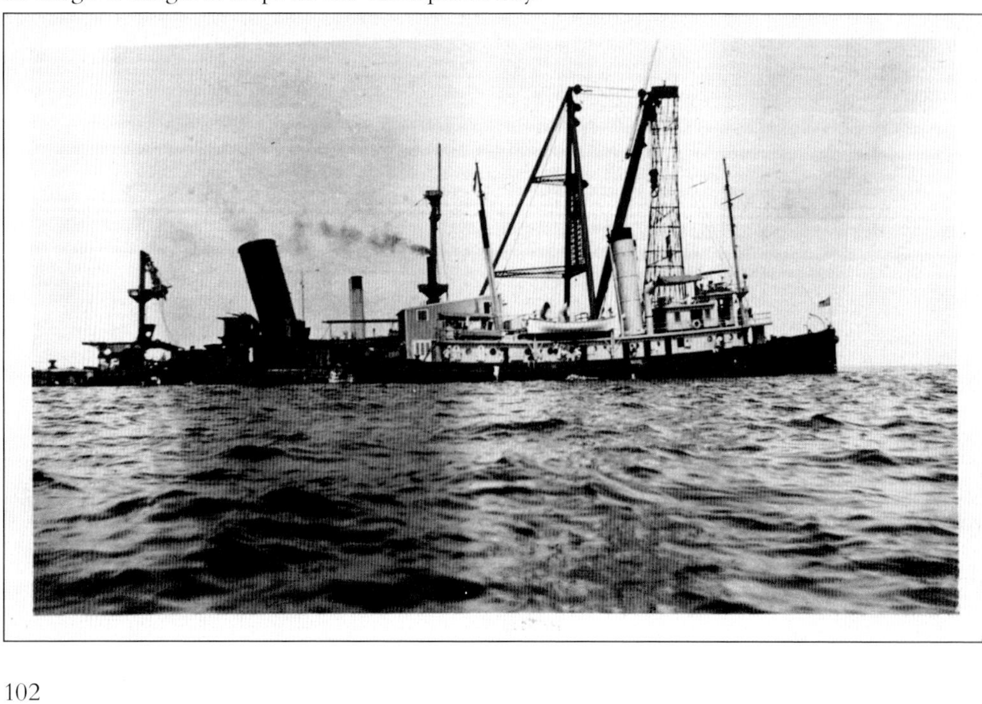

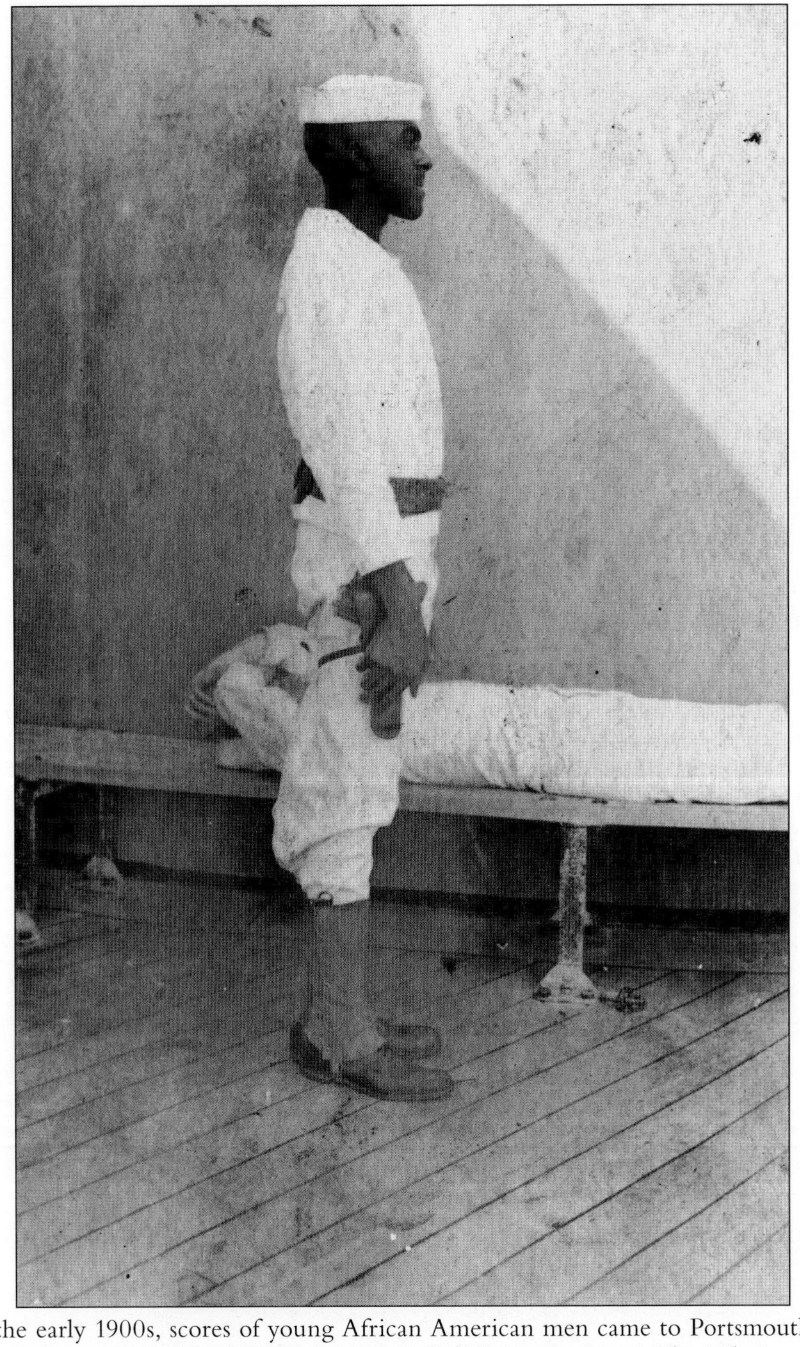

During the early 1900s, scores of young African American men came to Portsmouth seeking either employment at the Norfolk Navy Yard or to enlist in the Navy. The influx was so great during World War I that the federal government built a community for the African American workforce and named it "Truxton." This real photo postcard is of a young sailor who was a resident of the city. His mother, a laundress at the Norfolk Navy Yard, must have been truly proud to see her son in his Navy uniform. The sailor is pictured with an issued sidearm strapped to his hip and was most likely assigned to sentry duty. A number of African American sailors were posted at the St. Julian's Ordnance Depot to guard the munitions.

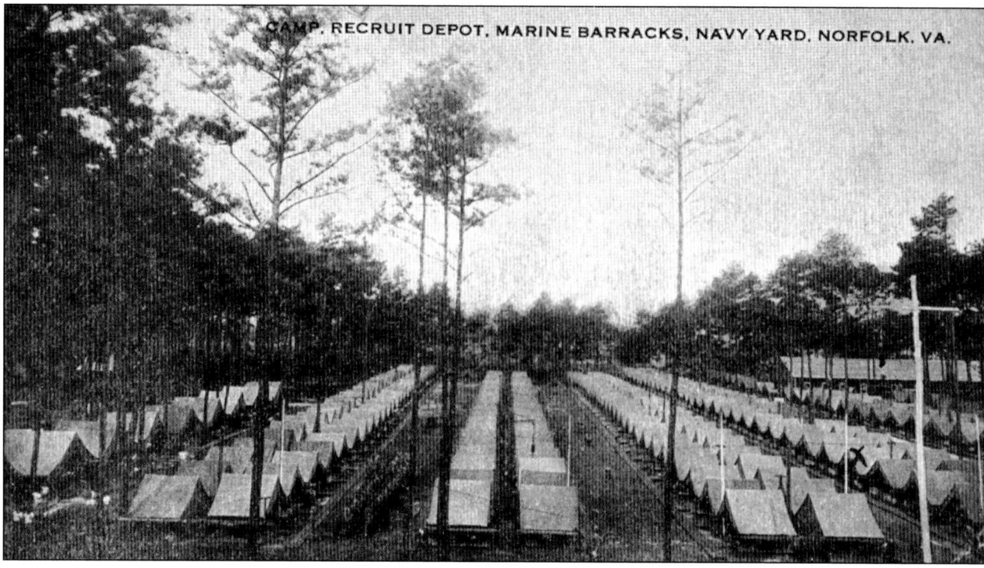

The wooded area between the Norfolk Navy Yard and Cradock came alive with fresh recruits who had enlisted in the Marines during World War I. Quartered in tent encampments and fed in a "slop" line, they drilled from sunup to sundown. The sender of this card, from 5th Company, writes, "I am getting along fine, am going to the range tomorrow."

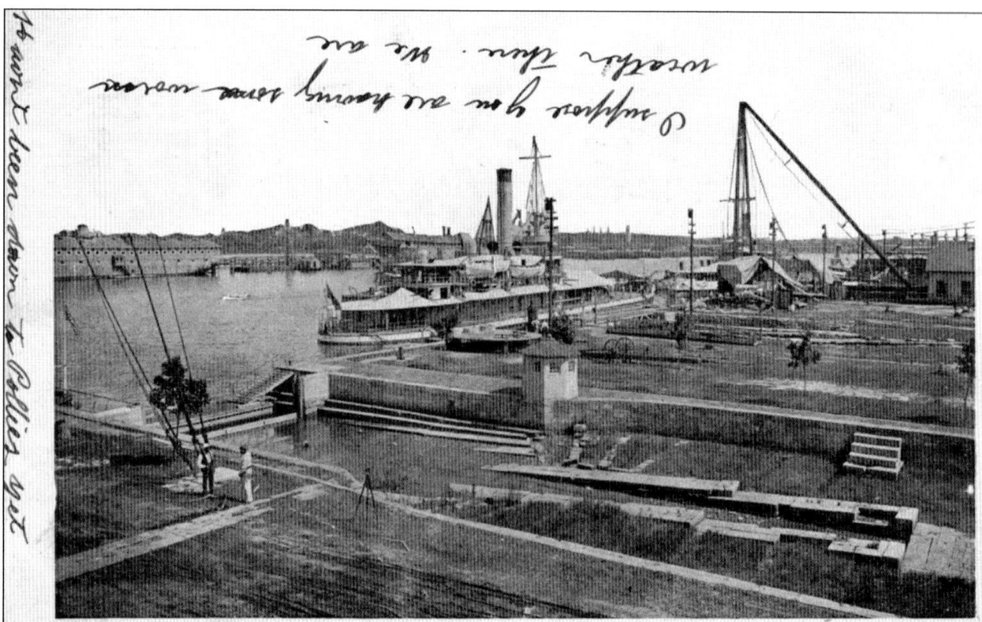

Sailors and visitors were often confused because the Naval hospital and Navy yard are located in Portsmouth, not Norfolk, as they were named. Imagine how befuddled people must have been when receiving this postcard of a "View of Navy Yard, Brooklyn, NY," when in fact it was the Norfolk Navy Yard in Portsmouth, Virginia.

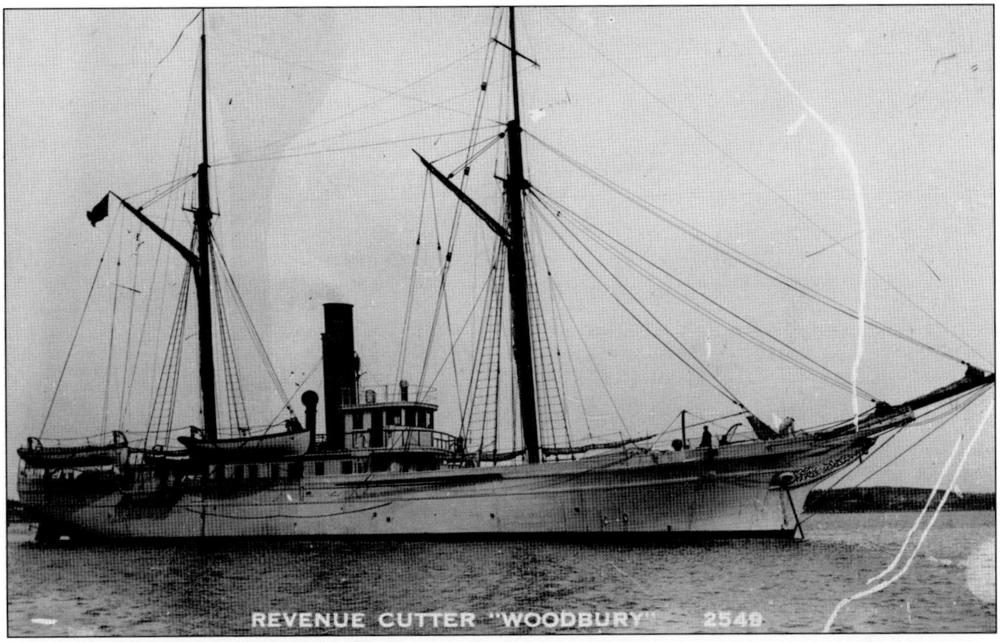

The Revenue Cutter *Woodbury* was assigned to the Auxiliary Naval Force at Norfolk Navy Yard during the spring of 1898. Capt. H.B. Rogers was the commanding officer of a crew of seven officers and 34 enlisted men, four of whom were African American stewards (listed as "colored" on the ship's roster), while the vessel was stationed in Portsmouth. For a brief time, until August 1898, the ship aided in the blockade of Cuba during the Spanish-American War.

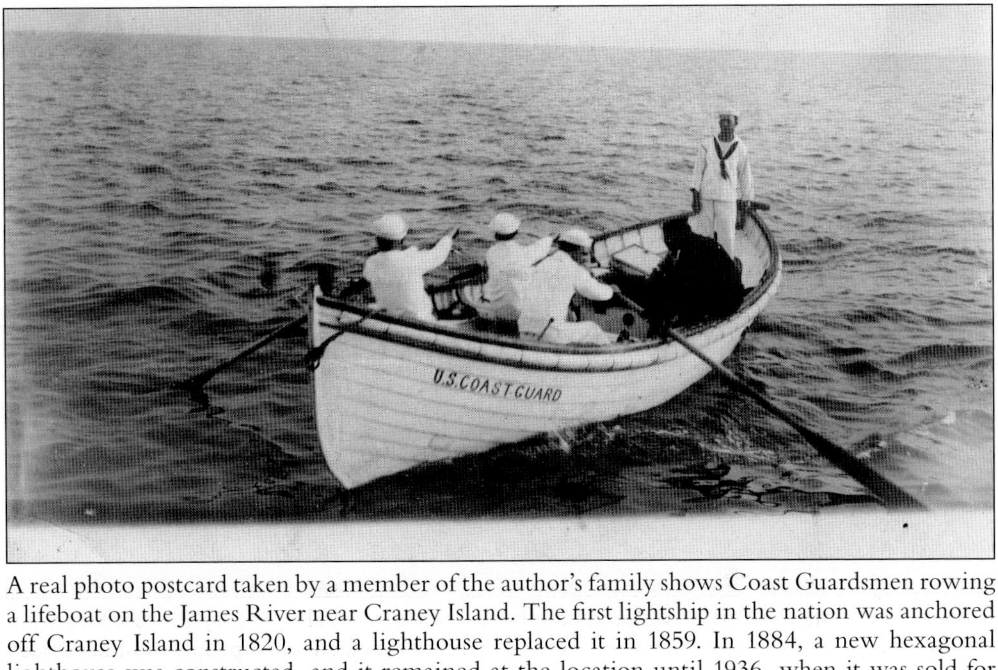

A real photo postcard taken by a member of the author's family shows Coast Guardsmen rowing a lifeboat on the James River near Craney Island. The first lightship in the nation was anchored off Craney Island in 1820, and a lighthouse replaced it in 1859. In 1884, a new hexagonal lighthouse was constructed, and it remained at the location until 1936, when it was sold for $1.07 to the Norfolk Sea Scouts according to an article in the *Portsmouth Star.*

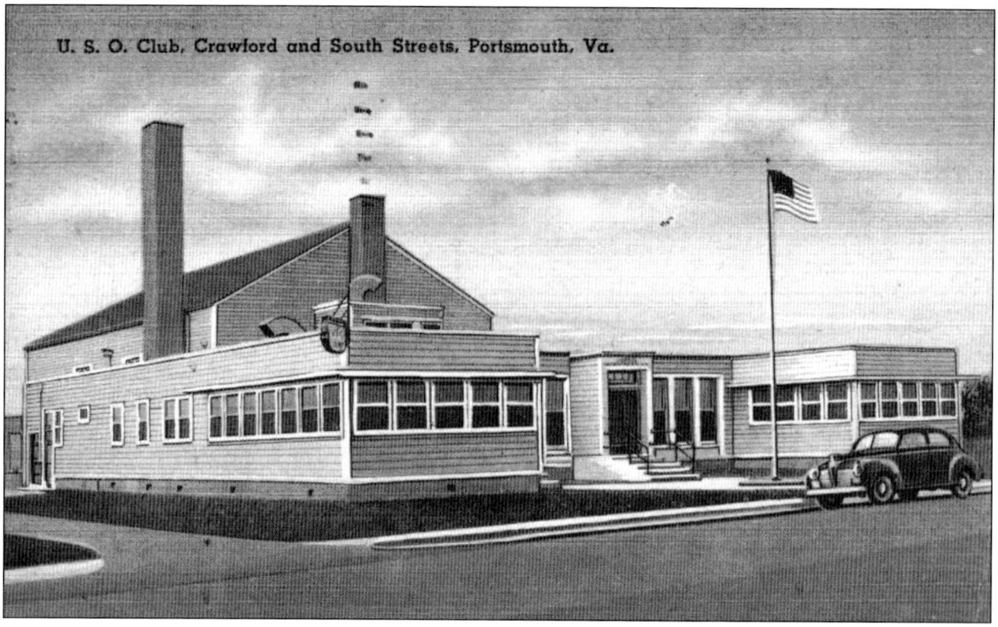

The USO Club at Crawford and South Streets for years provided a place for service personnel to relax and unwind. Members of all branches of the military were steadily coming or going on the Seaboard Airline Railway, which was close to the club. Stopping in for a break, they might have taken the time to shake a leg to the sound of Henry Divers's Big Band.

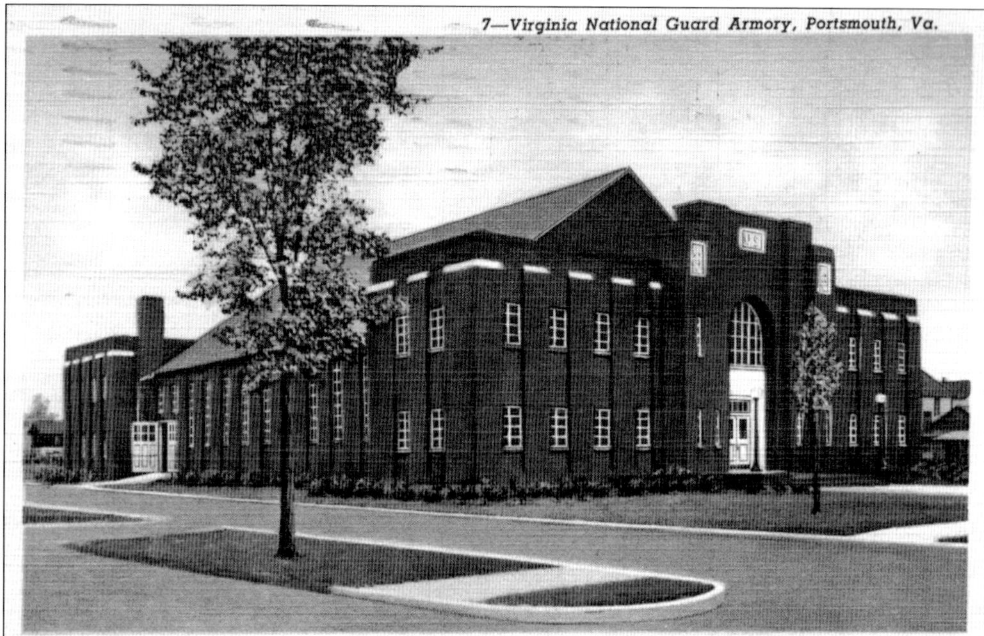

The Virginia Army National Guard Armory on Elm Avenue was built in 1934 for units of light artillery and cavalry that were trained to support the Army. The armory played host to dances where the big bands of Kirby Smith and His Orchestra and the Chic Ciccone Orchestra played into the late-night hours. When the guard relocated to a larger facility in 1970, it was converted into a community center.

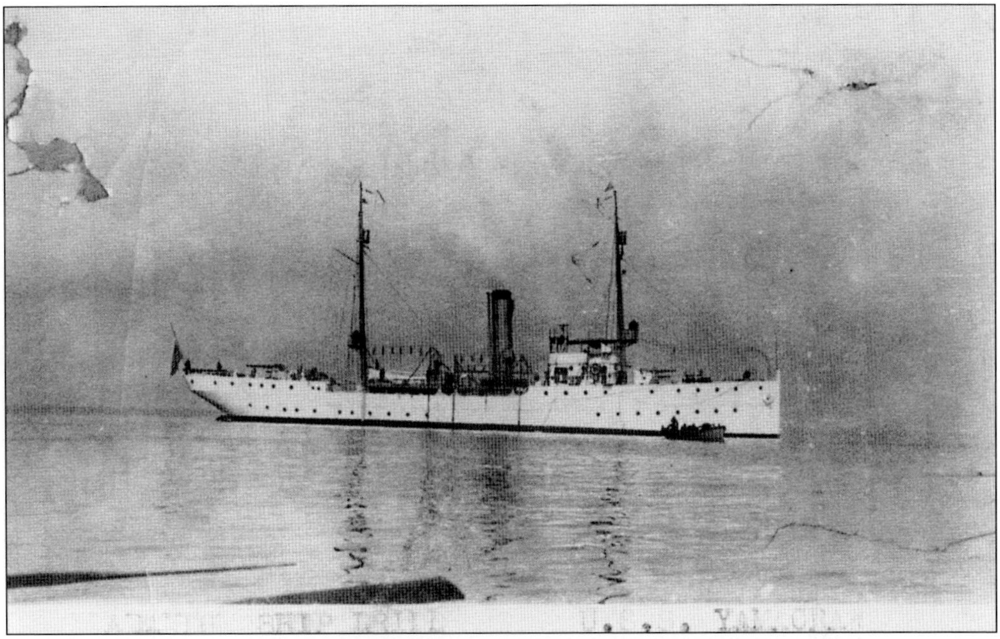

The real photo postcards pictured here are of the Revenue Cutter *Yamacraw* and its crew, which were stationed in Portsmouth during the early 1900s. The cutter is best known for a rescue attempt on March 3, 1917. Departing from port at 7:00 that fateful night, the captain, with only 60 percent of the crew onboard (the rest were on shore leave), set sail for the Chesapeake Bay in search of a British steamer needing assistance. While searching, an urgent distress call came from the SS *Louisiana*. After the *Louisiana* was found, the cutter crew made attempts to board the vessel and rescue the crew. By daylight on the 4th, the efforts had ended in the loss of 10 cutter crewmen and one crewman of the *Louisiana*. The cutter remained in the 5th Naval District until July 1917.

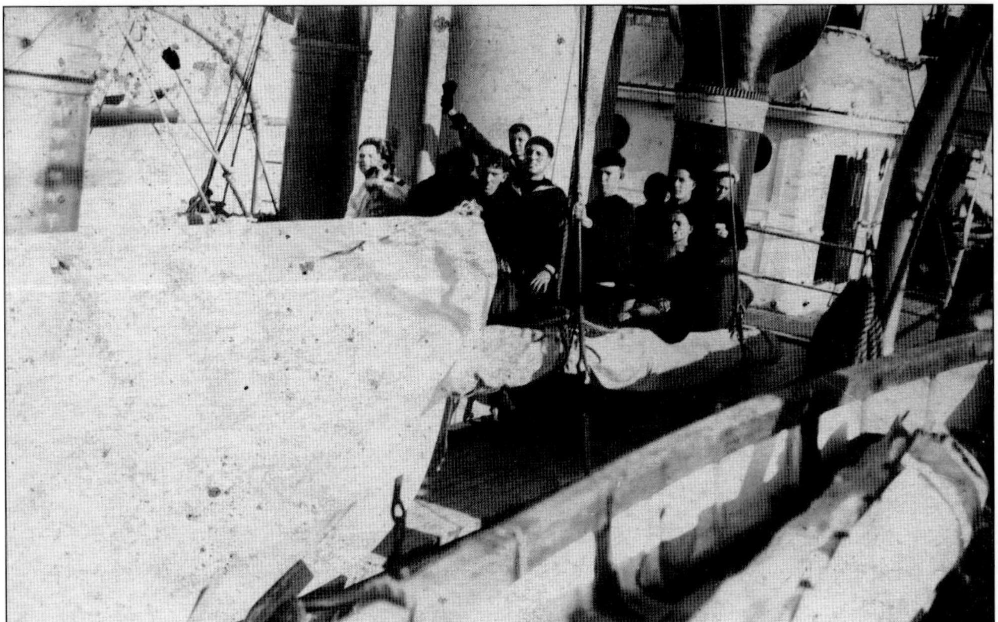

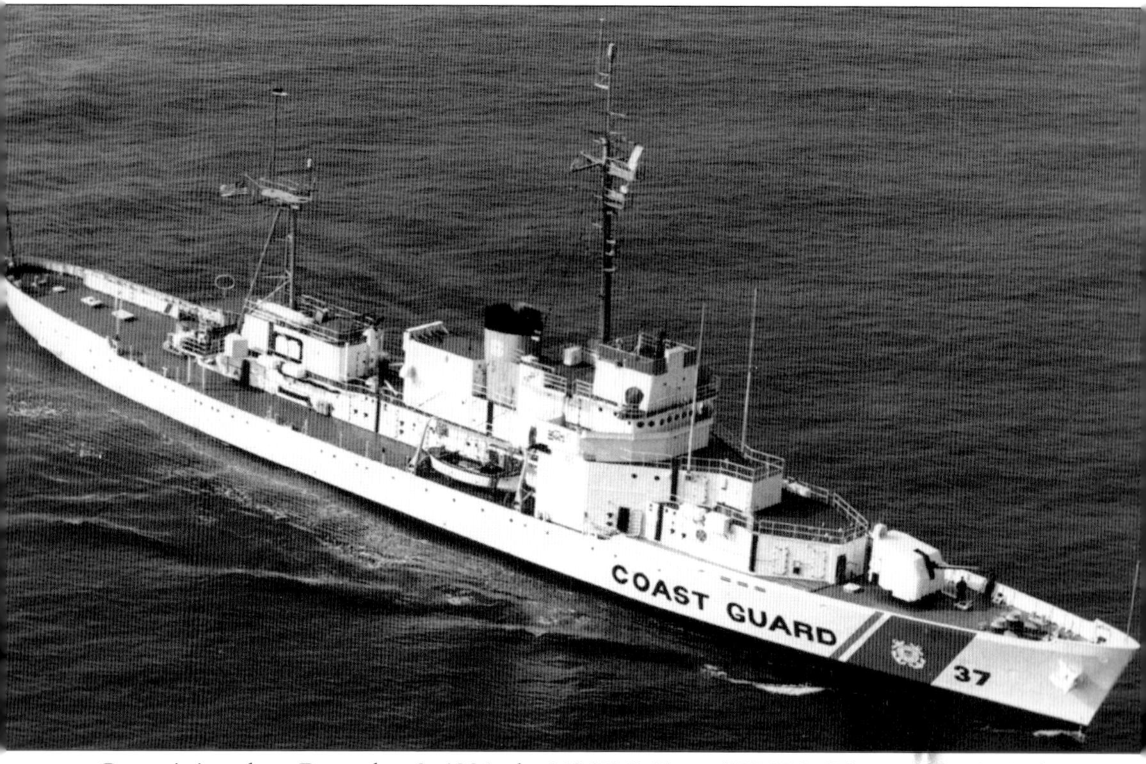

Commissioned on December 9, 1936, the USCGC *Taney* (WHEC-37) would begin its long cruise into maritime history. While stationed at Honolulu Harbor, the ship was transferred in July 1941 to the Navy but retained its Coast Guard crew. On the morning of December 7, 1941, the crew was startled when the call was sounded. "This is not a drill" was heard as the Japanese attacked Pearl Harbor. The ship saw action during the war in the Pacific, performing escort duty until March 31, 1944, when it arrived in Portsmouth and was assigned to the Atlantic Convoy Escort for the remainder of the war. By the 1960s, the *Taney* was the last commissioned vessel in service that had seen action at Pearl Harbor. In February 1972, the ship returned to the 5th Coast Guard District in Portsmouth and remained in service until decommissioned on December 7, 1986. The USCGC *Taney* is now a museum in the harbor at Baltimore, Maryland, and is on the National Register of Historic Landmarks. In 2009, the Coast Guard awarded the distinction of "Coast Guard City" to the city of Portsmouth.

Eight

They Have a Little Bit of Everything Here

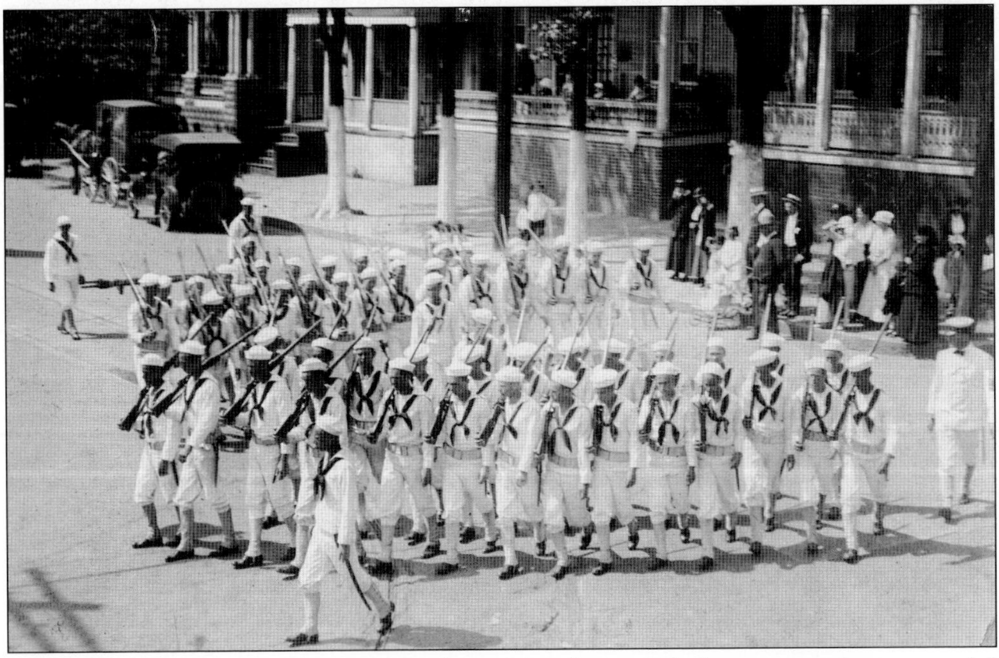

"It seems like we are always marching and practicing for a parade, but everyone loves a parade" was written under this postcard in the scrapbook it was taken from. Since 1884, the city of Portsmouth has held a Memorial Day (Decoration Day) celebration. It holds the distinction of having one of the oldest Memorial Day parades. This is a day to commemorate those who died while in military service; however, the official name was not declared until 1967. "Left flank, march!"

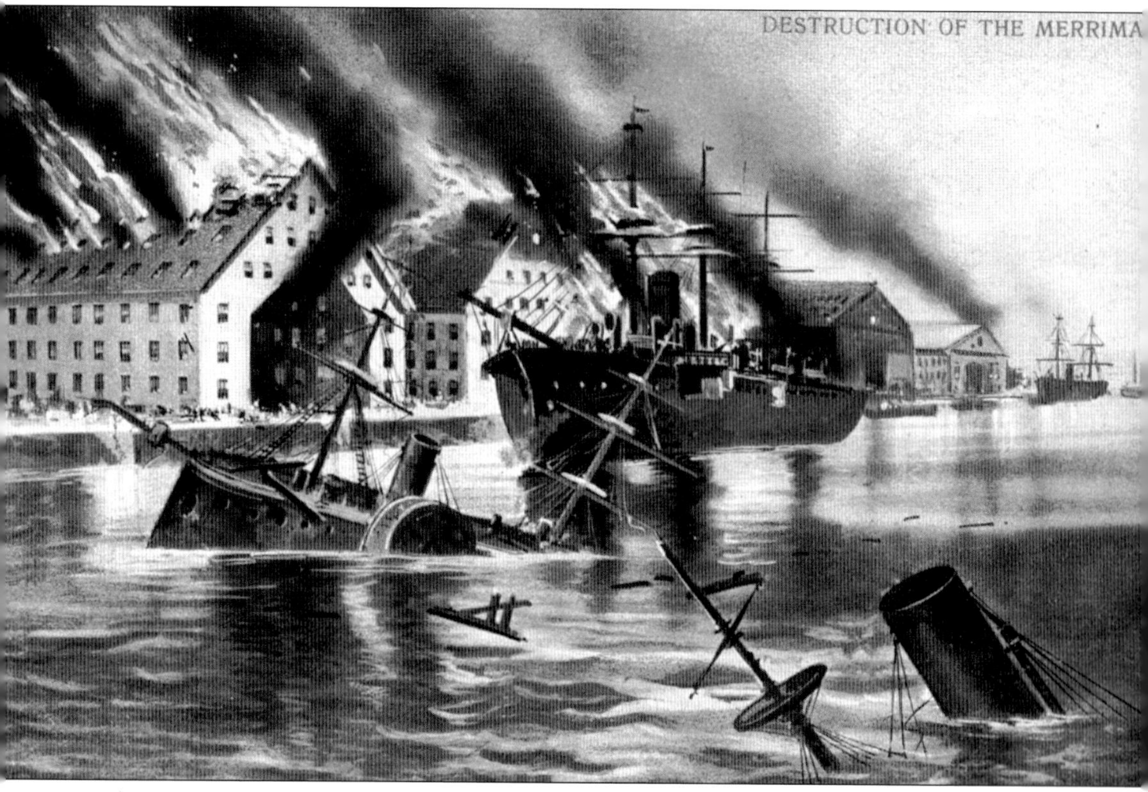

What started with a fire would end in a fire. On April 20, 1861, the order was given by Capt. Charles S. McCauley, the commanding officer of the Gosport Navy Yard, to destroy the buildings and ordnance and scuttle or burn all of the warships docked along the waterfront. The steam frigate USS *Merrimac* burned into the night, to the waterline, and sank at its moorings. Virginia militia forces under the command of Capt. Robert Pegram would occupy the shipyard the following day, and by late spring, the conversion of the USS *Merrimac* would begin. Confederate naval officers, along with ship designer and constructor John L. Porter, would begin the task of overseeing the burned-out steam frigate's conversion into the CSS *Virginia*, America's first ironclad. The burned hull of the *Merrimac* was pumped out and placed in Dry Dock No. 1, where the conversion work would begin. To meet the demands of Porter's designs, iron plates manufactured at Tredegar Iron Works steadily rolled in by rail. Work progressed rapidly, with labor provided by local shipyards.

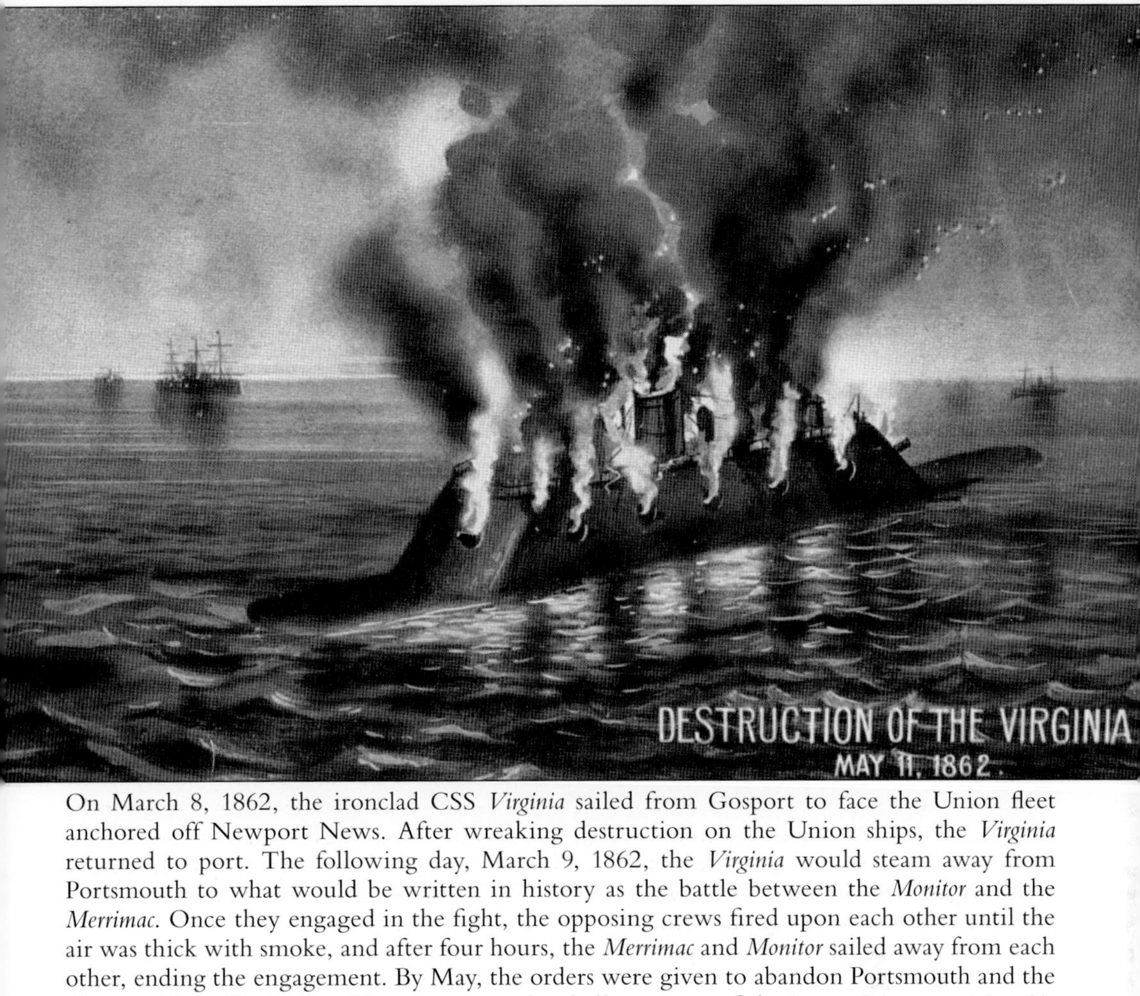

On March 8, 1862, the ironclad CSS *Virginia* sailed from Gosport to face the Union fleet anchored off Newport News. After wreaking destruction on the Union ships, the *Virginia* returned to port. The following day, March 9, 1862, the *Virginia* would steam away from Portsmouth to what would be written in history as the battle between the *Monitor* and the *Merrimac*. Once they engaged in the fight, the opposing crews fired upon each other until the air was thick with smoke, and after four hours, the *Merrimac* and *Monitor* sailed away from each other, ending the engagement. By May, the orders were given to abandon Portsmouth and the Gosport Navy Yard. Not able to navigate the shallow water of the James River, on May 11, 1862, the crew ran the *Virginia* aground at Craney Island and set the vessel ablaze.

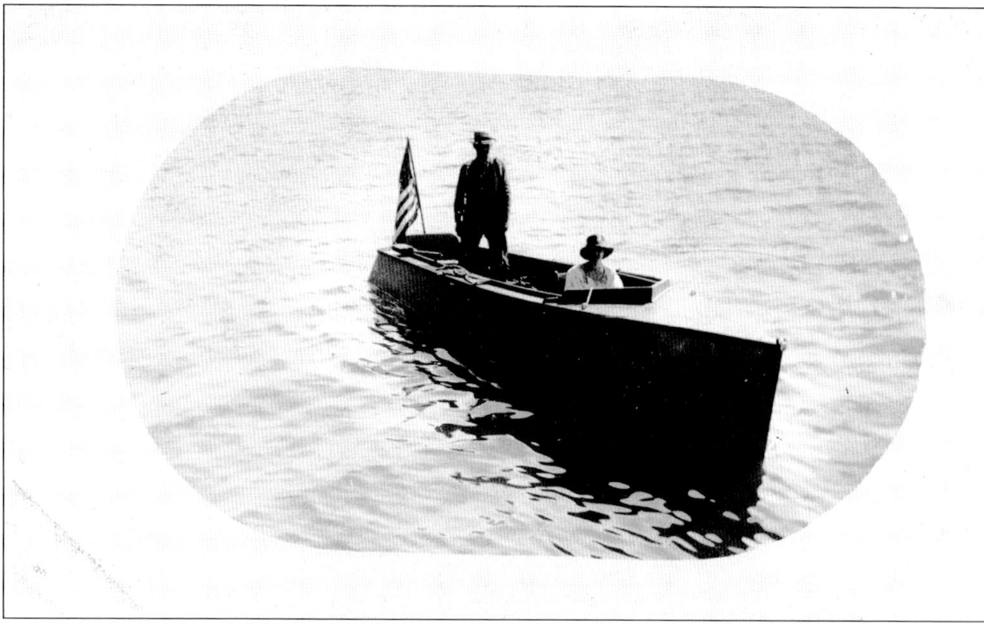

The Portsmouth Boat Club was incorporated on May 18, 1905, and prospered until 1919. Dr. Joseph Grice donated the clubhouse and docks located at Swimming Point along the shore, captured in postcard views from the past. The clubhouse was renovated in 1949 but was sold in the early 1970s, when the club disbanded. Reestablished in 1991, pleasure boating has remained a favorite pastime amongst residents like those in this real photo postcard view.

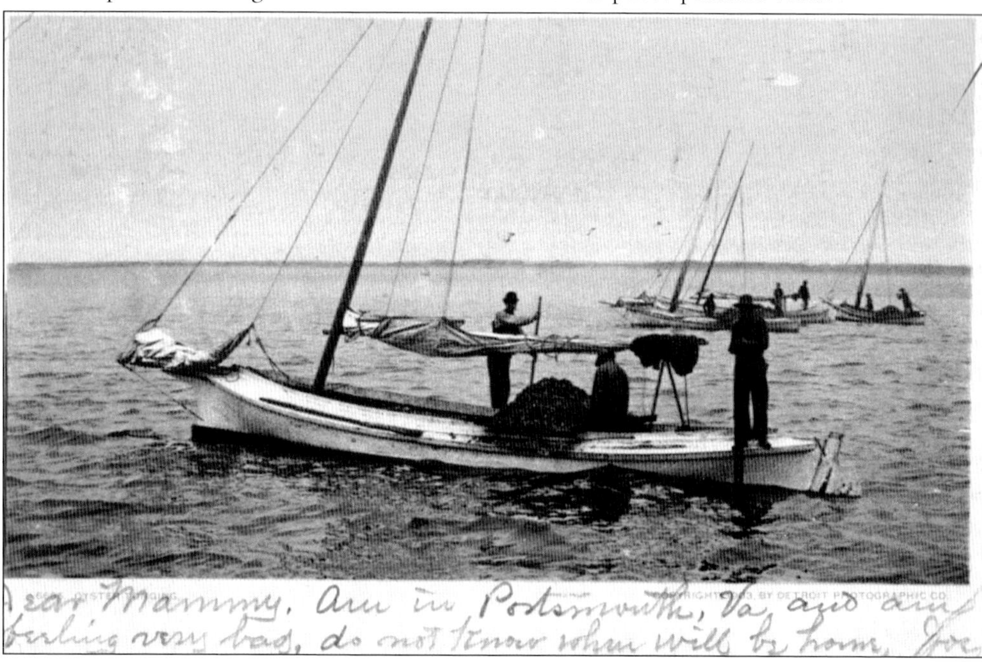

Tonging for oysters off the shores of Craney Island and Hoffler's Creek was common until the early 1930s. The oyster boats would sail to the docks, located on the western branch of the Elizabeth River (West Norfolk), to the plant where the oysters would be packed by the bushel or pickled by the gallon for shipment. The sender of this card most likely worked on an oyster boat.

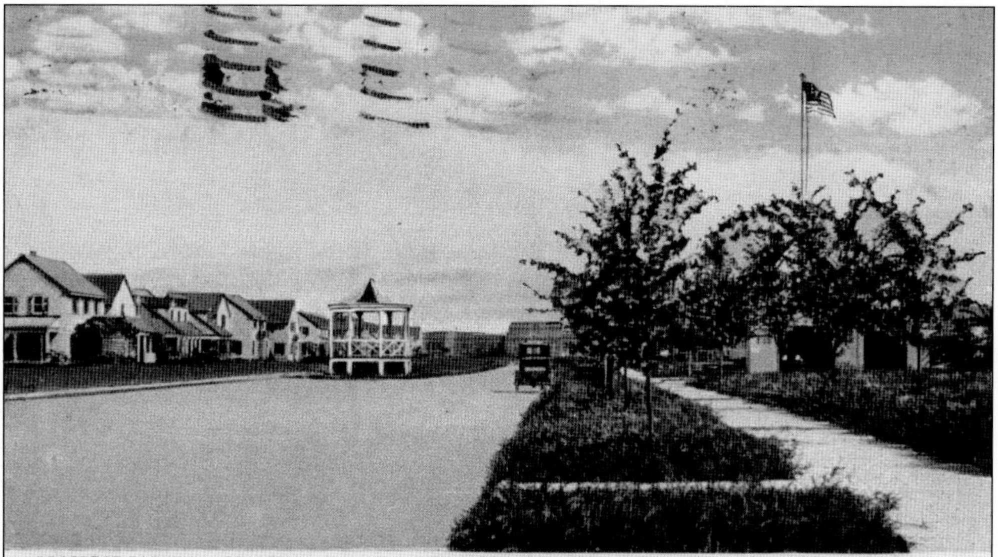

PROSPECT PARKWAY, CRADDOCK, SUBURB OF PORTSMOUTH, VA.

Built as housing for shipyard workers during World War I, Cradock was the nation's first planned housing project. Designed in the shape of an anchor, the community included a shopping center, schools, churches, and a fire station. After the war, before relinquishing control of the community, the government gave the residents the option to buy the houses that they were renting. The neighborhood is listed on the National Register of Historic Places.

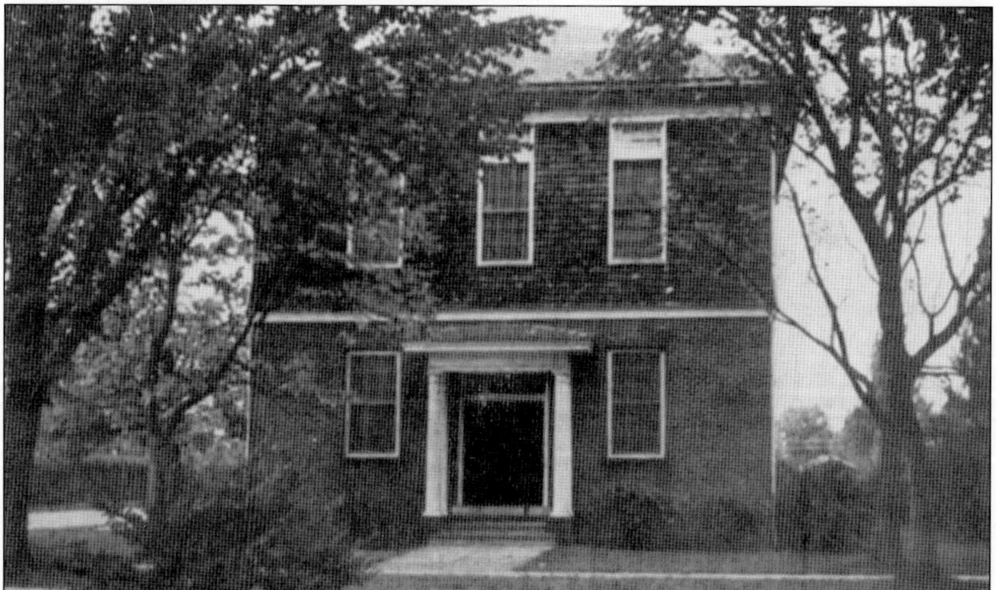

THE MASONIC TEMPLE, CRADOCK, VA.

Lake Drummond Masonic Lodge No. 178 purchased the site at 1 Afton Parkway (pictured) from the federal government in 1921. Construction began on the lodge, and the cornerstone was laid on December 3, 1921. The members, mostly residents of Cradock, held their first meeting on April 20, 1922, at this location. During the 1980s, a larger lodge was built, and this site was sold in 1985.

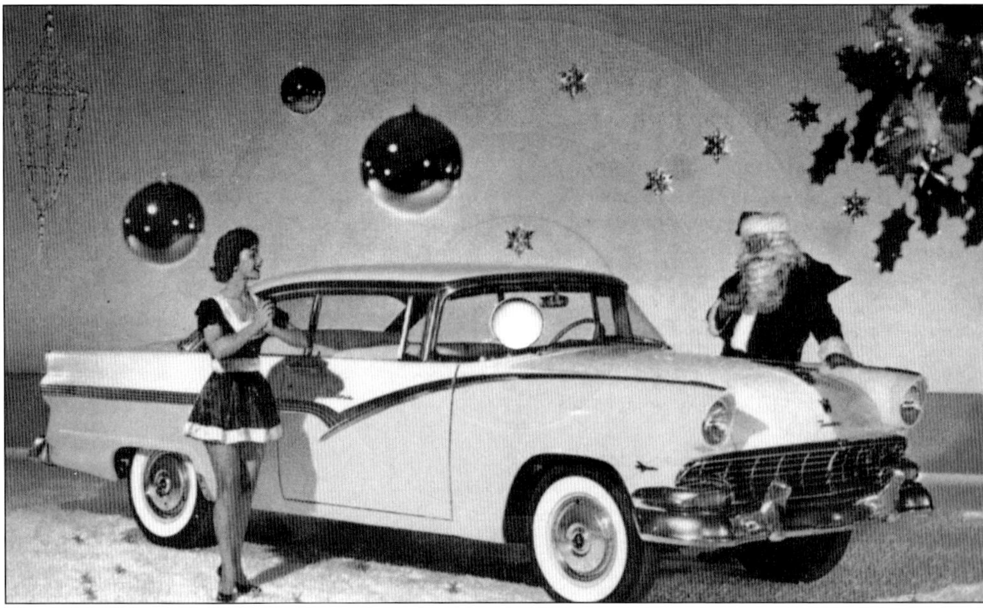

Tyree-Jones Motor Corporation was located at 1300 High Street and proclaimed to be "Portsmouth's oldest and largest automobile dealer." A promotional Christmas postcard from 1955 that advertised Ford's 1956 models was also a phonographic record. Played on any 78-rpm phonograph, Rosemary Clooney and Mitch Miller's Orchestra offered Christmas enjoyment, while the copy told one how to get in tune with the deal of a lifetime.

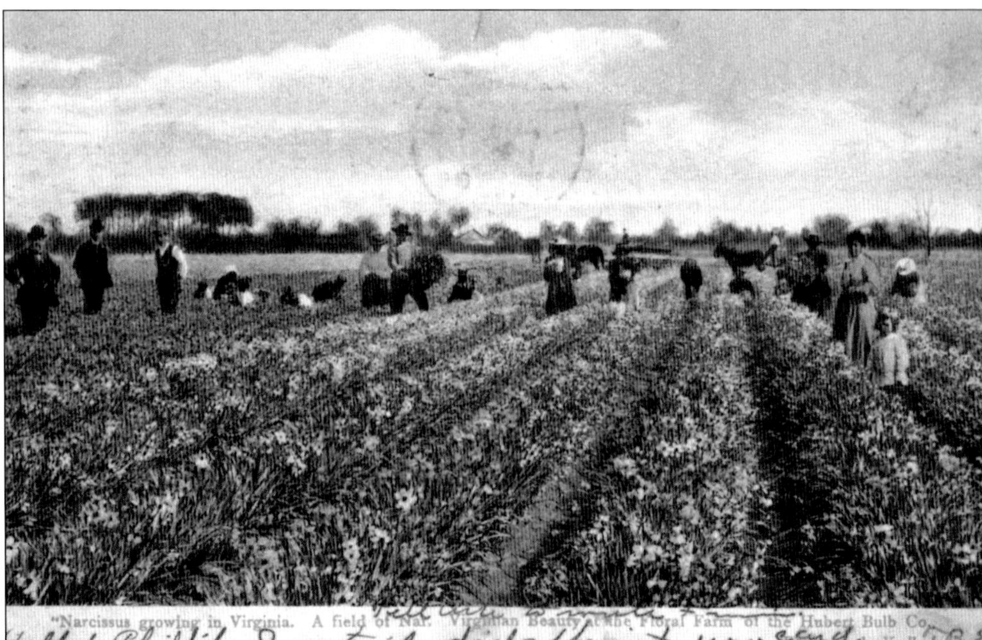

Churchland was known for the truck farms that grew collards, peanuts, sweet potatoes, and other crops throughout the seasons. Another popular crop that grew well was narcissus (daffodils), which were grown on acres of the Trotman farm. A Sunday drive along Rivershore Road past the blooming fields of flowers could make one think of the Netherlands.

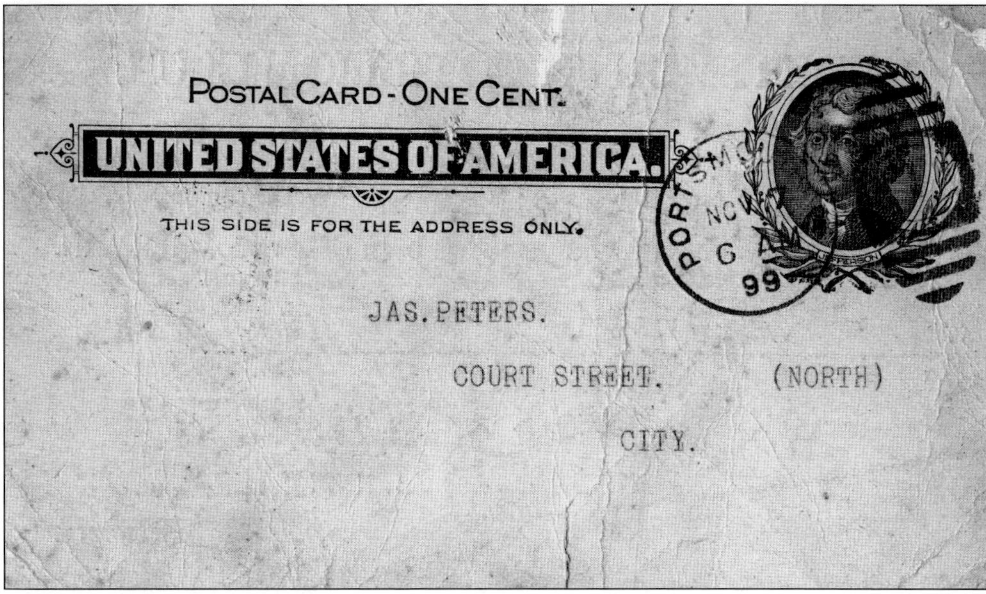
POSTAL CARD - ONE CENT.

UNITED STATES OF AMERICA.

THIS SIDE IS FOR THE ADDRESS ONLY.

PORTSMOUTH NOV 6 99

JAS. PETERS.

COURT STREET. (NORTH)

CITY.

Formal balls and semiformal dances have always been a favorite social event for the residents and guests of the city. To receive a notice by mail of an event sponsored by the Portsmouth Cotillion Club meant preparation for an evening of dining and dancing. The introduction and formal presentation of young ladies to "polite society" would be on the agenda, as well as dancing with young gentlemen. The couple best executing the dance would be given a prize. The theme for the dinner and dance scheduled on December 5, 1899, was German. Notable family names of Portsmouth residents can be recognized on the cards, and the house to which the card was sent remains in Olde Towne.

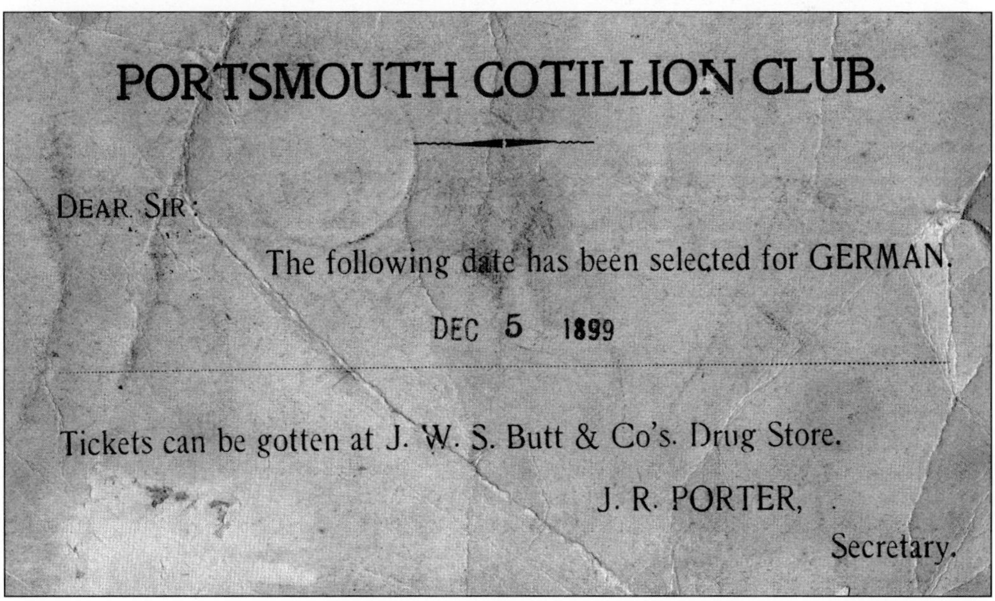
PORTSMOUTH COTILLION CLUB.

DEAR SIR:

The following date has been selected for GERMAN.

DEC 5 1899

Tickets can be gotten at J. W. S. Butt & Co's. Drug Store.

J. R. PORTER,

Secretary.

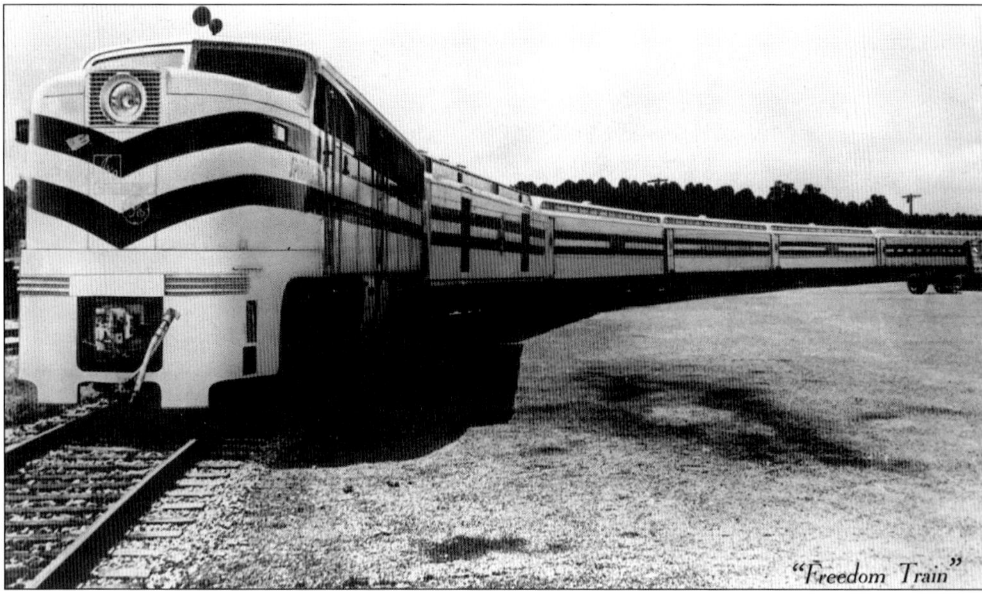

This souvenir postcard of 1947 shows the *Freedom Train* when the train visited the city while touring the United States. The train was painted in patriotic colors and displayed 127 historical documents, including the Declaration of Independence and one of the 13 copies of the Constitution. An elite group of Marines provided security for the rare cargo as well as filling the role of hosts and tour guides to visitors of the exhibit.

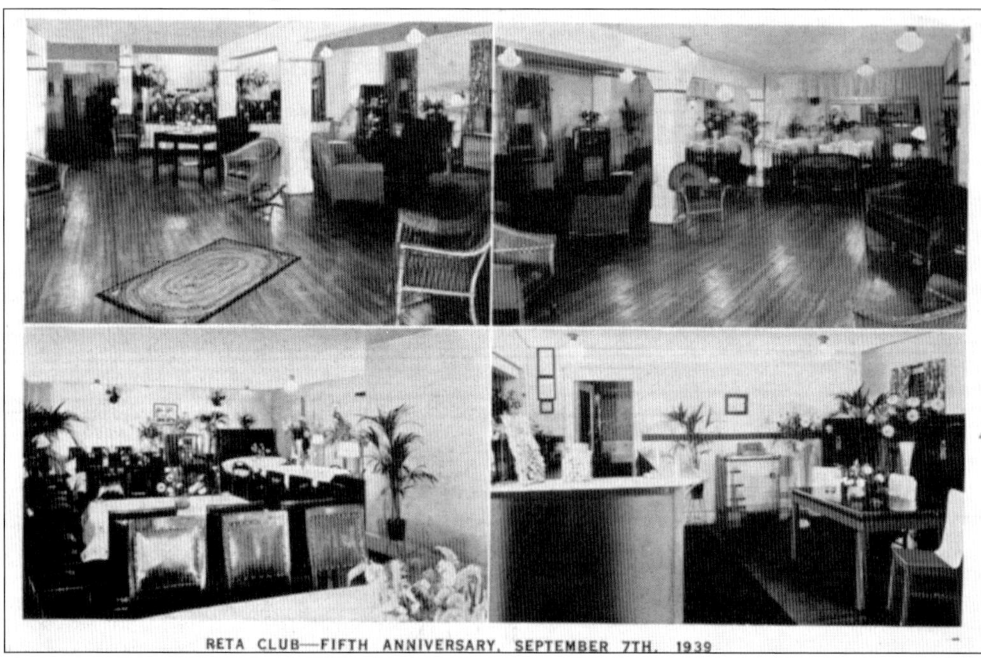

The Railway Employees and Taxpayers Association Club (RETA) was located on High Street from 1934 until the late 1940s. Club members could relax and unwind in the lounge or enjoy a meal in the dining room. Special activities and fundraising events were often on the calendar, as noted by the message on the reverse side of this card, "Come up Monday night and help the Fluoroscope Fund."

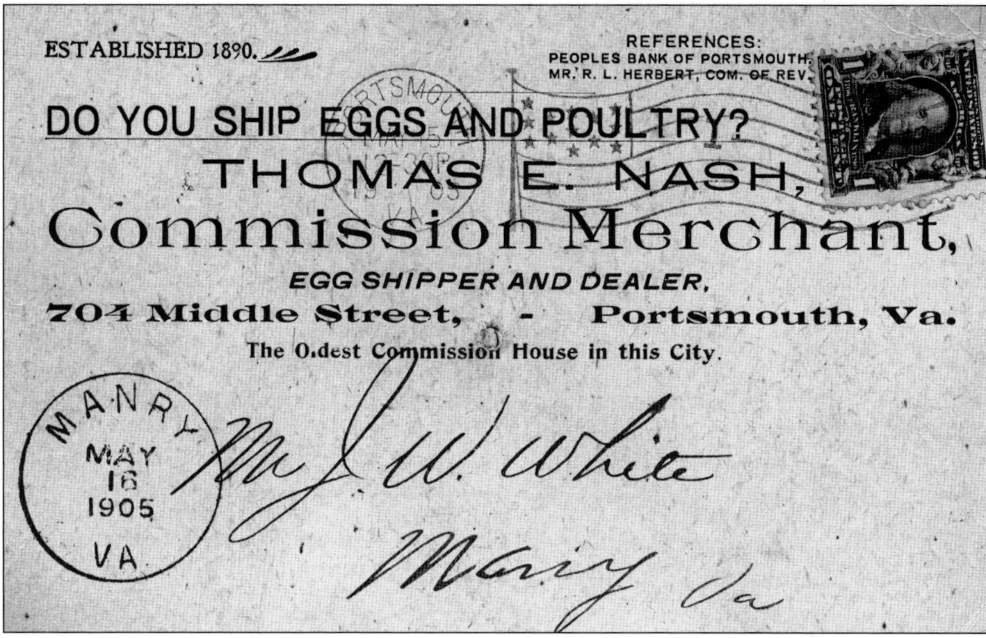

Thomas E. Nash was one of the nine commission merchants in the city during the 1800s and made a substantial living selling and shipping eggs. Located on Middle Street near the City Market, residents would deliver quantities of eggs to the Commission House, and in turn, Nash would sell and ship their eggs for a fee or commission. On the reverse side of this card, he advertises eggs for 15¢ a dozen.

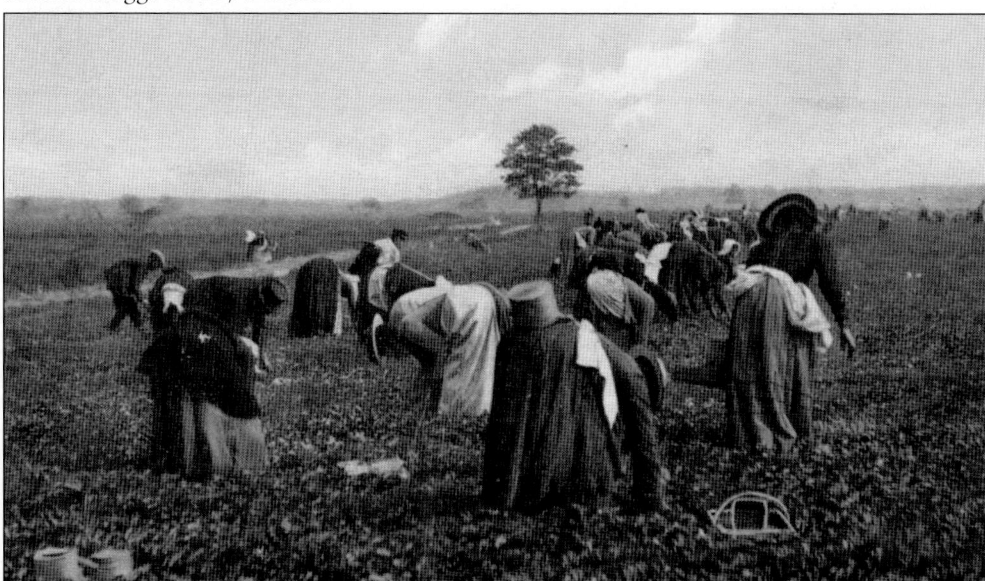

The Tidewater trucking section of Virginia included the truck farms in Churchland and Western Branch, both of which were located in Norfolk County. Farmers in both areas would grow strawberries, but it has been noted that the farms in Churchland would often plant alternating rows of strawberries and potatoes in their fields. Residents of the African American community of Twin Pines were often hired to help at harvest time.

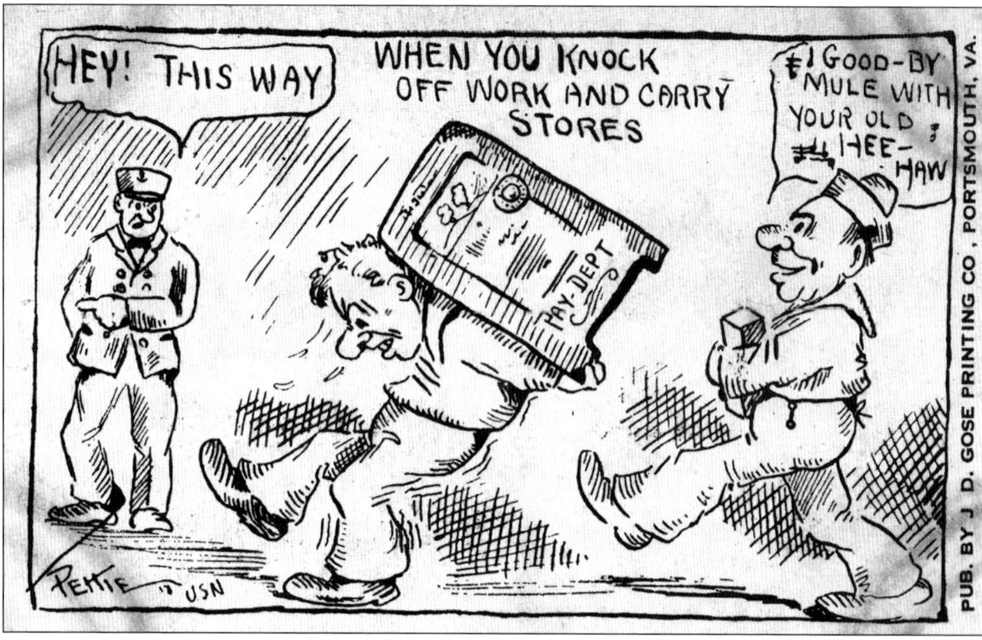

During 1918, the Naval hospital was overflowing with patients who were wounded and those suffering from the influenza pandemic. The hospital ship USNS *Mercy* was ordered to Portsmouth to help alleviate the overcrowding and to assist with ordinary medical treatment cases. One corpsman stationed aboard the *Mercy* liked to spend his spare time drawing comical and satirical cartoons of Navy life as he saw it each day. He had his work printed as postcards by local printer J.D. Gose, presumably to make a little extra money. This corpsman signed his artwork with only the word "Pettie." After research of the ship's roster, it can be assumed that he was a petty officer in the Naval Medical Corps who did not want to divulge his true identity.

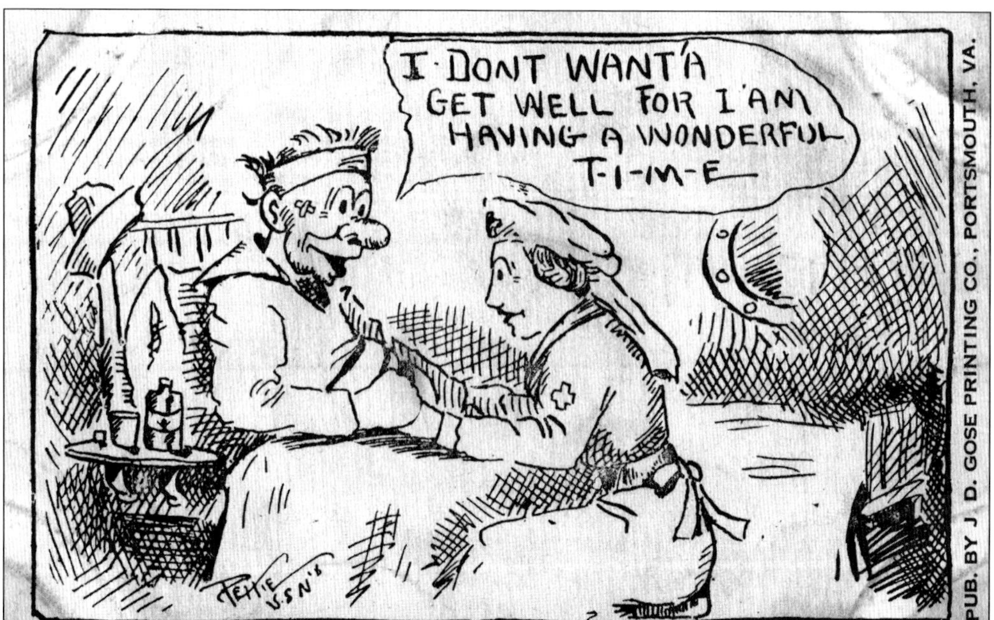

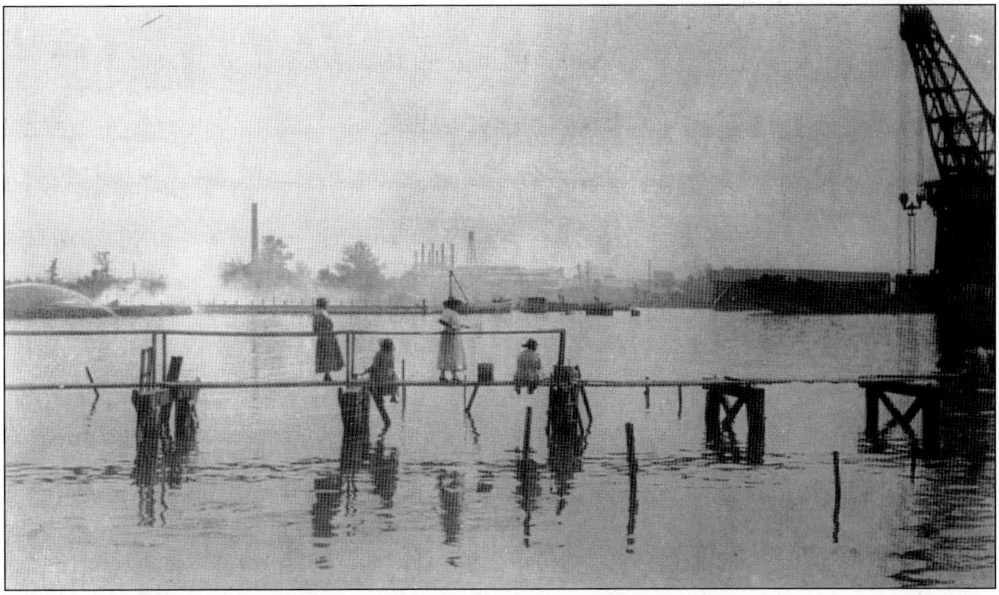

A real photo postcard from the early 1920s shows a pier on the south side of the Norfolk Navy Yard. The group of African American women on the pier is crabbing with the hopes of catching dinner or selling the excess outside the shipyard gate. On weekdays during the season, one would find someone at the wharves and piers along the city waterfront with a chicken neck on a string and a basket, just waiting for the right moment.

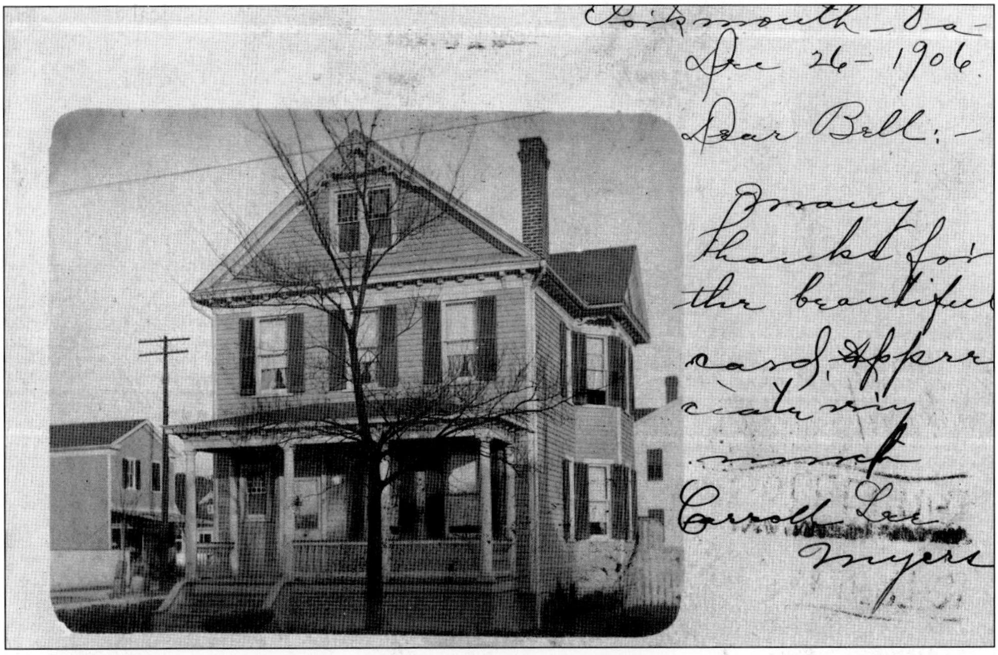

The neighborhood of Park View began development in the late 1800s with over 200 surveyed lots for sale. Multistoried homes were built in various architectural styles, with large front porches and ornate millwork trim. Some of the new homeowners were so proud that they would send real photo postcards of their homes to family members and friends, just as this family did in 1906.

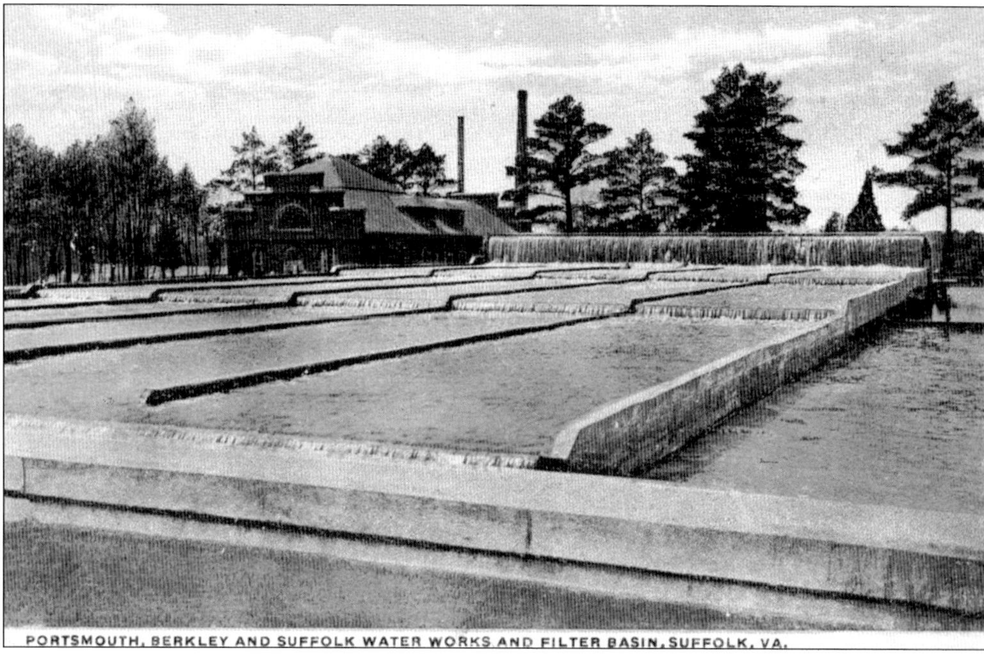

A postcard of the Portsmouth, Berkley, and Suffolk Water Works and Filter Basin shows its appearance in the early 1900s. In the 1920s, the city of Portsmouth bought the water rights from the private owners, and the facility still provides water to the residents of the city.

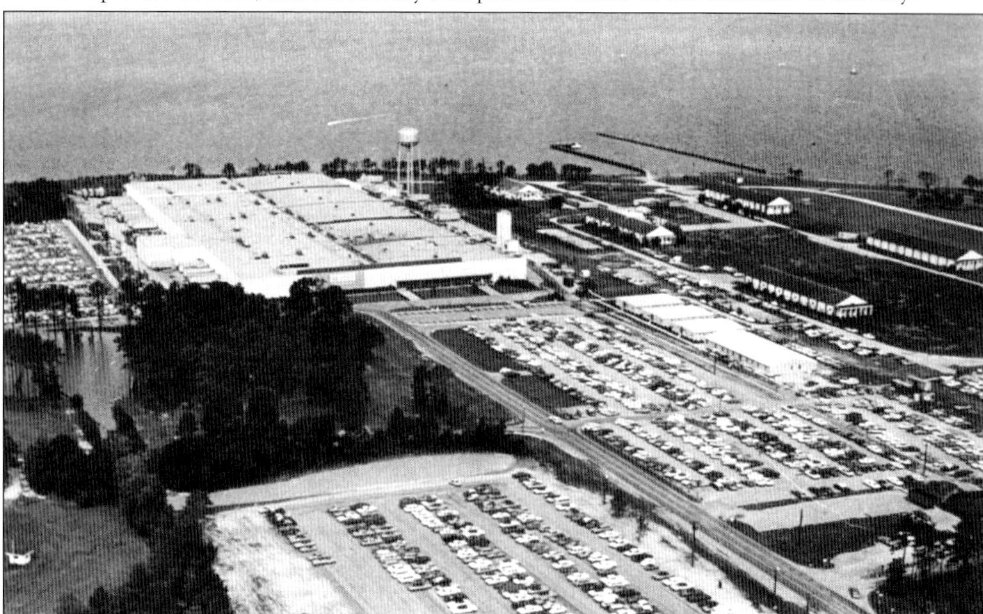

This aerial view from the 1960s shows the General Electric Plant and the campus of Frederick College, where workers assembled televisions and students rushed to class. Located at Pig Point, the buildings to the right were used in the past as barracks for the soldiers stationed at the ordnance depot, but by the 1960s, they were in use as college dorms. The college would close in July 1968, when the property was donated to the state, and the assembly line would cease operations in 1985.

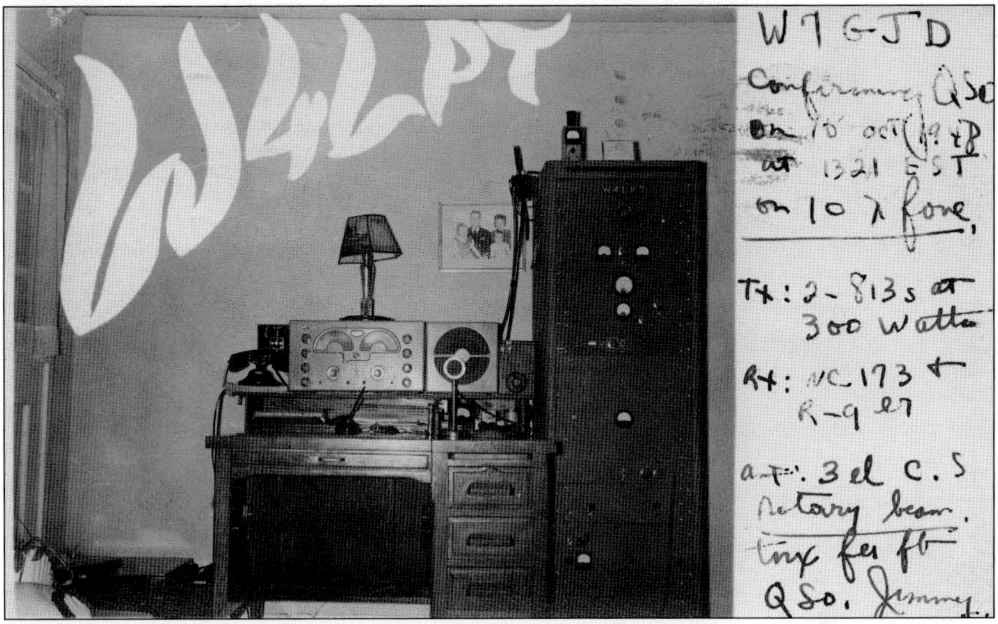

During the 1930s and 1940s, there was an abundance of ham radio operators within the city limits. Amateur radio operators would spend hours attempting to pick up signals from faraway places and to talk to other operators around the globe. This operator in Portsmouth was proud of his equipment and would send a QSL photograph postcard (Query Station Location, acknowledging receipt of communication between two amateur radio stations) to those with whom he had communicated and exchanged information.

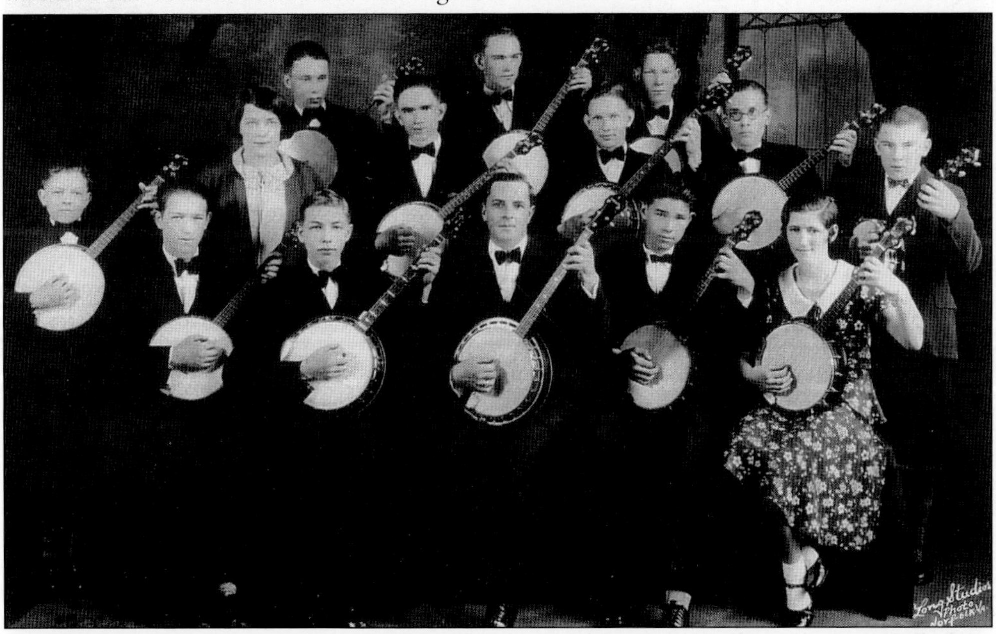

Before television, there was radio. Until the middle of the 20th century, most people were entertained by radio programs that provided music and the daily news. This real photo postcard is of the Tenor Banjo Ensemble at the State Music Studio in Portsmouth, broadcasting over WTAR radio of Norfolk in 1931. In 1943, WSAP became the first radio station to broadcast from the city.

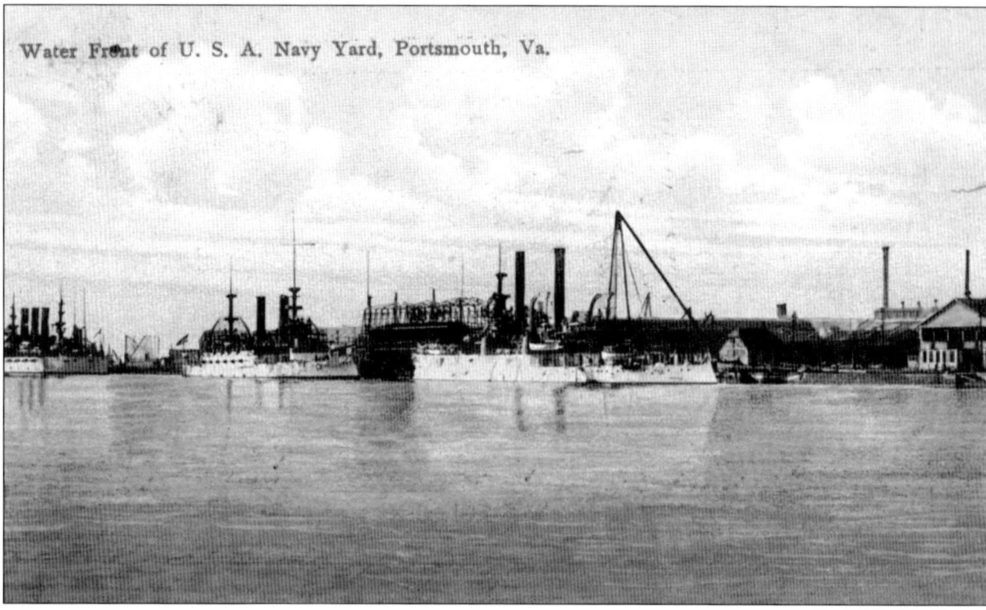

On April 26, 1907, Pres. Theodore Roosevelt and numerous dignitaries from around the globe visited the Jamestown Exposition. After his announcement of a global cruise by the entire fleet of battleships at the exposition, the Norfolk Navy Yard began the job of painting the battleships white. The Jamestown Exposition closed in early December; however, the president returned on December 16, 1907, to witness the Great White Fleet steaming out of port. A half-century later, Portsmouth again celebrated the anniversary of the founding of Jamestown. The Curtis-Dunn Marine Railway and Shipyard had the task of building replicas of the *Susan Constant*, *Godspeed*, and *Discovery* for the Jamestown Festival of 1957. The crowd along the shore in West Norfolk cheered when the three ships set sail for Jamestown, just as the crowd had cheered when the Great White Fleet set sail.

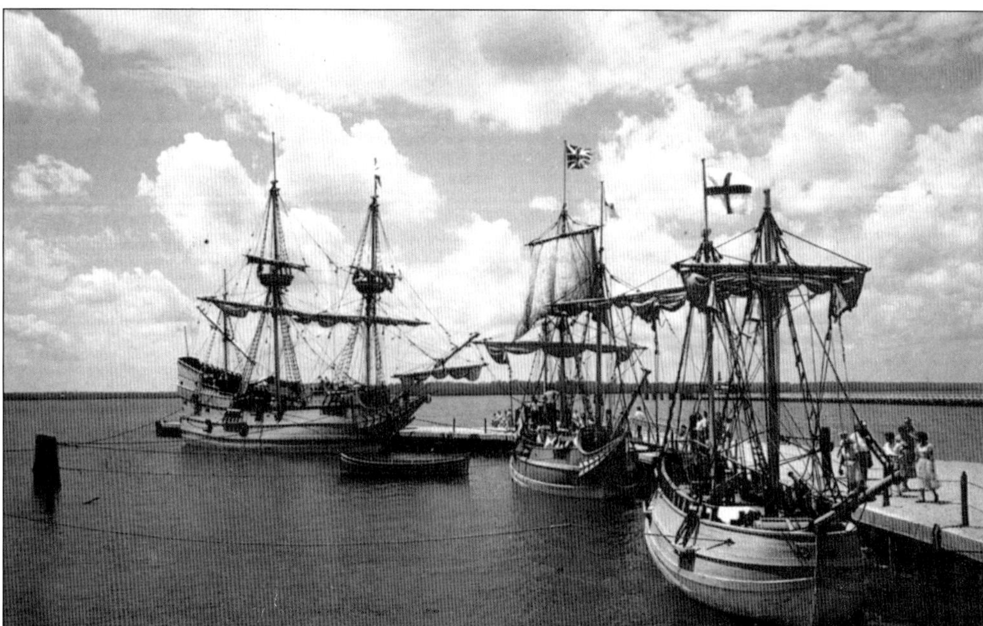

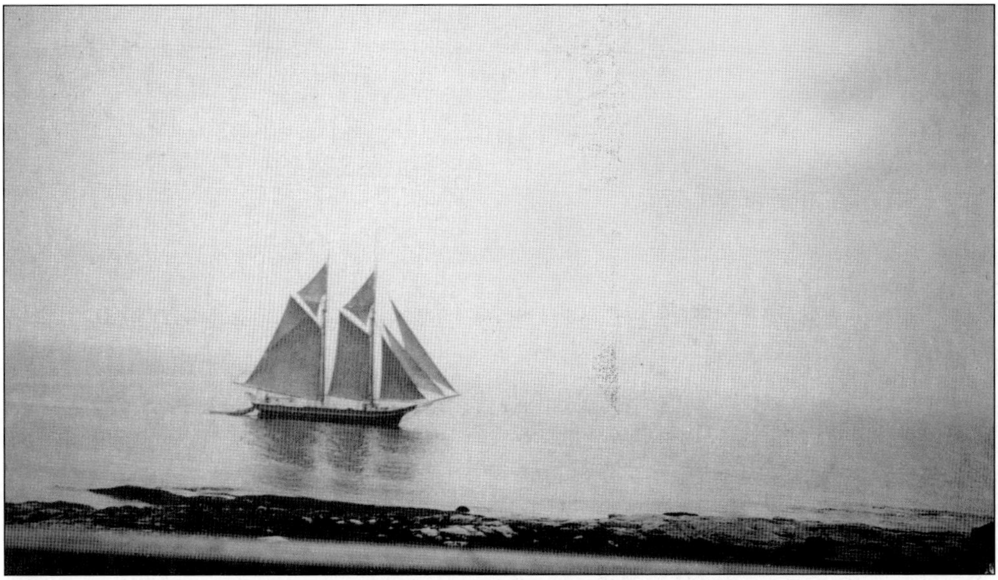

This real photo postcard offers a foggy view of a ship sailing past Floral Point near Hoffler's Creek. The waterfront between here and Craney Island would often be used by ships to sit in anchorage until they could dock in Portsmouth or Norfolk to unload and load cargo. It was also a well-known spot for digging clams at low tide and catching soft-shell crabs.

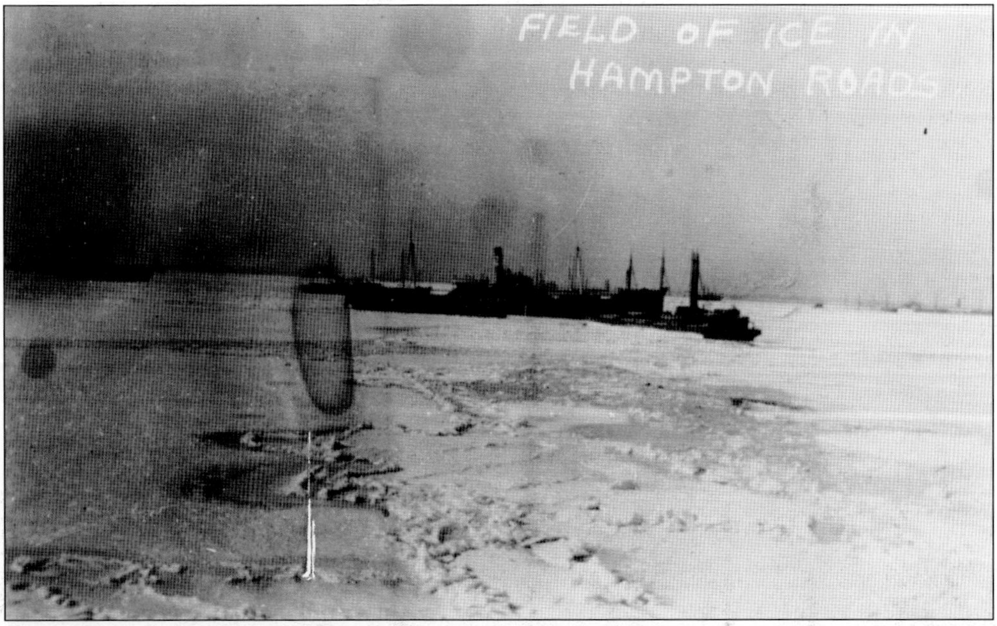

Through the years, the Elizabeth River has frozen solid between Portsmouth and Norfolk. The greatest freeze was in 1857, and one enterprising businessman opened a pub in the middle so those walking across the ice could stop and enjoy a drink. During the winter of 1917–1918, the river was frozen again, as seen on this postcard, and some have claimed that there are pictures of automobiles driving across the frozen ice.

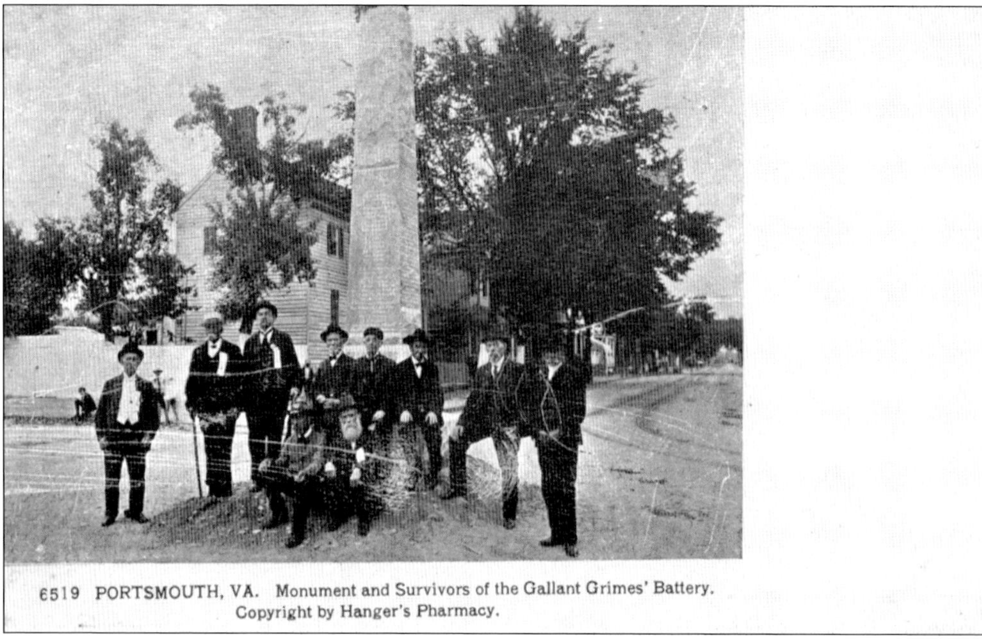

On June 8, 1906, the Confederate veterans and survivors of Grimes Battery gathered at the dedication of the monument honoring the Portsmouth Light Artillery. Grimes Battery was recognized for its bravery and being the second oldest artillery unit in the nation. Casualties were high, with 26 of the 100 that formed the battery at the onset of the war lost. The monument was moved from its original location, shown above, to a site in City Park.

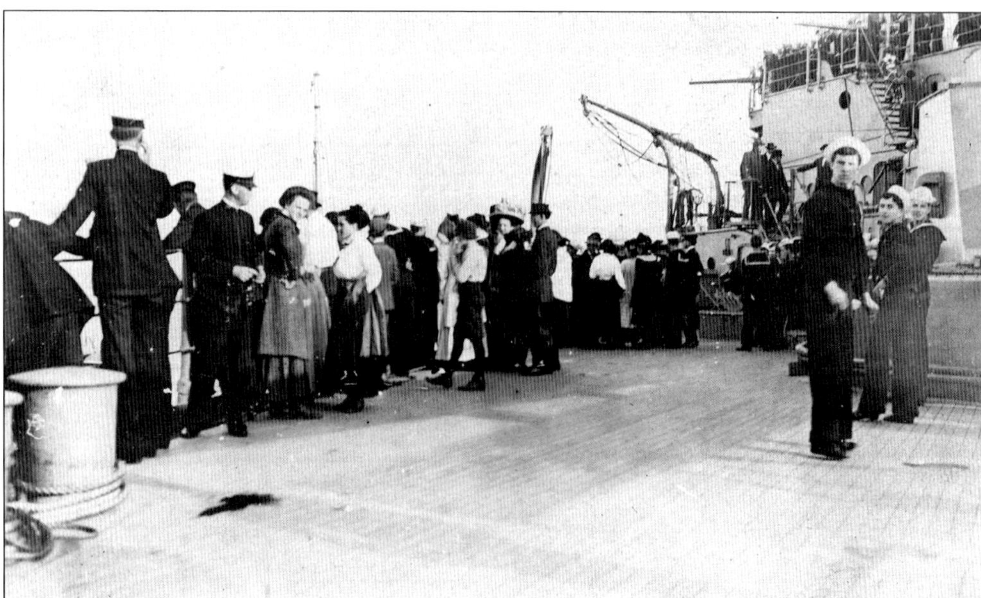

A common scene in earlier times was Visitors Day at the Norfolk Navy Yard. Local residents or family members and friends of the ship's crew could come to visit and be given tours of the shipyard and the ships. Upon entering World War I, the events were less frequent, but after the bombing of the World Trade Center, they have all but disappeared.

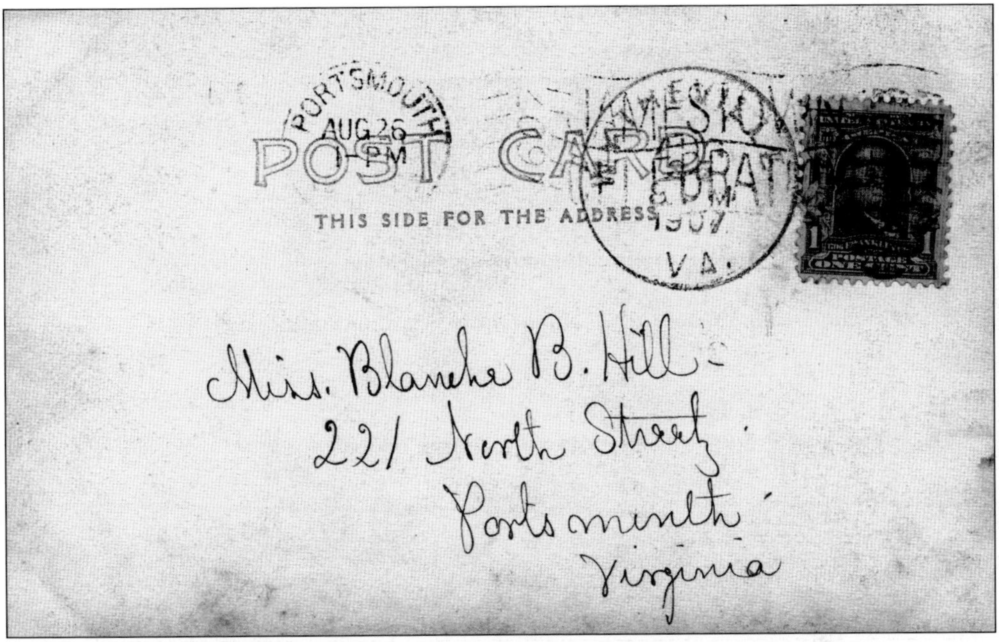

The address at 221 North Street is that of the Hill House. Built in the early 1800s, the four-story home with an English-style basement is now the home of the Portsmouth Historical Association. The house and all of the family belongings were conveyed by deed as a gift from Evelyn Hill, the last survivor of the family. Blanche B. Hill, to whom this postcard was sent, passed away in December 1949. The house is now a museum and is listed as a Virginia Historic Landmark.

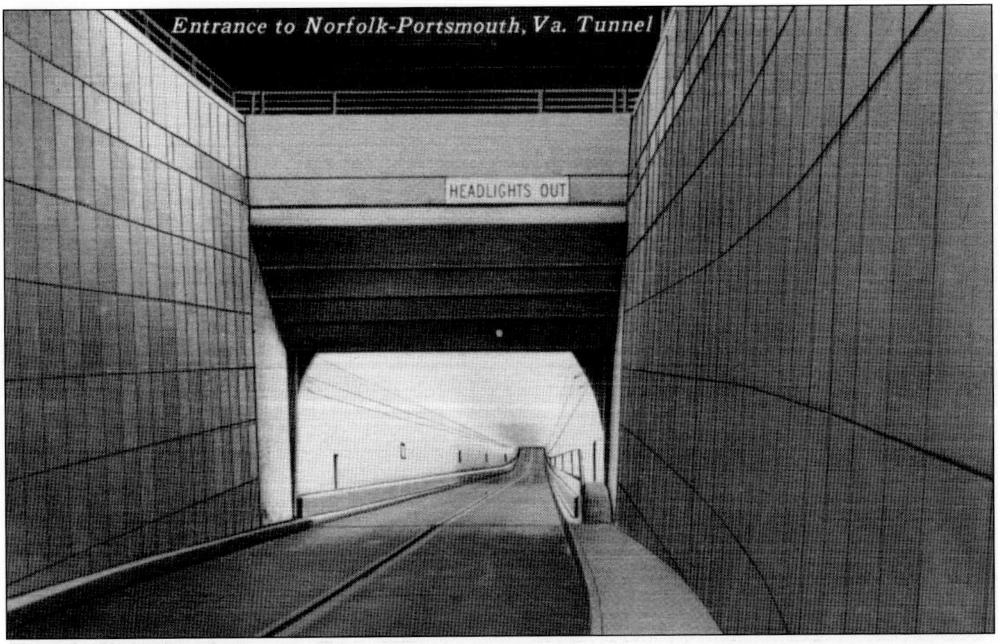

The tunnel between Norfolk and Portsmouth opened in 1952 to provide a faster route from city to city. As the population grew and traffic increased, a second tunnel was built. While sitting in traffic, one can sometimes spot a bumper sticker that reads, "Portsmouth—The Light at the Other End of the Tunnel."

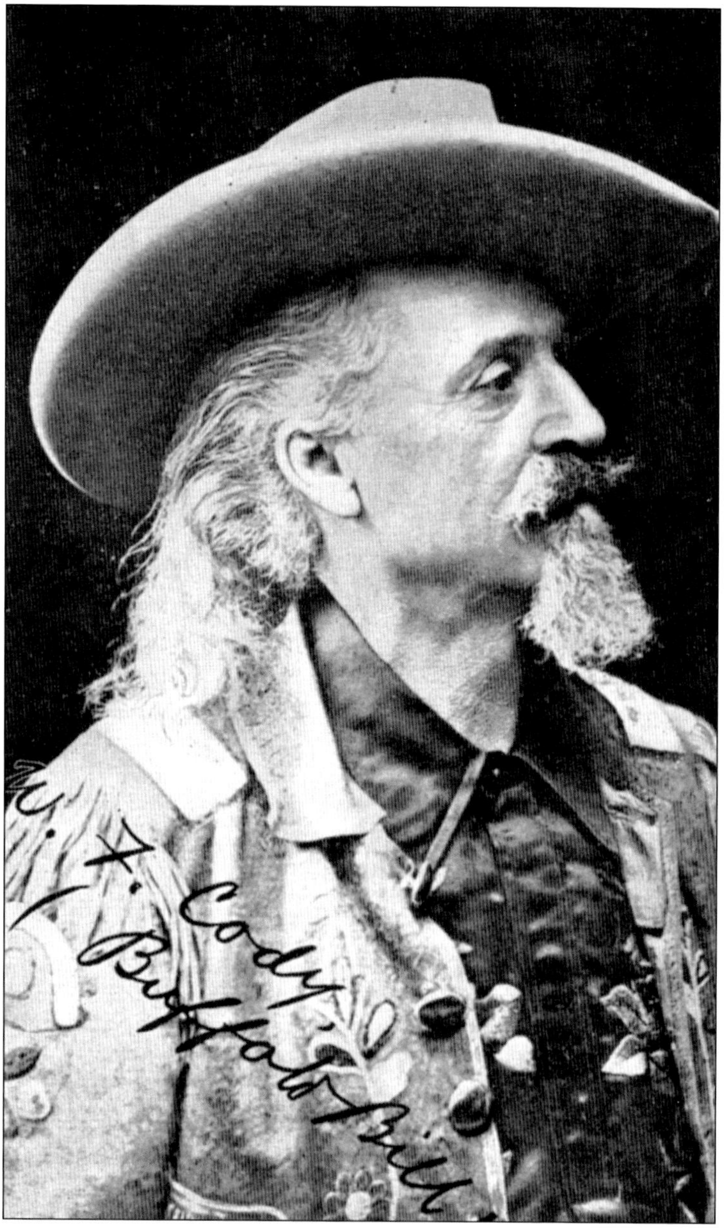

The show of shows had arrived in Portsmouth. "Buffalo Bill" Cody with the Miller Brothers and the Arlington 101 Wild West Show had come to town. As he stepped off the train, Cody was greeted by the mayor and other dignitaries. He then turned and waved his hat to the crowd of local residents, sailors, and children who had come to see a legend of the Wild West. At 70 years old, Cody was dressed in his knee-length cavalry boots and long fringed leather coat. He had grey hair that went past his shoulders, a curly mustache, and a goatee. The crowd knew they were in the presence of a living legend. The theme for the show on November 11, 1916, was "Military Preparedness," and it was held on the fairgrounds at Washington and Lincoln Streets. When Cody departed the city, he was ill with a cold. While en route to his home, he stopped in Denver to visit his sister. On January 10, 1917, he died of kidney failure, and the citizens of Portsmouth realized they had witnessed the grand finale for "Buffalo Bill" Cody.

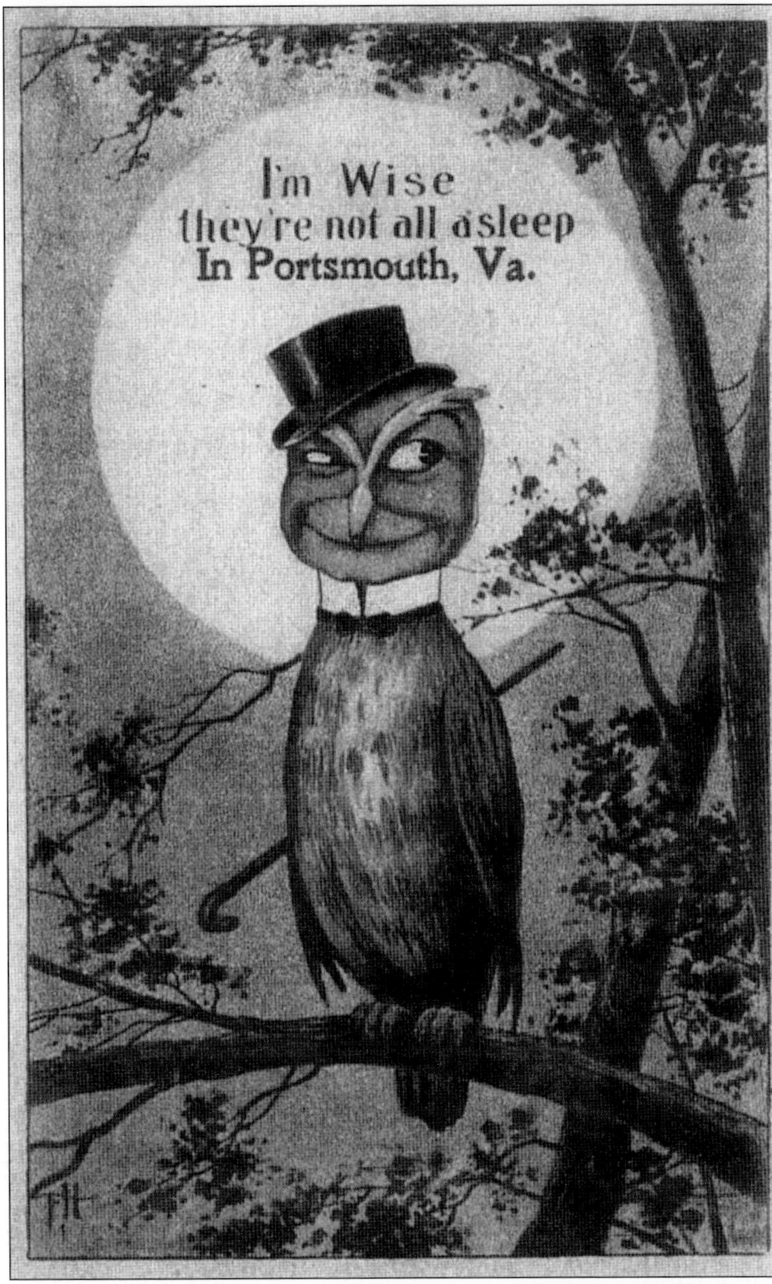

The caption on this card from the early 1900s is very true about the city of Portsmouth. While it may appear to be a sleepy little town, its citizens and members of the military have remained awake through 10 wars and heard the sound of four flags fluttering in the wind over the city. Always on guard and always prepared, Portsmouth has been there to meet the challenge. In times of peace and in times of war, the city provided whatever was needed to meet the task. Through the sound of ships being built at the Norfolk Naval Shipyard, Marines firing the nine o'clock gun, cargo ships unloading and loading, train whistles blowing at the crossings, church bells ringing, bands parading down the street, the Coast Guard patrolling the river, and the cheers at sporting events, the city of Portsmouth, Virginia, has always been, and remains, awake.

Consistent with our mission to preserve history on a local level, this book was printed in South Carolina on American-made paper and manufactured entirely in the United States. Products carrying the accredited Forest Stewardship Council (FSC) label are printed on 100 percent FSC-certified paper.

MADE IN THE USA